Journalism and Human Rights

This book is the first collection of original research to explore links between demographics and media coverage of emerging human rights issues. It covers cross-national reporting on human trafficking, HIV/AIDS, water contamination, and child labour; and same-sex marriage, Guantanamo detainee rights, immigration reform, and post-traumatic stress disorder in the United States. The research asks questions such as: What are the principal catalysts that propel rights issues into media agendas? Why do some surface more quickly than others? And how do the demographics of cross-national reporting differ from those driving multi-city US nationwide coverage of rights claims?

Using community structure theory and innovative Media Vector content analysis, the eight chapters of this book reveal three striking patterns that show how differences in female empowerment, social or economic vulnerability, and Midwestern newspaper geographic location link powerfully with variations in coverage of rights issues. The patterns connecting demographics and rights claims confirm that coverage of human rights can mirror the concerns of stakeholders and vulnerable groups, contrary to conventional assumptions that media typically serve as "guard dogs" reinforcing the interests of political and economic elites.

This book was originally published as a special issue of the *Atlantic Journal of Communication*.

John C. Pollock (PhD, Stanford) is Professor of Communication Studies at the College of New Jersey, Ewing Township NJ, USA. He is the author of *Tilted Mirrors: Media Alignment with Political and Social Change—a Community Structure Approach* (2007) and edited *Media and Social Inequality: Innovations in Community Structure Research* (2013). He is a media sociologist and pursues interests in health communication and media and human rights.

Journalism and Human Rights

How demographics drive media coverage

Edited by
John C. Pollock

Routledge
Taylor & Francis Group

LONDON AND NEW YORK

First published 2015
by Routledge
2 Park Square, Milton Park, Abingdon, Oxfordshire OX14 4RN

and by Routledge
711 Third Avenue, New York, NY 10017, USA

First issued in paperback 2016

Routledge is an imprint of the Taylor & Francis Group, an informa business

British Library Cataloguing in Publication Data
A catalogue record for this book is available from the British Library

ISBN 13: 978-1-138-21144-5 (pbk)
ISBN 13: 978-1-138-85789-6 (hbk)

Typeset in Times New Roman
by RefineCatch Limited, Bungay, Suffolk

Publisher's Note
The publisher accepts responsibility for any inconsistencies that may have
arisen during the conversion of this book from journal articles to book chapters,
namely the possible inclusion of journal terminology.

Disclaimer
Every effort has been made to contact copyright holders for their permission to
reprint material in this book. The publishers would be grateful to hear from any
copyright holder who is not here acknowledged and will undertake to rectify
any errors or omissions in future editions of this book.

To the many generations of students I have been privileged to teach, whose intelligence, enthusiasm, and creativity have given me great joy

Contents

Part I: Cross-National Coverage of Human Rights

Part II: Multi-City US Nationwide Coverage of Human Rights

CONTENTS

Citation Information

The chapters in this book were originally published in the *Atlantic Journal of Communication*, volume 22, issues 3–4 (July–October 2014). When citing this material, please use the original page numbering for each article, as follows:

Preface

Preface
Morton Winston
Atlantic Journal of Communication, volume 22, issues 3–4 (July–October 2014) pp. 139–140

Overview

Illuminating Human Rights: How Demographics Drive Media Coverage
John C. Pollock
Atlantic Journal of Communication, volume 22, issues 3–4 (July–October 2014) pp. 141–159

Chapter 1

Cross-National Coverage of Human Trafficking: A Community Structure Approach
Kelly Alexandre, Cynthia Sha, John C. Pollock, Kelsey Baier, and Jessica Johnson
Atlantic Journal of Communication, volume 22, issues 3–4 (July–October 2014) pp. 160–174

Chapter 2

Cross-National Coverage of HIV/AIDS: A Community Structure Approach
James Etheridge, Kelsey Zinck, John C. Pollock, Christina Santiago, Kristen Halicki, and Alec Badalamenti
Atlantic Journal of Communication, volume 22, issues 3–4 (July–October 2014) pp. 175–192

Chapter 3

Cross-National Coverage of Water Handling: A Community Structure Approach
Domenick Wissel, Kathleen Ward, John C. Pollock, Allura Hipper, Lauren Klein, and Stefanie Gratale
Atlantic Journal of Communication, volume 22, issues 3–4 (July–October 2014) pp. 193–210

CITATION INFORMATION

Chapter 4

Comparing Coverage of Child Labor and National Characteristics: A Cross-National Exploration
Jordan Gauthier Kohn and John C. Pollock
Atlantic Journal of Communication, volume 22, issues 3–4 (July–October 2014) pp. 211–228

Chapter 5

Nationwide Newspaper Coverage of Same-Sex Marriage: A Community Structure Approach
Victoria Vales, John C. Pollock, Victoria Scarfone, Carly Koziol, Amy Wilson, and Patrick Flanagan
Atlantic Journal of Communication, volume 22, issues 3–4 (July–October 2014) pp. 229–244

Chapter 6

Nationwide Newspaper Coverage of Detainee Rights at Guantanamo Bay: A Community Structure Approach
Kelsey Zinck, Maggie Rogers, John C. Pollock, and Matthew Salvatore
Atlantic Journal of Communication, volume 22, issues 3–4 (July–October 2014) pp. 245–258

Chapter 7

Nationwide Newspaper Coverage of Immigration Reform: A Community Structure Approach
John C. Pollock, Stefanie Gratale, Kevin Teta, Kyle Bauer, and Elyse Hoekstra
Atlantic Journal of Communication, volume 22, issues 3–4 (July–October 2014) pp. 259–274

Chapter 8

Nationwide Newspaper Coverage of Posttraumatic Stress: A Community Structure Approach
John C. Pollock, Stefanie Gratale, Angelica Anas, Emaleigh Kaithern, and Kelly Johnson
Atlantic Journal of Communication, volume 22, issues 3–4 (July–October 2014) pp. 275–291

Please direct any queries you may have about the citations to clsuk.permissions@cengage.com

Notes on Contributors

Kelly Alexandre is based in the Department of Communication Studies at the College of New Jersey, Ewing Township, NJ, USA.

Angelica Anas is based in the Department of Communication Studies at the College of New Jersey, Ewing Township, NJ, USA.

Alec Badalamenti is based in the Department of Communication Studies at the College of New Jersey, Ewing Township, NJ, USA.

Kelsey Baier is based in the Department of Communication Studies at the College of New Jersey, Ewing Township, NJ, USA.

Kyle Bauer is based in the Department of Communication Studies at the College of New Jersey, Ewing Township, NJ, USA.

James Etheridge is based in the Department of Communication Studies at the College of New Jersey, Ewing Township, NJ, USA.

Patrick Flanagan is based in the Department of Communication Studies at the College of New Jersey, Ewing Township, NJ, USA.

Stefanie Gratale (MPA, George Washington) earned a US Presidential Management Fellowship, a federal government rotational fellowship through which she worked at the Internal Revenue Service (IRS) and the Environmental Protection Agency. She now works in the facilities group at IRS, where her projects focus on improving energy efficiency, consolidating space, and reducing the environmental footprint of the agency's large facilities.

Kristen Halicki is based in the Department of Communication Studies at the College of New Jersey, Ewing Township, NJ, USA.

Allura Hipper is based in the Department of Communication Studies at the College of New Jersey, Ewing Township, NJ, USA.

Elyse Hoekstra is based in the Department of Communication Studies at the College of New Jersey, Ewing Township, NJ, USA.

Jessica Johnson is based in the Department of Communication Studies at the College of New Jersey, Ewing Township, NJ, USA.

NOTES ON CONTRIBUTORS

Kelly Johnson is based in the Department of Communication Studies at the College of New Jersey, Ewing Township, NJ, USA.

Emaleigh Kaithern is based in the Department of Communication Studies at the College of New Jersey, Ewing Township, NJ, USA.

Lauren Klein is based in the Department of Communication Studies at the College of New Jersey, Ewing Township, NJ, USA.

Jordan Gauthier Kohn is based in the Department of Communication Studies at the College of New Jersey, Ewing Township, NJ, USA.

Carly Koziol is based in the Department of Communication Studies at the College of New Jersey, Ewing Township, NJ, USA.

John C. Pollock (PhD, Stanford) is a Professor of Communication Studies at the College of New Jersey, Ewing Township, NJ, USA. He is the author of *Tilted Mirrors: Media Alignment with Political and Social Change—A Community Structure Approach* (2007) and edited *Media and Social Inequality: Innovations in Community Structure Research* (2013). He is a media sociologist and pursues interests in health communication and media and human rights.

Maggie Rogers is based in the Department of Communication Studies at the College of New Jersey, Ewing Township, NJ, USA.

Matthew Salvatore is based in the Department of Communication Studies at the College of New Jersey, Ewing Township, NJ, USA.

Christina Santiago is based in the Department of Communication Studies at the College of New Jersey, Ewing Township, NJ, USA.

Victoria Scarfone is based in the Department of Communication Studies at the College of New Jersey, Ewing Township, NJ, USA.

Cynthia Sha is based in the Department of Communication Studies at the College of New Jersey, Ewing Township, NJ, USA.

Kevin Teta is based in the Department of Communication Studies at the College of New Jersey, Ewing Township, NJ, USA.

Victoria Vales is based in the Department of Communication Studies at the College of New Jersey, Ewing Township, NJ, USA.

Kathleen Ward is based in the Department of Communication Studies at the College of New Jersey, Ewing Township, NJ, USA.

Amy Wilson is based in the Department of Communication Studies at the College of New Jersey, Ewing Township, NJ, USA.

Morton Winston (PhD, Illinois) is a Professor of Philosophy at the College of New Jersey, Ewing Township, NJ, USA, and a human rights activist. His areas of specialization include human rights theory and practice, biomedical ethics, political philosophy, and philosophy of technology. He is a member of the editorial boards of the *Journal of Human Rights* and *Human Rights Quarterly*.

NOTES ON CONTRIBUTORS

Domenick Wissel is based in the Department of Communication Studies at the College of New Jersey, Ewing Township, NJ, USA.

Kelsey Zinck is based in the Department of Communication Studies at the College of New Jersey, Ewing Township, NJ, USA.

Preface

Morton Winston

Department of Philosophy, Religion, and Classical Studies
The College of New Jersey

The case studies collected in this special issue of the *Atlantic Journal of Communication* address the important intersection between the right to health and the right to information. Mass communication, in particular journalism, is the primary means by which citizens around the globe gain access to information about health issues and health policies. The timely and accurate reporting of health matters is crucial to enabling people to safeguard their own health, and also to their ability to organize themselves to press their governments for national policies that better fulfill the human right to health.

However, as the case studies collected here demonstrate, the flow of information travels in both directions. Community activists, nongovernmental organizations (NGOs), and other civil society actors can influence the nature, extent, and direction of media coverage of their concerns and issues. This finding allows a more nuanced and accurate view of community structure theory and provides insight into how transnational activist networks are able to press their demands for better fulfillment of human rights, even those of the most vulnerable and marginalized members of society.

Human rights activists and scholars have long appreciated the importance of information politics in advancing human rights issues. The well-known global human rights NGOs such as Amnesty International and Human Rights Watch rely on journalists to deliver their reports on human rights violations to the public. When journalists are repressed or even killed, it is a serious form of human rights violation, because journalists are key players in the process of disseminating human rights information and promoting the diffusion of human rights norms and values.

But transnational activist networks operate most effectively when the international human rights NGOs have local NGO partners that work in their own countries on the same issues. Journalism that focuses public attention on human rights concerns within particular countries and regions is essential for empowering members of civil societies and allowing them to be more effective agents of social change in their own societies.

The empowerment of civil society actors is particularly important for categories of emerging human rights such as those that are the focus of these case studies. The campaigns for the recognition of the dignity and rights of people with HIV/AIDS of the 1980s were led by groups in the United States such as Gay Men's Health Crisis and the San Francisco AIDS Foundation. These campaigns led to major shifts in public policy with regard to human right issues such as mandatory testing, discrimination in employment and housing, immigration, and access to treatment.

Civil society actors were able to be successful in pressing governments to protect the human rights and dignity of people with AIDS, in large part because their concerns and their framing of these concerns as human rights issues were mirrored in local and national press coverage.

This phenomenon was also vividly demonstrated in countries like South Africa, where local NGOs and citizen groups led the struggle to have their government recognize and respond appropriately to the HIV/AIDS epidemic gripping that country in the 1990s. Had the new South African government followed the policy prescriptions adopted to deal with the epidemic in Western countries such as the United States and France, tens of thousands of lives could have been saved. Instead of following the best current scientific understanding of the disease and its effective treatment, however, President Thabo Mbeki subscribed to the view that HIV was not the cause of AIDS. So rather than treating HIV+ people with the triple retroviral cocktail that had been shown effective in preventing the progression of the disease, he recommended that HIV+ people eat beetroot, garlic, and olive oil to boost their immune systems. But again, due to initiatives by civil society groups such as the Treatment Action Campaign, and empowered individuals such as Zackie Achmat and Gugu Dlamini, the media profile of the concerns of vulnerable communities was raised. They lobbied pharmaceutical companies to allow South Africa to produce generic versions of basic HIV medicines. They also campaigned for the government to implement rights enshrined in the 1997 Constitution of the "New" South Africa that guaranteed citizens "the right to have access to health care services" including "reproductive health care" and "emergency medical treatment." As a result of these campaigns, combined with support from external human rights organizations, South Africa has largely reversed earlier misguided policies, and brought its policies more in line with those of other African states, such as Uganda and Botswana, which avoided the mistakes of the Mbeki era. Their struggle is what finally led the former national president Nelson Mandela to declare in 2003 that "AIDS is no longer a disease, it is a human rights issue."

These case studies extend and refine our understanding of exactly how media coverage can assist civil society actors in advancing human rights agendas on behalf of even the most marginalized groups in society. Although the story of HIV/AIDS is fairly well known, these studies examine the impact of coverage on lesser known issues such as human trafficking, child labor, water contamination, immigration reform, and mental health reform. Taken as a whole, these studies demonstrate that journalism can indeed function effectively as the "fourth estate" by holding governments accountable to human rights values and norms and by empowering civil society actors to press their demands that their governments respect their human dignity and rights.

Illuminating Human Rights: How Demographics Drive Media Coverage

John C. Pollock
Department of Communication Studies
The College of New Jersey

The case studies in this special issue of *Atlantic Journal of Communication* represent a broad spectrum of human rights issues of compelling interest both cross-nationally and nationally (inside the United States). This introduction addresses three topics that explain the significance and timing of a special issue on journalism and human rights: (a) an innovative use of community structure theory, examining how demographics are linked to variations in human rights coverage; (b) eight case studies, four focusing on cross-national perspectives and four on U.S. multicity comparisons; and (c) significant overall patterns in both cross-national and cross-city domestic research on news coverage of human rights conflicts, illustrating the striking contributions of gender and geography.

MEDIA COVERAGE OF EMERGING HUMAN RIGHTS DESERVES SYSTEMATIC, COMPARATIVE ANALYSIS

As a topic, "journalism" or "media coverage" and "human rights" is understudied and under-published. A quick review of communication studies databases such as Communication and Mass Media Complete and ComAbstracts reveals several shortcomings and gaps, including the following:

1. Scholarly work on coverage of human rights issues typically focuses on traditional topics such as combatants' rights, prisoners' rights, or freedom of the press, rights claims often

linked to issues of political and press freedom. Sometimes these traditional civil and political rights are covered selectively, connected somewhat to conditions or nation-states in which the United States has a strategic or, in an earlier time "Cold-War" interest (see, e.g., coverage by the *New York Times* across 50 countries: Caliendo, Gibney, & Payne, 1999).

2. Examinations of human rights coverage tend to focus on "micro-" or "macro-" levels of analysis, ignoring "meso-" levels or middle-level explorations. At the microlevel, studies might examine coverage of one issue in one or a few newspapers. At a macrolevel, studies might make broad generalizations about human rights coverage in large clusters of countries, such as "democracies" or "authoritarian" regimes. Little attention is given to the systematic comparison of human rights coverage in the "middle" range, comparing, for example, coverage of rights claims in multiple large cities, or a wide range of countries with varied demographic characteristics.

3. Relatively little attention is given to a broad spectrum of "emerging" rights issues: social, economic, and cultural rights (see Winston, 2001). Although some attention is paid to those living with HIV/AIDS and gay marriage, a vast array of rights issues are offered little attention in studies of human rights coverage, largely overlooking such topics as human trafficking, child labor, water handling, immigration reform, or mental health reform.

4. Studies of human rights coverage tend to focus on discrete issues such as the rights of those living with HIV/AIDS or gay marriage or political rights in authoritarian countries rather than on comparative frameworks for coverage of human rights generally. Such frameworks might seek and evaluate "patterns" in similarities and differences in rights coverage across different human rights categories.

As previous studies on media coverage of human rights fail to engage a full range of "emerging" human rights issues, the communication studies field is in a position to address that gap in coverage. Drawing on research conducted by students in classes in communication research methods and international communication at The College of New Jersey (TCNJ), the current collection attempts to redress that imbalance. This new scholarship offers systematic comparative investigations of rights coverage among a wide range of leading or database accessible newspapers in a large sample of nation-states, in particular in developing countries, and among major metropolitan areas in the United States.

AN INNOVATIVE USE OF COMMUNITY STRUCTURE RESEARCH

Until recently, it was expected that "visualization" of human rights abuses or atrocities would move populations and governments to action, that graphic evidence of abhorrent practices would prompt civilized groups to act to seek remedies. Indeed, after the photos of torture at Abu Ghraib surfaced, congressional hearings and national revulsion in the United States appeared to lead to some kind of responsive activity. Some military leaders were transferred and low-ranking enlisted personnel were court-martialed, and in some cases imprisoned. Yet overall expectations that visual horror generates efforts to ameliorate its roots have been recently challenged. A 2012 collection on "Media, Mobilization, and Human Rights: Mediating Suffering" finds little or no evidence that news stories, visual depictions of atrocities, or exposure to human rights violations in far-away countries prompt people to respond with activism (Borer, 2012). Indeed, an opinion editorial in the *New York Times* on "Advertising Torture" (Linfield, 2014, p. A23) documents the capacity of torturers in the Syrian civil war not to hide their activities but rather to display their skills and gruesome outcomes with bravado and triumphalism.

Evidence that graphic visualization of torture may not mobilize and that perpetrators can openly boast of their prowess suggests that those interested in finding a way to push back against human rights violations must cast a broad net in order to facilitate mobilization to stop atrocities. Specifically, to the extent that news media report on human rights issues and violations, variations in that reporting across countries and across cities deserve attention. How much variation in reporting on human rights claims is found in comparisons of different countries and cities? What characteristics of countries and cities are associated with reporting that holds governments responsible for addressing rights issues, or conversely that regards "society" as responsible for making a difference? Those are the key questions that animate this exploration of journalism and human rights.

The case studies in this collection all collect data from one specific news channel—newspapers—for several reasons. Newspapers are read by well-educated, economic, and politically influential decision makers who have a stake in major issues. In addition, newspapers are notorious agenda-setters for other sources of media (e.g., television, radio, Internet), all of which rely on newspapers to alert them to significant issues. Moreover, newspapers are community forums for discussion that keep citizens updated on the most pressing issues in their communities and how those issues relate to larger concerns regionally, nationwide, and throughout the world.

The Community Structure Approach

This collection of articles is united by two consistent elements: a shared theoretical framework and a shared methodology. To understand similarities and differences in article findings, explanations of both theory and methodology are useful.

Media scholars typically investigate the impact of media on society, often examining how media frames affect audience perspectives through "priming" some perspectives as more reasonable than others or setting issue "agendas" for audience consideration. This collection of articles, however, adopts a reverse perspective, asking how "society" affects "media." Specifically, the method applied in this study is the community structure approach, a research theory advanced by several communication scholars including Demers and Viswanath (1999); Hindman (1999); McLeod and Hertog (1999); Park (1922); Pollock (2007, 2013a, 2013b); and Tichenor, Donohue, and Olien (1973, 1980).

The current community structure approach as defined by Pollock (2007) is a "form of quantitative content analysis that focuses on the ways in which key characteristics of communities (such as cities) are related to the content coverage of newspapers in those communities" (p. 23). The approach can be further elaborated with its direct assessment of at least the following three tasks: the approach aims to explore a theory that has received little attention by other scholars. In addition, although the approach considers traditional media-centric descriptive approaches, it aims to go beyond traditional content analysis and connect theory with data collection, making a robust contribution to modern media sociology (Schudson, 2014; Shoemaker & Reese, 2013;

Waisbord, 2014). Finally, although the community structure approach has often been used to explore the relationship of media to society and political "control," it can be applied to evaluate the relationship of media to societal and political change (Pollock, 2007). The community structure approach will therefore be used to explore links between varied city (or national) demographics and coverage of emerging human rights issues in varied leading (or database accessible) newspapers in different nations or varied U.S. city newspapers, seeking patterns linking social characteristics and coverage of human rights across a wide range of issues.

The community structure concept can be traced to a leading founder of both sociology and communication studies at the University of Chicago, Robert Park. In his *The Immigrant Press and Its Control*, Park (1922) dedicated an entire chapter to the influence of society on local papers, "The Press Reflects Its Group," and urged scholars to consider the importance of this somewhat "reverse" view of the connection between society and media. That perspective was developed and elaborated at the University of Minnesota by modern scholars Tichenor, Donohue, and Olien, who called their research viewpoint "structural pluralism." Conducting studies mostly in Minnesota, one of the most homogeneous states in the nation, the Minnesota trio found that newspapers in larger, pluralistic metropolitan areas were generally more open to new ideas for change compared to papers in smaller, more homogeneous communities. The graduate students and intellectual offspring of the Minnesota giants focused on only a few cities but made several important contributions. Hindman (1999) found that larger proportions of ethnic groups in a community were linked to coverage favoring their interests. McLeod and Hertog (1999) found that the larger the size of a protest group, the more favorable the coverage of its concerns. The edited collection of Demers and Viswanath (1999) emphasized both the social control function of media and its opposite, the capacity of media to accommodate social change.

One of the approach's most recent "challenges" was offered by Donohue, Tichenor, and Olien (1995), later countered by Pollock and others (2007, 2008, 2013a, 2013b; Pollock & Yulis, 2004). The challenge of the Minnesota group was the assertion that local media often function less as "watchdogs" and more as "guard dogs" reinforcing and protecting the interests of local political, economic, and social elites (Olien, Donohue & Tichenor, 1995).

Pollock and colleagues have advanced the studies of the Minnesota team and its graduate students with three principal contributions to the community structure tradition. First, the Pollock et al. studies reach beyond simple measures of article "content" to collect measures of editorial judgment or "prominence," combining the two measures into a single composite score, a "Media Vector," resulting in highly sensitive scores of newspaper message "projection." Second, Pollock et al. researchers have conducted among the first systematic nationwide U.S. studies comparing multiple metropolitan area newspapers, as well as cross-national studies comparing leading or major accessible newspapers in multiple countries using the community structure approach. Third, the Pollock et al. studies often confirm that media are capable of reaching beyond the reinforcement of elite interests, beyond functioning as "guard dogs" to indeed mirror the interests of the most "vulnerable" populations (Pollock, 2007, 2008, 2013a, 2013b; Pollock & Yulis, 2004). For thorough explorations of both theoretical and empirical literature in the community structure tradition, refer to three recent contributions: (a) "Structural Pluralism in Journalism and Media Studies: A Concept Explication and Theory Construction" (Nah & Armstrong, 2011), (b) "Drug Abuse Violations in Communities: Community Newspapers as a Macro-Level Source of Social Control" (Yamamoto & Ran, 2013), and (c) an annotated online bibliography published by Oxford University Press Online (Pollock, 2013a).

The community structure approach will be used to address two main research questions:

RQ1: How much variation exists across different countries (or cities) in coverage of emerging human rights issues?

RQ2: How closely linked is that coverage variation to differences in national (or city) demographic characteristics?

Modern Community Structure Studies

Traditional community structure studies typically find that most media reinforce the existing social system, reflecting the interests and perspectives of social, political, and economic elites and privileged interests generally. More recent studies, however, reveal that media are capable of "mirroring" the interests and concerns of more "vulnerable" groups. The modern studies differ from previous studies in several ways.

Previous studies of human rights coverage often focused on legal, national security, or political definitions of human rights, often framed in the language and perspectives of the Cold War. The United States was often portrayed as "respecting" human rights, in particular the right to vote and the civil liberties described in the U.S. Bill of Rights, whereas the Soviet Union and countries associated with it were, by contrast, often viewed as violating that right. Modern perspectives on human rights have expanded the concept of "rights" to embrace a far broader array of issues, from security from gender-based abuse (human trafficking) to the right to choose a marriage partner to reasonable access to noncontaminated water, from shielding children from unreasonable working conditions (child labor) to pathways to citizenship (immigration reform) to expanded definitions of a right to health care (for mental health or posttraumatic stress [PTS] issues).

Instead of focusing on one or two cities or one state, modern community structure studies compare multiple cities or multiples states. The first nationwide studies using the community structure approach collected in a book were published in *Tilted Mirrors: Media Alignment With Political and Social Change* (Pollock, 2007). Modern media/newspaper databases, made widely available in the mid-1990s, have facilitated comparison of newspapers in a wide range of metropolitan areas in the United States.

Modern studies also use a far wider range of methodologies and measures compared to previous efforts. In some recent books, for example, whether in *Tilted Mirrors* (Pollock, 2007) or *Media and Social Inequality* (Pollock, 2013b), researchers combine measures of "content" with measures of editorial judgment or "prominence" (proximity of articles to the first page/first section of a paper or an inside front page, size of headline, length of article in words, presence or absence of graphics) to create single, highly sensitive composite scores or "Media Vectors" for newspapers for particular critical issues over a sampled period. More sophisticated measures of coverage have yielded substantively different results.

Recent studies pay more attention to measures likely to tap the concerns of historically underserved or invisible populations, such as poverty and unemployment levels, percentage of single-parent families, health care access (physicians/100,000, hospital beds/100,000, percentage of municipal spending on health care), crime rates, proportions of African Americans and Hispanics, percentage of foreign born, and number of organizations marketing to lesbian, gay, bisexual, and transgender (LGBT) communities. In cross-national studies, a wide range of measures have tapped concerns of the underserved, including infant mortality, longevity, and fertility rates, along with measures of undernourishment and changes in the prevalence and incidence of cholera and HIV/AIDS.

The two most recently published community structure books (Pollock, 2007, 2013b) stretch the boundaries of previous topics, which often focused on political access, political participation, and political self-efficacy, to explore variations in coverage of a wide range of issues and rights claims, for example: Anita Hill's harassment claims during the Clarence Thomas judicial hearings, physician-assisted suicide, stem cell research, ending capital punishment, gun control, drilling for oil in the Arctic National Wildlife Reserve, opposition to trying juveniles as adults, those living with HIV/AIDS in the late 80s and early 90s, gays in the Boy Scouts, "Occupy" Wall Street, universal health care, and so on.

A Methodology Combining Both "Direction" and "Prominence"

Most content analysis studies focus precisely on article "content." The articles in the current collection, however, add another dimension—editorial decisions about the "prominence" of each article. For each of the studies, all articles are indeed evaluated for the "direction" or "slant" of the headline and first few paragraphs. "Direction" is coded in three categories for each study, either "favorable/unfavorable/balanced-neutral" or "government responsibility/society responsibility/balanced-neutral." Article prominence deserves some elaboration. What makes these studies distinct, however, is that the measures of prominence and direction are not simply measured and presented separately. Rather, they are combined in a way that yields a single score.

The following paragraphs demonstrate the process of measuring two separate dimensions, then combining them into one composite score. For studies of cross-national coverage of human rights issues, each study sampled articles from between 18 and 21 leading or database-accessible papers in as many nations. For the studies of multicity coverage in the United States, each study sampled articles from between 21 and 35 newspapers nationwide. The number of newspapers selected varied with the number of coauthors per paper, but it also varied more importantly with the amount of coverage offered by each newspaper in the designated sample periods.

To qualify for inclusion in each study, newspapers were expected to publish at least 10 relevant articles, with a major focus on the topic in the headline and/or the lead paragraph, in the appropriate sample period. Although larger samples of newspapers were examined initially for each study, only those meeting the "10 article minimum" were selected. For cross-national studies, the NewsBank and AllAfrica databases were used; for U.S. nationwide studies, the NewsBank database was employed. Efforts were made to sample selections of newspapers from a variety of different regions worldwide and from each of four major regions inside the United States: Northeast, South, Midwest, and West. Across four cross-national studies, 78 newspaper samples were studied for a total of 1,195 articles, averaging 15.32 articles per newspaper. Across four U.S. multicity studies, 110 newspaper samples were studied for a total of 1,551 articles, averaging 14.1 articles per newspaper.

A sampling limitation of this collection merits mention. All targeted newspapers were found in major metropolitan areas in the United States or in a wide sample of countries. As a result, newspapers in medium-size and small cities were not included. The sampling guidelines therefore did not permit comparisons of newspapers in smaller and larger cities or smaller and larger population areas. The rationale for sampling large cities was twofold: First, every effort was made to maximize geographic diversity in the samples, and it was therefore reasonable to emphasize "breadth" in multiple locations over "depth" in just a few locations. Second, the databases employed typically contained records covering more years for larger papers than for smaller ones, so that selecting larger newspapers afforded samples of newspapers over longer time frames, essential for collecting sufficient quantities of articles to facilitate rigorous data analysis.

Article prominence.   Articles were assessed by two separate scores. The first determined "prominence," portraying editors' judgments on the importance of each article. A score ranging from 3 to 16 was assigned based on four factors: placement (front page, first section, etc.), headline size (number of words), article length (number of words), and any accompanying photographs and/or graphics. Articles that received a higher number of points were thought to obtain a higher attention score. All newspaper articles sampled in cross-national coverage contained a minimum of 250 words. All articles sampled in U.S. multicity, nationwide coverage also contained a minimum of 250 words, with one exception: the case study on PTS. That sample yielded so many articles in the sampled time frame that researchers increased the article size threshold to a minimum of 500 words to generate a manageable sample. Their word count parameters and coding are found in parentheses in the "article length" row in the prominence table. The prominence scoring system is detailed in Table 1.

Article direction.   After receiving a prominence score, each article was assigned a "direction" category based on the frame it used. "Direction" can indicate any of two sets of three-category codes: "favorable/unfavorable/balanced-neutral" regarding an issue (e.g., regarding same-sex marriage) or "government responsibility/society responsibility/balanced-neutral" (e.g., regarding addressing child labor issues internationally). Articles were coded for these directions, at least half of all articles in all studies were blind double-coded, and Scott's Pi coefficients of intercoder reliability were calculated. Scott's Pi coefficients for all case studies exceeded .70.

Media Vector calculation.   After analyzing multiple newspapers from distinct countries or cities, the Janis–Fadner Coefficient of Imbalance was applied to calculate a "Media Vector." Similar to a vector in physics, which combines the measures of two dimensions into a single score, the "Media Vector" was calculated by combining the prominence and directional scores

TABLE 1
Prominence Score (for Coding Databases)

Dimension	*4*	*3*	*2*	*1*
Placement	Front page first section	Front page inside section	Inside page first section	Other
Headline size (no. of words)	10+	9–8	7–6	5 or fewer
Article length (no. of words)	1,000+	750–999	500–749	250–499
	(1,250+)	(1,000–1,249)	(750–999)	(500–749)
Photos/graphics	2 or more	1		

Note. Prominence score, © John C. Pollock, 1994–2014.

TABLE 2a
Calculating a Media Vector (Favorable/Unfavorable)

f = sum of the prominence scores coded "favorable"
u = sum of the prominence scores coded "unfavorable"
n = sum of the prominence scores coded "balanced/neutral"
r = f + u + n

If f > u (the sum of the favorable prominence scores is greater than the sum of the unfavorable prominence scores), the following formula is used:

Favorable Media Vector: $\quad FMV = \dfrac{(f^2 - fu)}{r^2}$ $\qquad$ (Answer lies between 0 and +1.00)

If f < u (the sum of the unfavorable prominence scores is greater than the sum of the favorable prominence scores), the following formula is used:

Unfavorable Media Vector: $\quad UMV = \dfrac{(fu - u^2)}{r^2}$ $\qquad$ (Answer lies between 0 and −1.00)

Note. Media Vector, © John C. Pollock, 2000–2014.

TABLE 2b
Calculating a Media Vector (Government Responsibility/Societal Responsibility)

g = sum of the prominence scores coded "government responsibility"
s = sum of the prominence scores coded "societal responsibility"
n = sum of the prominence scores coded "balanced/neutral"
r = g + s + n

If g > s (the sum of the government prominence scores is greater than the sum of the society prominence scores), the following formula is used:

Government Media Vector: $\quad GMV = \dfrac{(g^2 - gs)}{r^2}$ $\qquad$ (Answer lies between 0 and +1.00)

If g < s (the sum of the "society" prominence scores is greater than the sum of the "government" scores), the following formula is used:

Society Media Vector: $\quad SMV = \dfrac{(gs - s^2)}{r^2}$ $\qquad$ (Answer lies between 0 and −1.00)

Note. Media Vector, © John C. Pollock, 2000–2014.

to measure article "projection" onto audiences (Pollock, 2007, p. 49). The "magnitude" of the media vector was measured by the article's prominence. The "direction" was defined by the article's direction. Media Vector scores range from +1.00 to −1.00. Coverage emphasizing "favorable" or "government responsibility" media frames of human rights issues had scores between +1.00 and 0, whereas coverage emphasizing "unfavorable" or "societal responsibility" media frames had scores between 0 and -1.00. The Media Vector formula is depicted in Tables 2a and 2b.

Correlations between national characteristics and Media Vectors were analyzed by means of Pearson correlations and regression analysis. Pearson correlations were employed to define which city or national characteristics were most strongly linked with Media Vectors. The strength and significance of each independent variable was further measured through regression analysis. Both procedures yielded strong associations between selected city or national characteristics and coverage of emerging human rights issues. Using the same theory and methodology for each of the eight case studies in this collection facilitates comparative evaluation and analysis.

ILLUMINATING HUMAN RIGHTS: EIGHT ISSUES

The eight articles included in this special double issue of *Atlantic Journal of Communication* include four cross-national studies and four nationwide U.S. multicity studies.

TABLE 3
Human Rights Issue Table

Title	Authors	Human Rights Issue
"Cross-National Coverage of Human Trafficking: A Community Structure Approach"	Kelly Alexandre, Cynthia Sha, John C. Pollock, Kelsey Baier, and Jessica Johnson	Right to avoid enslavement
"Cross-National Coverage of HIV/AIDS: A Community Structure Approach"	James Etheridge, Kelsey Zinck, John C. Pollock, Christina Santiago, Kristen Halicki, and Alec Badalamenti	Right to access health care services, in particular emergency medical treatment
"Cross-National Coverage of Water Handling: A Community Structure Approach"	Domenick Wissel, Kathleen Ward, John C. Pollock, Allura Hipper, Lauren Klein, and Stefanie Gratale	Right to access to uncontaminated water
"Comparing Coverage of Child Labor and National Characteristics: A Cross-National Exploration"	Jordan Gauthier Kohn and John C. Pollock	Right to freedom from harsh, inhumane working conditions
"Nationwide Newspaper Coverage of Same-Sex Marriage: A Community Structure Approach"	Victoria Vales, John C. Pollock, Victoria Scarfone, Carly Koziol, Amy Wilson, and Patrick Flanagan	Right to marry the person you love
"Nationwide Newspaper Coverage of Detainee Rights at Guantanamo Bay: A Community Structure Approach"	Kelsey Zinck, Maggie Rogers, John C. Pollock, and Matthew Salvatore	Right to due process
"Nationwide Newspaper Coverage of Immigration Reform: A Community Structure Approach"	John C. Pollock, Stefanie Gratale, Kevin Teta, Kyle Bauer, and Elyse Hoekstra	Right to live in "freedom from fear" or to pursue a path to citizenship
"Nationwide Newspaper Coverage of Posttraumatic Stress: A Community Structure Approach"	John C. Pollock, Stefanie Gratale, Angelica Anas, Emaleigh Kaithern, and Kelly Johnson	Right to mental health care

Cross-National Coverage of Human Rights Claims

The cross-national studies include coverage of human trafficking, HIV/AIDS, water handling/contamination, and child labor.

1. *Right to avoid enslavement.* "Cross-National Coverage of Human Trafficking: A Community Structure Approach," by Kelly Alexandre, Cynthia Sha, John C. Pollock, Kelsey Baier, and Jessica Johnson.

- Higher proportions of foreign investment in a country are associated in a regression analysis most strongly with coverage favoring more domestic government (as opposed to "society"—private organization, nongovernmental organization [NGO], etc.) intervention to reduce human trafficking. This finding suggests that foreign investment can be viewed as "leverage" to influence governments to address the issue of human trafficking.
- The higher the level of female empowerment in a country (measured by such indicators as female school life expectancy, with the highest Pearson correlation of any variable, female literacy rate, and—inversely with—female infant mortality), the greater the newspaper support for the intervention of "domestic governments" to address human trafficking challenges. This finding suggests that, for the issue of human trafficking, leading newspapers can generally be trusted (or at least expected) to mirror the interests of empowered women. Higher percentage foreign investment and empowerment of women together account for about 49% of the variance.
- Other significant variables associated with holding domestic governments accountable for human trafficking include GDP/capita and broadband subscriptions/100 people.

2. *Right to access health care services, in particular emergency medical treatment.* "Cross-National Coverage of HIV/AIDS: A Community Structure Approach," by James Etheridge, Kelsey Zinck, John C. Pollock, Christina Santiago, Kristen Halicki, and Alec Badalamenti.

- Some measures of privilege (female knowledge that consistent condom use prevents AIDS, similar male knowledge), along with one measure of health vulnerability (percentage undernourished) are associated with more media support for domestic government efforts to fight HIV/AIDS. Other measures of health vulnerability (such as cholera cases/100,000, AIDS incidence/rate of increase) are linked to less media support for domestic government responsibility for HIV/AIDS, more support for "societal" responsibility (NGOs, charities, and foreign assistance from the United Nations or the United States Agency for International Development [USAID]). Regression analysis confirms that measures of both vulnerability (e.g., percentage undernourished) and privilege (e.g., percentage of females in the workforce) are strongly associated with coverage holding domestic governments responsible for addressing HIV/AIDS issues.
- It is noteworthy that, consistent with other cross-national studies, "female empowerment" is a significant correlate of newspaper emphasis on domestic government responsibility for HIV/AIDS. The highest correlation is indeed "female knowledge that consistent condom use prevents AIDS." One of the most powerful regression variables in one regression equation is "percentage of females in the workforce." The larger the percentages of both indicators of female empowerment, the greater the media support for domestic government responsibility for HIV/AIDS.

3. *Right to access to uncontaminated water.* "Cross-National Coverage of Water Handling: A Community Structure Approach," by Domenick Wissel, Kathleen Ward, John C. Pollock, Allura Hipper, Lauren Klein, and Stefanie Gratale.

- Water handling (right to reasonable access to uncontaminated water) is one of the major international issues currently occupying the attention of the Johns Hopkins School of Public Health. Contaminated water kills far more people than AIDS worldwide each year. According to the authors in their introduction:

Lack of access to clean drinking water is an international health crisis demanding global attention. According to the World Health Organization (WHO; 2012), at least 11% of the world's population, or about 753 million people, lack access to clean drinking water. Clean drinking water is critical for healthy living, as more than 3,000 children die each day due to diarrheal diseases caused by contaminated water.

- The key finding: The higher the level of female empowerment in a country (measured by such indicators as female school life expectancy, female literacy rate, and—inversely with—female infant mortality), the greater the newspaper support for the intervention of "society" (individuals, organizations, NGOs, USAID, or the United Nations, and definitely not government) to address water access and contaminated water challenges. This finding suggests that, for the issue of water handling/water contamination, governments can generally not be trusted to mirror the interests of families without ready access to potable water, and that "society," in particular NGOs, are more trustworthy sources of credible advocacy. This finding from cross-national coverage of newspaper coverage mirrors many practices of United Nations and USAID assistance to developing countries, substantially bypassing governments to ensure that money reaches its intended destinations and purposes.
- This study is one of the first to link variations in female empowerment with significant variations in coverage of water handling, a major issue of interest to families everywhere (and to women everywhere because they often spend considerable time hauling water rather than attending school).

4. *Right to freedom from harsh, inhumane working conditions.* "Comparing Coverage of Child Labor and National Characteristics: A Cross-National Exploration," by Jordan Gauthier Kohn and John C. Pollock, with assistance from Christiana Nielsen and Dasia Stewart.

- The higher the level of broadband penetration (38% of the variance), and the higher the proportion of a nation's population younger than age 14 (10% of the variance), the more likely newspapers support "society" as opposed to "domestic government" efforts to address child labor issues (a total of 48% of the variance).
- Specifically, higher levels of broadband penetration (which may correspond with percentage engaged in manufacturing and a wide range of indicators of business activity), the more newspapers support "nongovernmental" efforts to deal with child labor. These findings are similar to those found in a study of cross-national coverage of "water handling" (this issue).

- In addition, the higher the level of female empowerment in a country (measured by such indicators as female school life expectancy, female life expectancy, and—inversely with—female infant mortality), the greater the newspaper support for the intervention of "society" (individuals, organizations, NGOs) and definitely not government to address child labor challenges. This finding suggests that, for the issue of child labor abuse, governments can generally not be trusted to mirror the interests of abused children and that "society," in particular NGOs, are more trustworthy sources of credible advocacy.

Multicity U.S. Coverage of Human Rights Claims

The four U.S. nationwide multicity studies included in the collection include ones on same-sex/gay marriage, detainee rights at Guantanamo, immigration reform, and PTS.

1. *Right to marry the person you love.* "Nationwide Newspaper Coverage of Same-Sex Marriage: A Community Structure Approach," by Victoria Vales, John C. Pollock, Victoria Scarfone, Carly Koziol, Amy Wilson, and Patrick Flanagan.

- The higher a city's score on an (original) "Gay Market Index" (measuring the number of businesses and organizations and services marketing to the LGBT community, an index developed and refined over many years by researchers at The College of New Jersey [TCNJ]), the more favorable the coverage of same-sex marriage. A varimax rotated factor analysis and subsequent regression analysis of factors against Media Vectors yielded two factor-variables accounting for more than 29% of the variance: privilege (family income of $100,000+)/gay marketing (Gay Market Index high score)/political identity (percentage voting Democratic), 24% (associated with support for same-sex marriage); and Evangelicals, 5% (associated with opposition).
- Metropolitan papers are clearly capable of "mirroring" stakeholders, in this case gays, in their metropolitan areas with remarkable precision. The Gay Market Index, an original construct developed at TCNJ, is revealed as an excellent indicator of sympathetic media coverage. The association of "privilege" with media support for gay rights reinforces previous findings confirming a "buffer" hypothesis: The larger the percentage privileged (or "buffered" from uncertainty) in a community (college education, family income, or professional occupational status), the more favorable the coverage of human rights claims. The association between voting Democratic and support for gay rights is, of course, expected. Among the many fascinating findings in this research project is that the region with the least support for gay marriage in a similar nationwide newspaper study a few years ago is now clearly the region with the greatest media support for gay marriage: the South!

2. *Right to due process.* "Nationwide Newspaper Coverage of Detainee Rights at Guantanamo Bay: A Community Structure Approach," by Kelsey Zinck, Maggie Rogers, John C. Pollock, and Matthew Salvatore.

- The higher the percentage of Mainline Protestants, and the higher the percentage of privileged (college educated), the more favorable the metropolitan coverage of detainee rights. A regression analysis confirmed a similar finding, Mainline Protestants (33% of the variance) and another measure of privilege, percentage with professional/technical occupational status (27% of the variance), both associated with more favorable coverage of detainee rights, together account for 59.9% of the variance. The association between college education or professional/technical occupational status, both indicators of "privilege," and support for detainee rights is expected, confirming the "buffer" hypothesis also found in the study of gay marriage. The Mainline Protestant finding, consistent with finding that higher percentages of Mainline Protestants are linked with favorable coverage of the "Occupy" protest movement (Pollock, 2013b), is an unusual, recent pattern, suggesting that belief systems may be associated with significant "rights" issues in modern community structure research. The significance of "belief system" is a fascinating finding, worthy of continuing study; in effect, a "breakthrough" in community structure studies. It suggests that protecting due process and prisoner rights, even those incarcerated at Guantanamo, is a "mainstream" issue.

- Another regional pattern is striking: The Midwest displays far greater support for detainee rights than does any other region, consistent with prominent regional support for the "Occupy" movement (Pollock, 2013b) and contrary to most previous studies manifesting the most "progressive" coverage of rights claims in the Northeast and Western newspapers, consistent with traditional voting patterns. Traditional regional reporting patterns may be in flux.

3. *Right to live in "freedom from fear" or to pursue a path to citizenship.* "Nationwide Newspaper Coverage of Immigration Reform: A Community Structure Approach," by John C. Pollock, Stefanie Gratale, Kevin Teta, Kyle Bauer, and Elyse Hoekstra.

- The "vulnerability" hypothesis, suggesting that media are capable of "mirroring" the interests of the most marginal or disadvantaged (Pollock, 2007, pp. 137–156), was essentially confirmed. The higher the percentage below the poverty line and the higher the crime rate, the more favorable the coverage of immigration reform. By contrast, the higher percentage of females in the workforce and the higher proportion of hate crimes, the less favorable coverage of immigration reform.
- Regression analysis revealed that the most powerful variable, accounting for 37.2% of the variance, was percentage living below the poverty line, further confirming the vulnerability hypothesis. Another compelling finding: the Midwest had the most favorable coverage of immigration reform, more than any other region in the United States, consistent with recent community structure studies on nationwide U.S. coverage of detainee rights at Guantanamo (Zinck, Rogers, Pollock, & Salvatore, this issue), and of the Occupy Wall Street movement (Pollock, 2013b, pp. 1–30).

4. *Right to mental health care.* "Nationwide Newspaper Coverage of Posttraumatic Stress: A Community Structure Approach," by John C. Pollock, Stefanie Gratale, Angelica Anas, Emaleigh Kaithern, and Kelly Johnson.

- Media Vectors revealed that 25 of the 26 newspapers studied in major metropolitan areas (96%) supported governmental responsibility for treatment of PTS in veterans. Curiously, however, Pearson correlations yielded nine significant findings, with all but one linked to "opposition" to government responsibility for treatment of PTS! All hypotheses under the buffer hypotheses (linking privilege with support for government responsibility) were disconfirmed. The greater the percentage of those with professional/technical occupational status, the greater the percentage of families with incomes of $100,000 or more, and the greater the percentage of college educated in a city, the *less* media support for government responsibility for PTS, revealing a "violated buffer" pattern. With a "violated buffer" pattern, coverage reflects a threat to a belief system or a cherished way of life (Pollock, 2007, pp. 101–136). The only confirmed hypothesis was that the greater the percentage age 65 and older in a city, the more coverage emphasized government responsibility for veterans' PTS treatment. This unusual finding may be due to an older generation living through the draft for the Vietnam War in the 1960s and early 1970s, a period when almost every family had a "stake" in the welfare of veterans.

- Regression analysis revealed that three variables had the most effect on the direction of coverage of PTS: Family Income $100K+ (26.4% of the variance), Hispanic (8%), and Professional/Technical Occupational status (5%), altogether accounting for 39.3% of the variance. All three of these variables were linked with newspaper coverage opposed to governmental responsibility for treatment of PTS. A regional finding was especially noteworthy: Coverage in the Midwest supported governmental responsibility more than in any other region, consistent with other recent studies of coverage of detainee rights and of immigration reform, both found in this collection, and of the Occupy Wall Street movement (Pollock, 2013b, pp. 1–30).

SIGNIFICANT OVERALL PATTERNS

The following patterns summarize some of the most important findings shared by the studies within each category: cross-national and U.S. nationwide/multicity.

Cross-National Coverage of Human Rights

A few key variables carry considerable weight in their association with variations in coverage of human rights issues. The cross-national studies revealed the recurring importance of a few key variables: Broadband penetration, GDP/capita, percentage foreign investment, and a composite of several indicators, female empowerment (in particular, female school life expectancy). In particular, "female empowerment" was the single concept found significant in all four cross national studies of coverage of human trafficking, HIV/AIDS, water handling, and child labor. The implication is that media can reach beyond the interests of the most powerful and beyond the "routines" of professional journalism to reflect the interests of vulnerable populations, in particular specific issue "stakeholders."

Women were stakeholders for all four issues. The interest of women in human trafficking is obvious. For water handling and water contamination, women do most of the work to find and bring potable water to their homes in developing countries, an effort so time consuming that it often prevents them from attending school. For HIV/AIDS, women are clear stakeholders because of the disparity in power, authority, and basic rights between the genders in many societies and nation-states, as well as the greater prevalence of HIV/AIDS worldwide among women compared to men. As one report noted, "In many ways, the inequity that women and girls suffer as a result of HIV/AIDS serves as a barometer of their general status in society and the discrimination they encounter in all fields, including health, education and employment" (Matlin & Spence, 2000, p. 1).

For child labor, because female children are far less likely to attend school than male children, female children are disproportionately likely to be employed as child laborers in developing countries. The capacity of media to represent the interests of these women/female stakeholders across all four issues studied is an astonishing finding.

In addition to female empowerment, broader indicators of both "vulnerability" and "privilege" were also found associated with cross-national coverage emphasizing government responsibility for several issues: For "vulnerability, the issues were HIV/AIDS, water handling, and child labor. Percentage of the population undernourished was linked to coverage extolling government responsibility for addressing HIV/AIDS. Similarly, a composite vulnerability scale—consisting of deaths due to diarrheal diseases, percentage without access to improved water services, infant mortality rate, and fertility rate indicators—was connected strongly to coverage emphasizing government responsibility for addressing water handling/contamination. Consistently, both infant mortality rate and percentage of the population younger than 14 years old were both associated strongly with coverage emphasizing government responsibility for child labor. Media are capable of mirroring the interests of a nation's most vulnerable populations.

Similarly, broad indicators of "privilege" were also linked to media support for government responsibility to address several issues (human trafficking, HIV/AIDS, and child labor), confirming what the community structure tradition calls a "violated buffer" pattern: privilege associated with empathic coverage of human rights claims. In addition to female school life expectancy, stock of direct foreign investment at home and GDP per capita all correlated significantly with media coverage emphasizing government responsibility to stop human trafficking. Percentage of women or men who know that consistent condom use prevents HIV/AIDS and percentage of females in the workforce were all associated strongly with media emphasis on government support for those with HIV/AIDS. A measure of "resource access," a nation's industrial production growth rate, was associated with more media support for government responsibility for child labor, as was broadband access.

Indeed, broadband subscriptions/100 people may be a "bell weather" indicator, perhaps a manifestation of a "consensus" on particular issues. For coverage of human trafficking, broadband penetration correlates positively with support for government responsibility, the main thrust of other significant variables. For coverage of child labor, broadband penetration is linked to the reverse: support for "society" responsibility for the issue, again mirroring the main thrust of other significant variables. Possible reasons for that variation, associated in one case study with support for government responsibility (human trafficking), in another with support for societal responsibility (child labor), deserve further exploration.

"Societal responsibility" as a concept and source of responsibility for social and policy issues deserves more thorough exploration. Under what conditions or levels of development do media turn to "societal" responsibility for help? Are there "thresholds" or "pre-conditions" for media to regard "societal responsibility" as a viable repository of responsibility for human rights issues? Specifically, how much evidence for a "civic society" or "civic culture" must exist for media to consider that area of human endeavor a reasonable locus of help for rights claims?

These and similar questions will help scholars "unpack" the concept of "societal responsibility" to assist researchers and policymakers understand the conditions in which "society" can play a constructive role in addressing emerging human rights concerns.

U.S. Nationwide Multi-City Coverage of Human Rights

Regional differences are important, and traditional regional identities may be shifting. The Midwest manifests the greatest media support for detainee rights at Guantanamo and immigration reform and for government responsibility for helping those suffering from PTS. In an astonishing finding, one of the most traditional regions of the United States, the South, manifests greater newspaper support for same-sex marriage than do papers from any other region.

Privilege is associated with support for human rights claims, sometimes called the "buffer" hypothesis. It expects that metropolitan areas with higher percentages "buffered" from economic uncertainty (whether through benefit of college education, high family income, or professional/ technical occupational status) are likely to manifest favorable coverage of human rights claims. The buffer hypothesis is indeed confirmed for all three measures of privilege, and in particular, using a factor analysis, for family income of $100,000 or more in its association with favorable coverage of same-sex marriage. Another buffer indicator, professional/technical occupational status, is strongly associated with support for detainee rights at Guantanamo.

The "vulnerability" hypothesis was also confirmed for several U.S. case studies, confirming the capacity of media to mirror the interests of the most vulnerable or marginal social groups. The higher the percentage below the poverty level, or the higher the crime rate, the more favorable the nationwide coverage of immigration reform. An original "Gay Market Index," using the Gayellow Pages to measure number of organizations marketing to the LGBT community in major metropolitan areas, was confirmed as strongly associated with support for gay rights, in this case, same-sex marriage. Previous research (Pollock, 2007, pp. 231–248) confirmed a similar association between high scores on the Gay Market Index and media support for gay membership in the Boy Scouts of America.

The belief system category "Mainline Protestant" in its association with support for detainee rights (reprising a previous finding about its link to media support for the Occupy Wall Street movement in Pollock, 2013b, pp. 1–30) deserves further investigation. Over more than 16 previous years of community structure research, prior to 2011, the year the "Occupy" movement first appeared, percentage of Mainline Protestant had not been found associated with any variations in coverage of critical public issues. The emergence of this variable after the economic crisis of 2008, and in particular with support for the Occupy movement, suggests less about membership in a particular older form of Protestant worship than about a deeply held value perspective, articulated by Max Weber in *The Protestant Ethic and the Spirit of Capitalism*.

In that classic work, Weber noted the extraordinary optimism and confidence of the pilgrims who made their way to North America, bringing little with them and flourishing in the face of overwhelming obstacles. Perhaps that older, historic belief that individuals can prevail against overwhelming obstacles (such as predatory lenders, banks too big to fail, and governments relatively insensitive to the employment difficulties of so many) finds resonance with both the obvious protests of the Occupy movement against the big banks of Wall Street and the unwillingness of the U.S. government to grant prisoners held in U.S.-controlled prisons the basic legal rights most Americans believe every prisoner in our legal system deserves to be accorded.

CONCLUSION

Viewed collectively, the case studies reveal relationships between national or city characteristics and coverage variation that confirm four umbrella patterns and raise fascinating questions for ongoing research. The umbrella patterns include the following:

1. Privilege can be associated with responsive coverage of human rights claims, whether through privilege linked to a "buffer" pattern, with privileged groups linked to "positive" coverage of a claim (e.g., immigration reform) or a "violated buffer" pattern, with privileged groups associated with fearful or "negative" coverage of a circumstance (e.g., human trafficking, HIV/AIDS), reinforcing rights claims.
2. Vulnerability can also be connected to responsive coverage of human rights claims, evident especially in coverage of those with HIV/AIDS, water handling, and child labor in cross-national studies, and for immigration reform and same-sex marriage in U.S. multicity studies.
3. Female empowerment is associated strongly with cross-national coverage of a wide range of rights claims regarding several issues, including human trafficking, HIV/AIDS, water handling, and child labor.
4. Regional identities may change. The Midwest, often viewed in recent decades, through newspaper coverage and public opinion polls, as manifesting less progressive policy perspectives than either Northeastern or Western regions, has emerged as capable of yielding supportive news coverage at the forefront of issues such as detainee rights at Guantanamo, immigration reform, and PTS.

Patterns apart, the eight case studies in this collection pose fascinating questions as well. What are the catalysts for putting human rights on the public agenda and into the media's "sights"? When human rights emerge on the public agenda, what are the principal drivers: demographics (in the absence of city-level or national-level surveys, sometimes a proxy for public opinion), political and social leaders, or editors/journalists themselves? Why do some human rights issues emerge more quickly than others onto media agendas at the city or national level? Are there "thresholds" or "tipping points" that help determine whether the prevalence of some human rights issues makes them more likely than others to gain access to media attention?

For example, is it easier for those suffering from mental health disorders to acquire media coverage if they engage in some kind of antisocial or violent activity? Similarly, is it easier for those who live with HIV/AIDS than those who suffer from contaminated water to gain access to media agendas, even though more people die each year from contaminated water than from HIV/AIDS? More broadly, what is the "mechanism" that transforms national or city-level characteristics into coverage reflecting those characteristics? What are the most likely explanatory pathways for scholars to pursue? Several demographic "reflecting" patterns are clear, but how and why do media function as the "tilted mirrors" they appear to resemble? These questions continue to arouse the curiosity of scholars and policy analysts alike.

These and similar questions deserve the attention of scholars, policymakers, and human rights activists. By exploring connections between city or national demographics and variations in human rights coverage, the community structure approach adds value to the effort to understand how emerging human rights issues gain access to national and metropolitan public agendas.

ACKNOWLEDGMENTS

I express deep appreciation to the other contributors to this collection of articles on "Illuminating Human Rights: How Demographics Drive Media Coverage." All are either current students or alumni of the Department of Communication Studies at The College of New Jersey. Without the dedication of these students and former students, none of the articles in this collection would have been possible. In addition, I wish to express warm appreciation for the "Preface" written by internationally renown human rights expert Dr. Morton Winston, and for substantial editorial assistance and expert coauthorship on several articles by Stefanie Gratale, a graduate of the communication studies program at The College of New Jersey, who earned a master of public affairs from George Washington University.

Finally, I wish to acknowledge the invaluable help of three scholars who reviewed the articles in this collection, providing excellent advice for revision: Dr. Michael McCluskey of American University, Dr. Seungahn Nah of the University of Kentucky, and Dr. Masahiro Yamamoto of the University of Wisconsin–LaCrosse.

REFERENCES

Borer, T. A. (Ed.). (2012). *Media, mobilization, and human rights: Mediating suffering*. New York, NY: Zed Books.

Caliendo, S. M., Gibney, M. P., & Payne, A. (1999). All the news that's fit to print? "New York Times" coverage of human-rights violations. *Harvard International Journal of Press Politics, 4*, 48–69.

Demers, D., & Viswanath, K., (Eds.). (1999). *Mass media, social control, and social change: A macrosocial perspective*. Ames, IA: Iowa State University Press.

Donohue, G. A., Tichenor, P. J., & Olien, C. N. (1995). A guard dog perspective on the role of media. *Journal of Communication, 45*, 115–132.

Hindman, D. B. (1999). Social control, social change and local mass media. In D. Demers & K. Viswanath (Eds.), *Mass media, social control, and social change: A macrosocial perspective* (pp. 99–116). Ames, IA: Iowa State University Press.

Linfield, S. (2014, January 29). Advertising torture. *The New York Times*, p. A23.

Matlin, S., & Spence, N. (2000, November). *The gender aspects of the HIV/AIDS pandemic.* Paper presented at the Expert Group Meeting on "The HIV/AIDS Pandemic and its Gender Implications," Division for the Advancement of Women (DAW)/World Health Organization (WHO)/Joint United Nations Programme on HIV/AIDS (UNAIDS), Windhoek, Namibia.

McLeod, D. M., & Hertog, J. K. (1999). Social control, social change, and the mass media's role in the regulation of protest groups. In D. Demers & K. Viswanath (Eds.), *Mass media, social control, and social change: A macrosocial perspective* (pp. 305–331). Ames, IA: Iowa State University Press.

Nah, S., & Armstrong, C. (2011). Structural pluralism in journalism and media studies: A concept explication and theory construction. *Mass Communication and Society, 14*, 857–878.

Olien, C. N., Donohue, G. A., & Tichenor, P. J. (1995). Conflict, consensus and public opinion. In T. L. Glaser & C. T. Salmon (Eds.), *Public opinion and the communication of consent* (pp. 301–322). New York, NY: Guilford.

Park, R. (1922). *The immigrant press and its control.* New York, NY: Harper.

Pollock, J. C. (2007). *Tilted mirrors: Media alignment with political and social change—A community structure approach.* Cresskill, NJ: Hampton Press.

Pollock, J. C. (2008). Community structure model. In W. Donsbach (Ed.), *International encyclopedia of communication* (pp. 870–873). London, UK: Blackwell.

Pollock, J. C. (2013a). Community structure research. In P. Moy (Ed.), *Oxford Bibliographies Online.* New York, NY: Oxford University Press.

Pollock, J. C. (Ed.). (2013b). *Media and social inequality: Innovations in community structure research* (pp. 1–30). New York, NY: Routledge.

Pollock, J. C., & Yulis, S. (2004). Nationwide newspaper coverage of physician-assisted suicide: A community structure approach. *Journal of Health Communication, 9*, 281–307.

Schudson, M. (2014). Linking media sociology to political development in trans-legislative democracies. In S. Waisbord (Ed.), *Media sociology. A reappraisal* (pp. 46–62). Cambridge, UK: Polity Press.

Shoemaker, P. J., & Reese, S. D. (2013). *Mediating the message in the 21st century: A media sociology perspective.* New York, NY: Routledge.

Tichenor, P. J., Donohue, G., & Olien, C. (1973). Mass communication research: Evolution of a structural model. *Journalism Quarterly 50*, 419–425.

Tichenor, P. J., Donohue, G., & Olien, C. (1980). *Community conflict and the press.* Beverly Hills, CA: Sage.

Waisbord, S. (Ed.). (2014). *Media sociology: A reappraisal.* Cambridge, UK: Polity Press.

Weber, M. (2010). *The Protestant ethic and the spirit of capitalism.* New York, NY: CreateSpace.

Winston, M. E. (2001). Assessing the effectiveness of human rights NGOs: Amnesty International. In C. E. Welch, Jr. (Ed.), *NGOs and human rights: Promise and performance* (pp. 25–54). Philadelphia, PA: University of Pennsylvania Press.

Yamamoto, M., & Ran, W. (2013). Drug abuse violations in communities: Community newspapers as a macro-level source of social control. *Journalism & Mass Communication Quarterly, 90*, 629–651.

Part I

Cross-National Coverage of Human Rights

Cross-National Coverage of Human Trafficking: A Community Structure Approach

Kelly Alexandre, Cynthia Sha, John C. Pollock, Kelsey Baier, and
Jessica Johnson
Department of Communication Studies
The College of New Jersey

A community structure analysis compared cross-national coverage of human trafficking in 250+ word articles in newspapers in 18 countries for a 12-year period: July 27, 2000 to July 27, 2012. The resulting 266 articles were coded for "prominence" and "direction" ("government responsibility," "society responsibility," or "balanced/neutral"), then combined into a composite "Media Vector" score for each newspaper (range = .5167 to −.0214). Seventeen of 18 Media Vectors reflected media emphasis on government responsibility to end human trafficking. Pearson correlations identified that two characteristic clusters had significant relationships with media coverage: privilege (the "buffer" hypothesis associates higher levels of privilege with coverage emphasizing government action to reduce human trafficking) and stakeholders (associating larger proportions of groups with a stake in human trafficking with coverage emphasizing government action to reduce it). Pearson correlations revealed that female school life expectancy ($r = .478, p = .022$), stock of direct foreign investment at home ($r = .467, p = .026$), broadband subscriptions/100 people ($r = −.41, p = .045$), and gross domestic product per capita ($r = .467, p = .025$) all correlated significantly with media coverage of human trafficking. Regression analysis reinforced the role of stakeholders, with stock of direct foreign investment and female school life expectancy significant. Foreign influence and female empowerment matter.

INTRODUCTION

Human sex trafficking is a horrific social problem both domestically and abroad, with estimates of victims in the millions. The Federal Bureau of Investigation has documented the issue as the fastest growing business of organized crime and third-largest criminal enterprise in the world

(Hill & Walker-Rodriguez, 2011). The United Nations Office on Drugs and Crime (2012) defines trafficking as the

> recruitment, transportation, transfer, harboring, or receipt of persons through threat or use of force, coercion, abduction, fraud, deception, abuse or power or vulnerability, or giving payments of benefits to a person in control of the victim for the purpose of exploitation, which includes exploiting the prostitution of others, sexual exploitation, forced labour, slavery or similar practices and the removal of organs. (United Nations Convention against Transnational Organized Crime, 2003)[1]

Although many victims are women and children, men also fall victim to trafficking. Due to the grievous nature and growing prevalence of this problem, this study seeks to explore media coverage of the issue and identify any links between national characteristics and media coverage of human trafficking.

The way that media frame a social issue can influence how the public views that issue and believes the problem should be addressed. In terms of media coverage of human trafficking, two frames are analyzed to determine which is most prominent in newspapers. The government responsibility frame suggests that it is the responsibility of governments to impose harsh punishments on the perpetrators of trafficking in order to end human trafficking. In contrast, the societal responsibility frame suggests that society or nongovernmental groups should be responsible for ending human trafficking and recommends that private organizations increase awareness of the problem and offer support to victims.

This study focuses specifically on cross-national newspaper coverage of human trafficking. It utilizes the community structure approach in its investigation of media coverage, examining how society impacts reporting on human trafficking, by considering two research questions:

RQ1: How much variation is there in cross-national coverage of human trafficking?
RQ2: How closely linked is variation in cross-national coverage of human trafficking with the characteristics of different nations?

To address these research questions, several hypotheses regarding national demographics and media coverage of human trafficking are tested.

LITERATURE REVIEW

Human trafficking has received little scholarly attention in the field of communication studies. Scholarly research is especially scant regarding media coverage of the issue, which should be particularly relevant to the field. Yet trafficking has been explored in greater depth by other fields, such as women and gender studies, sociology, and history.

---

[1] In its resolution 55/25 of November 15, 2000, the General Assembly adopted the United Nations Convention against Transnational Organized Crime and one of its supplementary Protocols, namely: the Protocol to Prevent, Suppress and Punish Trafficking in Persons, Especially Women and Children. It entered into force on December 25, 2003. It is the first global legally binding instrument with an agreed definition on trafficking in persons. The intention behind this definition is to facilitate convergence in national approaches with regard to the establishment of domestic criminal offenses that would support efficient international cooperation in investigating and prosecuting trafficking in persons cases. An additional objective of the Protocol is to protect and assist the victims of trafficking in persons with full respect for their human rights.

Multiple searches of the communications studies databases yielded relatively few results. Searching "trafficking" AND "human" in the Communication and Mass Media database returned 44 results, but searching "trafficking" AND "women" in the same database returned only one. Using the terms "trafficking" AND "media" produced just 23 results. In the ComAbstracts, searches using "human" AND "trafficking," and then "trafficking" AND "women" produced just one article, whereas "trafficking" AND "media" yielded no results. This paucity of citations is especially telling for the communication field because of the recent attention the subject has received from President Obama, who in 2012 declared January "National Human Trafficking Awareness Month" in an effort to raise awareness of the problem (Jesionka, 2012).

One communication studies article examined the world of international web-based marriage agencies, arguing that governments facilitate trafficking of young women and children from economically poor areas to advanced economies and profit in the process (Jones, 2011). Another article discussed the role of journalists in mobilizing global action, citing a panel discussion of the United Nations and 2008 Vienna Forum to Fight Human Trafficking, which focused on media's role and how it could help advance attention to the issue (Ricchiardi, 2010). In addition, another article documented a photojournalist on a journey to cover human trafficking by conveying South African victims' stories through the use of visuals, rather than through text, to elicit a stronger reaction from the public (Hamman, 2010). Although some of these studies touched on media and human trafficking, little systematic scholarly analysis was undertaken on media coverage of the issue.

In contrast to the scarcity of articles on human trafficking in communication studies, searching "human" AND "trafficking" and "trafficking" AND "women" in the sociological JSTOR database returned 442 results, including studies discussing such issues as lack of government intervention regarding trafficking and financial hardships contributing to women's embroilment in forced prostitution (Stone & Vandenberg, 1999). Similarly, in the gender studies field, the search terms "human" AND "trafficking" produced 560 articles in the GenderWatch database, exploring topics like recent laws passed to combat trafficking and the prevalence of trafficking internationally (Bangladesh, 2012). In the history field, the combination of "human" AND "trafficking" AND "women" in the ProQuest database produced an overwhelming 6,000 articles, discussing such topics as domestic trafficking in Africa (Okojie, 2009). Furthermore, the combination of "human" AND "trafficking" AND "children" in ProQuest produced roughly 1,000 articles, which discussed the relationship between poverty and trafficking of children (Kessler, 2007), the expansions of the legal definition of trafficking in the United States (106th Congress, 2000), and other relevant subjects.

The sociology, women and gender studies, and history disciplines have all produced a vast amount of research regarding the topic of human trafficking. Yet the same cannot be said about the communication studies field, as communications scholars have given little attention to the topic of human trafficking, particularly as it relates to media coverage. This article attempts to address this imbalance by exploring links between variations in national characteristics and differences in cross-national newspaper coverage of human trafficking.

HYPOTHESES

Utilizing the community structure approach, researchers tested individual hypotheses that can be grouped into three categories: buffer, vulnerability, and stakeholder. Each of these categories represents an important demographic dimension in human trafficking.

Privilege: The "Buffer Hypothesis"

The buffer hypothesis expects that in communities with a high level of privilege, media coverage of human rights issues will be more favorable, due to the privileged being "buffered" from economic and occupational uncertainty, and therefore likely displaying sympathy for those who are not (Pollock, 2007, p. 62). In cross-national research, privilege is often defined as high gross domestic product (GDP)/GDP per capita, literacy rate, and life expectancy. The buffer hypothesis has been supported by research from previous cross-national studies. Gratale et al. (2005) examined cross-national newspaper coverage of the United Nation's effort to combat AIDS, finding that the higher the level of GDP in a nation, the more favorable the coverage was of UN efforts to fight AIDS. Another study focused on cross national newspaper coverage of NGO efforts and discovered a positive correlation between higher GDP in a nation and more favorable coverage of non-governmental organization's efforts to fight AIDS (Eisenberg, Kester, Caputo, Sierra, & Pollock, 2006). Consistently, preliminary previous research on coverage across 13 countries reveals that the higher the proportion of privileged groups in a nation (higher GDP/capita, lower infant mortality rate), the greater the media emphasis on government action to reduce human trafficking (Pollock & Koerner, 2010). Thus, the following is predicted:

H1: The higher a nation's GDP, the more coverage emphasizes government responsibility to end human trafficking (Central Intelligence Agency [CIA], 2011).

H2: The higher a nation's GDP per capita, the more coverage emphasizes government responsibility to end human trafficking (CIA, 2011).

H3: The higher a nation's literacy rate, the more coverage emphasizes government responsibility to end human trafficking (CIA, 2011).

H4: The higher a nation's male life expectancy at birth, the more coverage emphasizes government responsibility to end human trafficking (CIA, 2011).

H5: The higher a nation's female life expectancy at birth, the more coverage emphasizes government responsibility to end human trafficking (CIA, 2011).

Health care access.   Another indicator of privilege in a country is the availability of health care. Like other measures of privilege, health care access has also been tied to favorable coverage of human rights claims. A study by Pollock (2007, pp. 89–100) revealed a positive correlation between the number of physicians per 100,000 people in a city and favorable coverage of expanding stem cell research, as well as favorable coverage pertaining to physician-assisted suicide (Pollock, 2007, pp. 75–88). Similarly, cross-national studies discovered that the greater the number of hospital beds or physicians per 100,000 inhabitants, the greater media support for government involvement in reducing human trafficking (Pollock & Koerner, 2010) and in addressing climate change (Pollock, Reda, Bosland, Hindi, & Zhu, 2010). Therefore, the following can be expected:

H6: The greater the number of physicians/100,000 in a country, the more coverage emphasizes government action against human trafficking (United Nations Statistics Division,
2011).

H7: The greater the number of hospital beds per 100,000 in a country, the more coverage emphasizes government responsibility to end human trafficking (United Nations
Statistics Division, 2011).

Vulnerability Hypothesis

The vulnerability hypothesis expects that in more "vulnerable" areas, newspapers devote more
attention to "vulnerable" populations such as the poor, unemployed, minority groups, and people
in high crime areas. The higher percentage of people below the poverty level in a city, the more
likely newspaper coverage will be directed toward the "vulnerable group's concerns" (Pollock,
2007, p. 137). The vulnerability hypothesis opposes the "guard dog" hypothesis articulated by
Olien, Donohue, and Tichenor (1995), claiming that media representations generally favor or
reinforce the interests of elite groups (Pollock, 2007, p. 24).

Several previous community structure approach studies have reinforced the vulnerability
hypothesis. For example, higher levels of poverty in a city correlated with more favorable
coverage of legalization of abortion at the time of the *Roe v. Wade* decision (Pollock &
Robinson, 1977; Pollock, Robinson, & Murray, 1978, p. 137). Another study found that the
"higher the poverty or unemployment levels in a city, the less inflammatory or ethnocentric"
the coverage of major conflicts between Caribbean American and Hasidic Jews in Brooklyn,
New York in 1978 (Pollock & Whitney, 1997, p. 138), and the "greater the media support for
genetically-modified food" (Pollock, Maltese-Nehrbass, Corbin, & Fascanella, 2010, pp. 51–
75). Curiously, another study also found that the higher the homicide rate, the more favorable
the coverage of same-sex marriage (Pollock, Davies, Effingham, & Heisler, 2012). Furthermore,
in another study, communities with higher proportions below the poverty level manifested less
favorable coverage of capital punishment and more favorable coverage of legislation supporting
a Patients' Bill of Rights (Pollock, 2007, pp. 137–156). Clearly, in many cases, media coverage
of vulnerable communities can reflect favorable coverage of vulnerable groups' own concerns.

The findings of the prior domestic studies might suggest that media in areas with more
vulnerable populations would emphasize government action against human trafficking, but
initial hypotheses regarding this issue are framed in the opposite direction. The very sensitive
nature of this cross-national issue could affect coverage in a manner inconsistent with the
vulnerability hypothesis. Specifically, countries with higher prevalence of human trafficking
and greater proportions of vulnerable groups may have governments that do not strongly defend
the interests and rights of such groups, nor may they be likely to respect media rights. As a
result, media in such nations may have less faith and trust in their government to respect media
or to take necessary action to combat trafficking. Consequently, media support of human rights
claims could actually manifest itself in an emphasis on societal responsibility. Therefore, the
following is predicted:

H8: The greater the percent living below the poverty line, the less coverage emphasizes
government responsibility to end human trafficking (United Nations Statistics Division, 2011).

H9: The higher the infant mortality rate, the less coverage emphasizes government responsibility to end human trafficking (United Nations Statistics Division, 2011).

H10: The higher a nation's fertility rate, the less coverage emphasizes government responsibility to end human trafficking (United Nations Statistics Division, 2011).

H11: The greater the thefts/100,000, the less coverage emphasizes government responsibility to end human trafficking (The Financial Times World, 2004).

H12: The higher the mortality rate, the less coverage emphasizes government responsibility to end human trafficking (United Nations Statistics Division, 2011).

H13: The greater percentage of a nation's population that is undernourished, the less coverage emphasizes government responsibility to end human trafficking (United Nations Statistics Division, 2011).

H14: The higher a nation's Gini inequality index, the less coverage emphasizes government responsibility to end human trafficking (CIA, 2011).

H15: The greater percentage of a nation's population without access to improved water services, the less coverage emphasizes government responsibility to end human trafficking (United Nations Development Programme, 2010).

H16: The greater number of deaths due to diarrheal diseases per 100,000 in a nation, the less coverage emphasizes government responsibility to end human trafficking (CIA, 2011).

H17: The greater the number of cases of cholera per 100,000 in a nation, the less coverage emphasizes government responsibility to end human trafficking (CIA, 2011).

H18: The higher the percentage of the population younger than 20, the less coverage emphasizes government responsibility to end human trafficking (United Nations Statistics Division, 2011).

Stakeholder Hypothesis

The stakeholder hypothesis states that the larger the presence of citizens with a stake in an issue, the more favorable the coverage of claims affecting those stakeholders (Pollock, 2007, p. 172). Consistently, McLeod and Hertog (1999) confirmed that larger protest groups gain more attention and favorable coverage than smaller groups. The stakeholder categories investigated in this study are female empowerment, energy production and consumption, communication penetration and press freedom, and stock of direct foreign investment at home.

Female empowerment. An important aspect of human trafficking coverage is reporting associated with gender, particularly females. Workforce presence typically indicates economic influence in family matters and is one index of the relative economic influence and authority of women in a community (Pollock, 2007, p. 69). A community structure study confirmed a link between percentage of women in the workforce and relatively favorable newspaper coverage of human cloning (Pollock, Dudzak, Richards, Norton, & Miller, 2000). Another study on the Beijing conference's efforts to promote women's rights suggested that one measure of women's strength is stakeholder female life expectancy. The study found that the higher the percentage of female life expectancy at birth, the more favorable the coverage of women's rights (Hammer, Mitchell, Shields, & Pollock, 2006, p. 29). Because human trafficking is a women's rights issue, it is reasonable to expect that the higher the proportion of empowered female stakeholders in a country, the more coverage will emphasize government responsibility to end human trafficking. Thus, the following hypotheses are predicted:

H19: The higher the percentage of working women in a nation, the more coverage emphasizes government responsibility to end human trafficking (United Nations Statistics Division, 2011).

H20: The higher the female literacy rate, the more coverage emphasizes government responsibility to end human trafficking (United Nations Statistics Division, 2011).

H21: The higher the abortion rate, the more coverage emphasizes government responsibility to end human trafficking (United Nations Statistics Division, 2011).

H22: The higher the years of female school life expectancy, the more coverage emphasizes government responsibility to end human trafficking (CIA, 2011).

H23: The higher a nation's percentage of females who are satisfied with their freedom of choice, the more coverage emphasizes government responsibility to end human trafficking (United Nations Development Programme, 2010).

Energy production/consumption and infrastructure. Influential stakeholder groups include those who produce or consume large quantities of energy. Studies have shown an association between such stakeholder groups and media coverage supporting government efforts to address energy issues. Pollock, Reda, Bosland, Hindi, and Zhu (2010) found that the greater oil/natural gas production and natural gas consumption in a nation, the greater emphasis on government activity addressing climate change. Therefore, in areas that consume and produce more gas and oil, coverage may favor government intervention to end human trafficking. The following is expected:

H24: The higher a nation's natural gas consumption, the more coverage emphasizes government responsibility to end human trafficking (CIA, 2011).

H25: The higher a nation's natural gas production, the more coverage emphasizes government responsibility to end human trafficking (CIA, 2011).

H26: The higher a nation's oil consumption, the more coverage emphasizes government responsibility to end human trafficking (CIA, 2011).

H27: The higher a nation's oil production, the more coverage emphasizes government responsibility to end human trafficking (CIA, 2011).

Another case study, Wright et al. (2008), found that greater terawatt hours of electricity production was associated with less favorable coverage of Muslim immigration. Muslim immigration may not be perceived by some media as a human rights issue to the extent that human trafficking is considered a human rights issue. As a result, the following is expected:

H28: The higher a nation's electricity consumption, the more coverage emphasizes government responsibility to end human trafficking (CIA, 2011).

H29: The higher a nation's electricity production, the more coverage emphasizes government responsibility to end human trafficking (CIA, 2011).

H30: The higher a nation's coal consumption, the more coverage emphasizes government responsibility to end human trafficking (CIA, 2011).

H31: The higher a nation's coal production, the more coverage emphasizes government responsibility to end human trafficking (CIA, 2011).

It is important to consider a nation's infrastructure when analyzing the trafficking issue. Nations with stronger infrastructure, which facilitates resource production, likely display similar coverage as those with high energy production/consumption. Thus, the following is expected:

H32: The higher the total length of a nation's road network, the more coverage emphasizes government responsibility to end human trafficking (CIA, 2011).

H33: The higher a nation's industrial production growth rate, the more coverage emphasizes government responsibility to end human trafficking (CIA, 2011).

Communication penetration and press freedom. Freedom of expression is the concept that individuals may express themselves without fear of punishment, and in the United States, this right goes hand in hand with freedom of the press. Freedom of the press is an important issue affecting cross-national coverage. Pollock, D'Angelo, and colleagues (2010) showed the significance of press freedom, finding that the higher the level of press freedom in a nation, the greater the media support for government assistance to fight AIDS (see also D'Angelo, Pollock, Kiernicki, & Shaw, 2013). Freedom of the press thus correlates with coverage supporting human rights, so the following is predicted:

H34: The greater the number of daily newspapers per 1,000 people in a nation, the more coverage emphasizes government responsibility to end human trafficking (United Nations Development Programme, 2010).

H35: The greater the percentage of a population covered by a mobile phone network in a nation, the more coverage emphasizes government responsibility to end human trafficking (United Nations Development Programme, 2010).

H36: The greater the number of broadband subscriptions per 100 people in a nation, the more coverage emphasizes government responsibility to end human trafficking (United Nations Development Programme, 2010).

H37: The greater a nation's freedom of the press, the more coverage emphasizes government responsibility to end human trafficking (Freedom House, 2011).

Stock of direct foreign investment at home. Stock of direct foreign investment at home is the money value of all investments in the home country made directly by nonresidents, primarily companies of other countries. Many countries are economically interdependent and look to others for aid, so it is reasonable to assume that the greater a nation's stock of direct foreign investment at home, the more coverage will emphasize government responsibility regarding human rights claims. The following can be expected:

H38: The greater a nation's stock of direct investment at home, the more coverage emphasizes government responsibility to end human trafficking (CIA, 2011).

METHODOLOGY

To investigate the topic of human trafficking cross-nationally, a sample of 18 major newspapers in as many nation-states was selected from the NewsBank and AllAfrica databases. The researchers included all relevant articles of 250 words or more from the sample period, yielding 266 articles. The compilation of articles was taken from the following publications: the *Sydney Morning Herald*, the *Times*, the *New York Times, Turkish Daily News, This Day*, the *Times of India, El Universal, New Straits Times*, the *Namibian*, the *Daily Nation, El Mercurio, China Daily*, the *Herald, Accra Mail*, the *Japan Times*, the *Toronto Star, Times of Zambia*, and *Daily News Egypt*.

The sample ranged from July 27, 2000, to July 27, 2012, a 12-year period. On July 27, 2000, the United States Senate passed its first legislation to prevent international human trafficking. Before this law was enacted, minimal preventative measures existed to stop human trafficking overseas, to help victims rebuild their lives in the U.S. with federal and state support, or to prosecute traffickers under stiff federal penalties. This study focuses on the period after the Trafficking Victims Protection Act of 2000 was enacted until a period 12 years later.

Article Coding and Procedures

All articles were assigned two separate scores: prominence (representing editorial decisions about how significantly the article was positioned in the newspaper) and direction (the frame represented in the article: government responsibility, societal responsibility, or balanced/neutral). Articles were coded as "government responsibility" if human trafficking was portrayed as an international problem that needs to be confronted by domestic governments. An article from *China Daily* stated, "China plans to ratify a United Nations protocol on human trafficking as part of its ongoing fight against cross-border crime" ("China Set to Ratify," 2008, para. 1). Also, an article from the *Times of Zambia* about amendments regarding criminalizing human trafficking stated that the "government was working hard to ensure that the code was amended before the end of the year and that measures were being put in place to ensure that an Act of Parliament incorporated the protocol into Zambia's domestic laws" ("Criminalisation," 2005, para. 2). These articles were coded as "government responsibility" because they focused on the efforts of domestic governments to prevent human trafficking.

On the other hand, articles were coded as "societal responsibility" if nongovernment groups, such as nongovernmental organizations, were regarded as appropriate vehicles to prevent human trafficking, increase awareness about the issue, and help survivors. For example, an article from Malaysia's *New Straits Times* stated, "100 activists marched to the ministry in Putrajaya and presented its minister, Datuk Seri Hishammuddin Hussein, with 10,000 signatures calling for a stop to child trafficking" ("Put an End to Trafficking," 2011, para. 2). In addition, an article from the *Japan Times* stated, "Human rights groups and researchers presented a draft set of proposals Thursday aimed at addressing the problem of human trafficking, saying that a government plan to beef up punishment for the crime is not enough to combat the problem" (Shmoyachi, 2004, para. 1). These articles expressed how nongovernmental organizations are becoming involved in the efforts to end human trafficking.

Finally, coverage of human trafficking was coded as "balanced/neutral" if both government responsibility and societal responsibility were discussed equally, or if the article assigned no specific responsibility for the problem. In South Africa's *The Herald*, a reporter told of her experience interviewing 30 girls younger than 13 who were working as prostitutes, as the interviews gave the reporter a broader insight into the workings of the sex trafficking industry. The article discussed human trafficking without stating how the issue could be resolved by the government or society (Mphande, 2010).

All of the articles were read by two coders, resulting in a Scott's Pi coefficient of intercoder reliability of .877. Media Vectors were then calculated, combining both prominence and direction scores. The researchers utilized Pearson correlations and regression analysis to assess connections between national demographic indicators and Media Vectors.

RESULTS

Media Vectors revealed considerable variation in cross-national coverage of human trafficking, with scores from .5167 (Australia) to −.0214 (Egypt), a range of .5381. All except one of the Media Vectors were positive, favoring governmental action (see Table 1). To explore any links between country characteristics and variations in coverage, Pearson correlations were calculated (see Table 2). All four significant correlations linked national characteristics with media emphasis on government responsibility for human trafficking.

TABLE 1
Media Vector by Nation

Country	Newspaper	Media Vector
Australia	The Sydney Morning Herald	.5167
United Kingdom	The Times	.4948
United States	The New York Times	.4688
Turkey	Turkish Daily News	.3235
Nigeria	This Day	.3087
India	The Times of India	.3013
Mexico	El Universal	.2575
Malaysia	New Straits Times	.2382
Namibia	The Namibian	.1957
Kenya	The Daily Nation	.1824
Chile	El Mercurio	.1394
China	China Daily	.1190
South Africa	The Herald	.1034
Ghana	Accra Mail	.0966
Japan	The Japan Times	.0746
Canada	The Toronto Star	.0428
Zambia	Times of Zambia	.0238
Egypt	Daily News Egypt	−.0214

TABLE 2
Pearson Correlation Results

Country Characteristics	Pearson Correlation	Significance
Female school life expectancy	.478	.022*
GDP/capita	.467	.025*
Stock of direct foreign investment at home	.467	.026*
Broadband subscriptions/100 people in a nation	.410	.045*
Natural gas consumption	.377	.061
Natural gas production	.360	.071
Physicians/10,000	.360	.071
Freedom of the Press report	−.330	.090
Oil production	.319	.098
Length of nation's road network	.318	.099
Oil consumption	.297	.115
Male life expectancy	.280	.130
% of nation's citizens satisfied with water	.273	.136
GDP	.274	.136
Female life expectancy	.270	.140
Deaths due to DD/100,000	−.320	.155
% undernourished	−.247	.161
Infant mortality/1,000	−.320	.155
% of population covered by a mobile phone network	.237	.172
Fertility rate	−.217	.194
Poverty level	−.212	.199
Literacy rate per 100	.211	.200
Nation's industrial production growth rate	−.205	.208
Electricity production	.198	.215
Electricity consumption	.202	.219
% of nation's population w/o access to improved water services	−.194	.220
% female literacy rate	.192	.222
Journalists imprisoned in a nation	−.181	.237
% population <14	−.175	.244
% of females who are satisfied with their freedom of choice	.138	.292
Hospital beds/10,000	.127	.308
Daily newspapers/1,000 people	.140	.332
Gini inequality index	−.109	.333
Coal production	.058	.410
% of females in the workforce	−.045	.430
Cases of cholera	.040	.444
Coal consumption	.011	.482

Note. GDP = gross domestic product, DD = diarrheal diseases.
*$p < .05$.

Stakeholder Significant: Female School Expectancy and Stock of Direct Foreign Investment at Home

Female empowerment (confirmed). According to the United Nations Interregional Crime and Justice Research Institute, at least six nongovernmental agencies have been trying to address the issue of human trafficking through female empowerment activities. The aim of this effort is to empower young women and minors to improve their socioeconomic status and find means of supporting themselves, so that they do not fall victim to trafficking (United Nations Interregional Crime and Justice Research Institute, 2012). On the other hand, an article in *This Day* from Nigeria stated, "Many of these women are naïve, and those who perpetrate this evil capitalise on their naivety to wreak havoc on their lives" (Financial Times Information Limited, 2008, para. 4). Female empowerment seems to be an issue that organizations and media see as important in discussions of human trafficking.

Consequently, this study hypothesized that indicators of female empowerment would correlate with media emphasis on government responsibility to end human trafficking. Pearson correlations found a significant relationship between higher female school life expectancy and media support for government responsibility to end human trafficking ($r = .478$, $p = .022$). School life expectancy was defined as the total number of years of schooling (primary to tertiary) that a child can expect to receive, assuming that the probability of someone being enrolled in school at any particular future age is equal to the current enrollment at that age (CIA, 2011).

Stock of direct foreign investment at home (confirmed). The initial hypothesis was confirmed, finding that the greater a nation's stock of direct foreign investment at home, the more coverage emphasized government responsibility to end human trafficking. This hypothesis was confirmed and found to be significant ($r = .510$, $p = .026$). This finding can potentially be attributed to nations with more ability to invest in countries outside their own being more aware of human trafficking issues and their need for government intervention.

Privilege and Media Access Significant

GDP/capita and broadband subscriptions per 100 people (confirmed). Two buffer hypotheses were confirmed. Higher GDP per capita correlated with more media emphasis on government responsibility to end human trafficking ($r = .478$, $p = .025$), as did higher numbers of broadband subscriptions per 100 people in a nation ($r = .41$, $p = .045$).

Regression Analysis

Regression analysis linking the four significant national characteristics with Media Vector scores revealed that stakeholders play a role in media coverage of human trafficking, with both stock of direct foreign investment at home and female school life expectancy emerging as significant. A surprising pattern emerged when testing for significant variables. When all four of the most important indicators where entered, stock of direct foreign investment at home was confirmed as the only significant variable. However, when stock of direct foreign investment at home was eliminated, female school life expectancy emerged as the only significant variable. Therefore, two regression analyses were conducted—one that included stock of direct foreign investment at home and one that did not. The first regression revealed that stock of direct foreign investment at home accounted for 26% of the variance, and the second showed that female school life expectancy accounted for 22.8% of the variance, both correlating with media coverage emphasizing government responsibility to end human trafficking (see Tables 3 and 4).

TABLE 3
Regression Analysis of Human Trafficking

Model	R (equation)	R^2 (cumulative)	R^2 Change	F Change	Significance of F Change
Stock of direct foreign investment at home	.510	.260	.260	4.575	.052

TABLE 4
Regression Analysis of Human Trafficking

Model	R (equation)	R^2 (cumulative)	R^2 Change	F Change	Significance of F Change
Female school life expectancy	.478	.228	.228	4.730	.045

IMPLICATIONS FOR FURTHER RESEARCH

This study explored the cross-national newspaper coverage of human trafficking, a major issue affecting many nations. To expand upon this endeavor, future researchers could examine more newspapers, such as those in South America or Europe. Because human trafficking occurs all over the world, expanding the range of nations would be useful to obtain a better overview of the issue. Utilizing the community structure approach to examine newspaper coverage of human trafficking yielded significant results. The connections found between country-level charactcristics and framing of articles on human trafficking suggest that national demographics are connected to variations in coverage of human trafficking, and further research on this issue is warranted.

ACKNOWLEDGMENT

A previous version of this article was presented at the annual conference of the New Jersey Communication Association (NJCA), April 2013, where it won the award for best NJCA conference undergraduate paper.

REFERENCES

Bangladesh: New ways to crack down on human trafficking. (2012, June 4). *Women's Feature Service*. Retrieved from http://search.proquest.com/genderwatch/docview/1020902972/1392AF36DCA55D32652/4?accountid=10216

Central Intelligence Agency (CIA). (2011). *The world factbook*. Retrieved from https://www.cia.gov/library/publica tions/the-world-factbook/

China set to ratify trafficking protocol. (2008, October 24). *China Daily*. Retrieved from NewsBank database.

Criminalisation of human trafficking. (2005, June 5). *Times of Zambia*. Retrieved from NewsBank database.

D'Angelo, P., Pollock, J. C., Kiernicki, K., & Shaw, D. (2013). Framing of AIDS in Africa: Press-state relations, HIV/AIDS news, and journalistic advocacy in four sub-Saharan Anglophone newspapers. *Politics and the Life Sciences, 33*, 100–125.

Eisenberg, D., Kester, A., Caputo, L., Sierra, J., & Pollock, J. C. (2006, November). *Cross-national coverage of NGO's efforts to fight AIDS: A community structure approach.* Paper presented at the annual conference of the National Communication Association, San Antonio, TX.

Financial Times Information Limited. (2008, July 14). Senator decries high human trafficking. *This Day*, pp. 1–2. Retrieved from the World NewsBank database.

The Financial Times World. (2004). *World desk reference homepage.* Retrieved from http://dev.prenhall.com/divisions/hss/worldreference/

Freedom House. (2011). *Freedom of the Press 2011.* Retrieved from http://www.freedomhouse.org/report/freedom-press/freedom-press-2011#.U5zL6tdOXIU

Gratale, S., Hagert, J., Dey, L., Pollock, J., D'Angelo, P., Braddock, P., . . . Montgomery, A. (2005, May). *International coverage of United Nations' efforts to combat AIDS: A structural approach.* Paper presented at the annual conference of the International Communication Association, New York, NY.

Hamman, M. (2010). Visual stories of human trafficking's victims. *Nieman Reports, 64*, 41–45. Retrieved from http://ezproxy.tcnj.edu:2417/ehost/detail?vid=3&hid=21&sid=a185d91d-1883-49c8-8390-50911650f487%40sessionmgr12&bdata=JnNpdGU9ZWhvc3QtbGl2ZQ%3d%3d#db=ufh&AN=57676398

Hammer, B., Mitchell, E., Shields, A., & Pollock, J.C. (2006, November). *Cross-national coverage of "Beijing Plus Ten": Women's rights in the ten years after the 1995 Beijing Conference.* Paper presented at the annual conference of the National Communication Association, San Antonio, TX.

Hill, R., & Walker-Rodriguez, A. (2011). Human sex trafficking. *FBI Law Enforcement Bulletin, 80*, 1–9. Retrieved from http://ezproxy.tcnj.edu:2417/ehost/detail?vid=3&hid=18&sid=116308d6-86ed-4c5b-b0ca-dff215fb5eaf%40sessionmgr11&bdata=JnNpdGU9ZWhvc3QtbGl2ZQ%3d%3d#db=aph&AN=64392758

Jesionka, N. (2012, January 24). *Human trafficking: The myths and the realities.* Retrieved from http://www.forbes.com/sites/dailymuse/2012/01/24/human-trafficking-the-myths-and-the-realities/

Jones, J. (2011). Trafficking Internet brides. *Information & Communications Technology Law, 20*, 19–33. Retrieved from http://ezproxy.tcnj.edu:2417/ehost/detail?vid=3&hid=105&sid=b02e8f4c-8844-45c5-8410-ceecb613f023%40sessionmgr113&bdata=JnNpdGU9ZWhvc3QtbGl2ZQ%3d%3d#db=ufh&AN=59792934

Kessler, J. (2007, March/April). Human trafficking and sexual exploitation of children. *Catholic women.* Retrieved from http://ezproxy.tcnj.edu:4776/news/docview/220807639/fulltext/13936A2D69029FBD8EA/12?acaccount=10216

McLeod, D. M., & Hertog, J. K. (1999). Social control, social change, and the mass media's role in the regulation of protest groups. In D. Demers & K. Viswanath (Eds.), *Mass media, social control, and social change: A macrosocial perspective* (pp. 305–331). Ames, IA: Iowa State University Press.

Mphande, H. (2010, September 16). Girls as young as 13 made to be prostitutes. *The Herald.* Retrieved from NewsBank database.

Okojie, C. E. E. (2009). International trafficking of women for the purpose of sexual exploitation and prostitution the Nigerian case. *Pakistan Journal of Women's Studies, 16*, 147–178. Retrieved from http://ezproxy.tcnj.edu:4776/news/docview/237264786/fulltextPDF/13936A2D69029FBD8EA/4?accounacc=10216

Olien, C. N., Donohue, G. A., & Tichenor, P. J. (1995). Conflict, consensus, and public opinion. In T. L. Glaser & C. T. Salmon (Eds.), *Public opinion and the communication of consent* (pp. 301–322). New York, NY: Guilford

106th Congress. (2000). *Victims of trafficking and violence protection act of 2000* (3244). Retrieved from http://www.state.gov/documents/organization/10492.pdf

Pollock, J. C. (2007). *Titled mirrors: Media alignment with political and social change—A community structure approach.* Cresskill, NJ: Hampton Press.

Pollock, J. C., D'Angelo, P., Shaw, D., Burd, A., Kiernicki, K., & Raudenbush, J. (2010, June). *African newspaper coverage of AIDS: Comparing new models of press-state relations and structural factors in sub-Saharan Anglophone Africa.* Paper presented at the annual conference of the International Communication Association, Singapore.

Pollock, J. C., Davies, M., Effingham, A., & Heisler, B. (2012, November). *Nationwide coverage of same-sex marriage after New York legalization: A community structure approach.* Paper presented at the annual conference of the National Communication Association, Orlando, Florida.

Pollock, J. C., Dudzak, M., Richards, K., Norton, S., & Miller, R. (2000, June). *Nationwide newspaper coverage of human cloning: A community structure approach.* Paper presented at the annual conference of the International Communication Association, Acapulco, Mexico.

Pollock, J. C., & Koerner, M. (2010). Cross-national coverage of human trafficking: A community structure approach (Documento de Trabajo # 2). Departamento de Derecho y Ciencia Política/Universidad Nacional de La Matanza (UNLaM), Buenos Aires, Argentina.

Pollock, J. C., Maltese-Nehrbass, M., Corbin, P., & Fascanella, P. B. (2010). Nationwide newspaper coverage of genetically-modified food in the United States: A community structure approach. *Ecos de la Comunicación, 3*, 51–75.

Pollock, J. C., Reda, E., Bosland, A., Hindi, M., & Zhu, D. (2010, June). *Cross-national coverage of climate change: A community structure approach.* Paper presented at the annual conference of the International Communication Association, Singapore.

Pollock, J. C., & Robinson, J. L. (1977). Reporting rights conflicts. *Society, 13*, 44–47.

Pollock, J. C., Robinson, J. L., & Murray, M. C. (1978). Media agendas and human rights: The Supreme Court decision on abortion. *Journalism Quarterly, 53*, 545–548, 561.

Pollock, J. C., & Whitney, L. (1997). Newspapers and racial/ethnic conflict: Comparing city demographics and nationwide reporting on the Crown Heights (Brooklyn, NY) incidents. *The New Jersey Journal of Communication, 5*, 127–149.

Put an end to trafficking in children. (2011, March 31). *New Straits Times.* Retrieved from NewsBank database.

Ricchiardi, S. (2010). Navigating the underworld of human trafficking. *Global Journalist, 16*, 20–23. Retrieved from http://ezproxy.tcnj.edu:2417/ehost/detail?vid=5&hid=105&sid=b02e8f4c-8844-45c5-8410-beecb613f023%40sessionmgr113&bdata=JnNpdGU9ZWhvc3QtbGl2ZQ%3d%3d#db=ufh&AN=55605429

Shmoyachi, N. (2004, October 15). Government's human trafficking plan 'inadequate.' *The Japan Times.* Retrieved from NewsBank database.

Stone, A., & Vandenberg, M. (1999). How the sex trade becomes a slave trade: The trafficking of women to Israel. *Middle East Report, 112*, 36–38.

United Nations Convention against Transnational Organized Crime. (2003). *Protocol to Prevent, Suppress, and Punish Trafficking in Persons:* Article 3, paragraph (a). UN General Assembly resolution 55/25, adopted November 15, 2000; entered into force on December 25, 2003. Retrieved from http://www.unodc.org/unodc/en/human-trafficking/what-is-human-trafficking.html?ref=menuside

United Nations Development Programme. (2010). *Human development report: The real wealth of nations, pathways to human development* (20th ed.). Retrieved from http://hdr.undp.org/en/reports/global/hdr2010/

United Nations Interregional Crime and Justice Research Institute. (2012). *Emerging crimes: Trafficking in human beings.* Retrieved from http://www.unicri.it/emerging_crimes/human_trafficking/nigeria2/activities.php

United Nations Office on Drugs and Crime. (2012). *Human trafficking.* Retrieved from http://www.unodc.org/unodc/en/human-trafficking/what-is-human-trafficking.html

United Nations Statistics Division. (2011). *UNSD statistical databases.* Retrieved from http://unstats.un.org/unsd/databases.htm

Wright, J. B., Giovenco, D., DiMarco, G., Dato, A., Holmes, A. C., & Pollock, J. C. (2008, November). *International newspaper coverage of Muslim immigration since September 11, 2001: A community structure approach.* Paper presented at the annual conference of the National Communication Association, San Diego, CA.

Cross-National Coverage of HIV/AIDS: A Community Structure Approach

James Etheridge, Kelsey Zinck, John C. Pollock, Christina Santiago,
Kristen Halicki, and Alec Badalamenti

Department of Communication Studies
The College of New Jersey

Community structure analysis compared cross-national coverage of responsibility to fight HIV/AIDS in newspapers in 18 countries, selecting articles of 250+ words from May 7, 2003, to September 13, 2013. The resulting 291 articles were coded for "prominence" and "direction" ("government," "society," including nongovernmental organizations [NGOs]/foreign aid or "balanced/neutral" coverage), and combined for composite scores in each newspaper's "Media Vector" (range = .4974 to −.1465). Newspaper support for governmental versus societal involvement was 9 to 9 (50/50). Pearson correlations revealed significant relationships in privilege and vulnerability categories: public knowledge of HIV/AIDS preventative measures and general health of the population. Regression of national characteristics against Media Vectors yielded percentage of women who know condom use prevents HIV (63.7% of variance), percentage of men who know condom use prevents HIV, and percentage of population undernourished, collectively totaling 84.8% of variance, all correlated with support for government intervention. A second regression analysis excluding self-report variables found that "% population undernourished" and "% females in the workforce" (combined 52.8% of variance) were linked to coverage supporting government responsibility. "AIDS incidence" (13.6% of variance) was linked to support for "societal" intervention. Most of the variance was linked to coverage supporting government responsibility for HIV/AIDS.

INTRODUCTION

In the last decade alone, monumental strides have been made in the fight against HIV and its resulting condition, AIDS. For instance, in 2009 the White House released the National HIV/AIDS Strategy as the nation's first-ever comprehensive coordinated HIV/AIDS roadmap. Then the world was stunned in 2012 when an individual in Germany suffering from both AIDS and advanced leukemia was allegedly cured of AIDS with a stem-cell-based treatment

(Tubeza, 2012). In addition, in 2012, various new treatment regimens for HIV began undergoing clinical trials. One of these medications was mutation-resistant dolutegravir, a treatment that could forever change the approach to treating patients with HIV. Dolutegravir helps fight other viruses, protecting the infected patient's immune system, and requires only one daily dose, as compared to raltegravir, which patients had to take twice a day (Sax, 2013). It is important to note that the "fight" has included not only efforts to research a cure but also efforts to impede the spread of HIV/AIDS via dissemination of educational media. Notwithstanding the recent progress combating HIV/AIDS, according to the World Health Organization (WHO, 2011), about 34 million people worldwide still suffer from HIV/AIDS. Therefore, HIV/AIDS continues to be an international crisis demanding global attention.

When reporting on the fight against HIV/AIDS, journalists' interpretations of the efforts can often be divided into two divergent media perspectives. In the field of communication and journalism, scholars often classify such divisions as "frames." The frames of HIV/AIDS sometimes focus on the effectiveness of the fight, but this study aims to explore the frames involving ownership in the fight against HIV/AIDS. One frame argues that domestic governments and their agencies should assume primary responsibility for the fight against HIV/AIDS, advocating that governments have a duty to protect their citizens. Conversely, the other frame emphasizes responsibility on the part of "society," which includes international organizations and relief agencies, such as the United States Agency for International Development (USAID), the President's Emergency Plan for AIDS Relief (PEPFAR), the Red Ribbon Foundation, and the United Nations.

This study examines cross-national media framing of responsibility for the fight against HIV/AIDS, specifically in newspaper coverage. Using the community structure approach, it will explore differing positions in newspapers and how they are influenced by national demographic indicators. Community structure theory will be used to address two main research questions to investigate connections between national characteristics and newspaper coverage of the fight against HIV/AIDS:

RQ1: How much variation exists in cross-national coverage of the fight against HIV/AIDS?
RQ2: How closely linked is that coverage variation to differences in national characteristics?

In the exploration of these research questions, the study tests several hypotheses regarding newspaper coverage and national demographics.

LITERATURE REVIEW

The fight against HIV/AIDS has been extensively studied in various fields, such as social sciences, nursing, and humanities. Although media coverage on HIV/AIDS would be particularly relevant to the field of communication studies, this discipline has largely disregarded the topic of HIV/AIDS in the media. Communication Studies databases such as Communication and Mass Media Complete and Communication Institute for Online Scholarship ComAbstracts were accessed to solicit articles relevant to the topic area. Search terms included "HIV/AIDS" and "HIV/AIDS AND media coverage." Twenty-three relevant articles were found out of 707 articles that were returned via these two databases.

Many of the relevant articles discussed either statistics related to HIV/AIDS worldwide or parties responsible for addressing the problem. Several of the articles within the communication studies databases were not relevant, covering such topics as the use of communication theories to help solve other health issues or the significance of particular social groups such as teens.

The most relevant articles encountered could be sorted into four major categories: assessments of media coverage of HIV/AIDS, media coverage of HIV/AIDS prevention strategies, media coverage of the stigma associated with HIV/AIDS, and media coverage of improvements in treating HIV/AIDS. One sample article assessing media coverage of HIV/AIDS examined coverage in the United States, Portugal, Spain, and Brazil from October to December 1993, showing that governments dominated coverage (Traquina, 2004). Another article examined which channels are most effective for HIV/AIDS-related messages (Kingdon et al., 2013). Regarding HIV/AIDS prevention strategies, one study explored the WHO NGO Life Skills Education curriculum and its effort to increase behavior change, working in tandem with health materials put in a multiliteracy framework (Higgins, 2010). Another analyzed United Nations Millennium Development Goals and their impact on the hard-hit sub-Saharan African region, with particular emphasis on prevention strategies associated with Goal 6 (Muturi & Mwangi, 2011).

In terms of coverage of the stigma associated with HIV/AIDS, one media study of 182 articles analyzed between January 1, 2005, and December 31, 2009, revealed that 60% of the articles omitted stigma associated with the AIDS virus and the other 40% acknowledged the stigma without promoting it (D'Silva, Leichty, & Agarwal, 2011). A second study reviewed Chinese media coverage and found that 59% of the articles examined declared that it was society's responsibility to reduce stigma surrounding HIV/AIDS (Ren, Hust, & Zhang, 2010). Fewer articles were encountered regarding coverage of improvements in treating HIV/AIDS, but one found that the Internet was a main source for information on treatment and control of HIV/AIDS for those recently diagnosed and was utilized to find resources, access information about antiretrovirals, and talk to other HIV-positive individuals in anonymous outlets (Horvath et al., 2010). Despite the aforementioned articles, overall few studies within the communication studies field analyzed media coverage of HIV/AIDS.

In contrast to communication studies, the field of social sciences returned 53 relevant articles in a search on the EBSCO database for "HIV/AIDS" and "coverage," illuminating such topics as media framing of HIV/AIDS in sub-Saharan Africa (Pratt, Ha, & Pratt, 2002), the marginalization of HIV-positive voices in the mainstream, versus the "alternative" press (Altheide, 2004), and the "heterocentric" bias in media and news production (Hallett & Cannella, 1997).

The nursing field produced staggering results, returning 22,209 results in a PubMed search of "HIV/AIDS," with results covering such subjects as HIV/AIDS discourse and framing in South Korean media (Jung, 2013) and emerging patterns in treatment-focused news stories about HIV/AIDS in China (Gao et al., 2013). The humanities field also outpaced communication studies in the study of AIDS, with a search of the EBSCO database Humanities Full Text for "AIDS and media" yielding 86 results. One article chronicled a timeline of major events in the disease's history (Rosario, 2013), whereas another humanities article explored how art in South Africa represented HIV/AIDS (Allara, 2012). It is evident that the communication studies field, unlike other fields, has not devoted significant scholarly attention to HIV/AIDS, particularly in reference to media coverage. As a result, this study attempts to help bridge this gap in communication studies literature.

HYPOTHESES

The following 45 hypotheses regarding coverage of HIV/AIDS were developed using the community structure approach. These hypotheses can be categorized into three subgroups: violated buffer, vulnerability, and stakeholder.

Violated Buffer Hypothesis

The violated buffer hypothesis is an outgrowth of the buffer hypothesis, which asserts that higher proportions of privileged groups in a city correlate with favorable coverage of human rights claims (Pollock, 2007, p. 53). Privilege can be measured cross-nationally thorough gross domestic product (GDP), GDP per capita, literacy rates, and life expectancy. However, the violated buffer hypothesis suggests that "the greater the proportion of privileged citizens in a community, the more unfavorable newspaper reporting is likely to be on issues framed as 'ominous,' hazardous to physical safety or a secure, predictable way of life" (Pollock, 2007, p. 53).

Previous community structure studies have confirmed the validity of the violated buffer hypothesis. For instance, a study by Pollock (2007, p. 223) that focused on Magic Johnson's HIV announcement linked relative privilege in a city to less favorable coverage of both Magic Johnson and those living with HIV/AIDS generally. Likewise, Pollock, Mink, Puma, Shuhala, and Ostrander (2001) found that media coverage of women in combat was less favorable in cities with higher levels of privilege. An article on cross-national coverage by Alexandre, Sha, Pollock, Baier, and Johnson (this issue) found that the higher a nation's GDP per capita, the greater the media emphasis on government responsibility to end human trafficking. The violated buffer hypothesis is likely to apply to the case of HIV/AIDS, because, as confirmed by Pollock (2007, pp. 211–229) in the Magic Johnson study, HIV/AIDS can be framed as a threat to privileged lifestyles in any developed country. An article by Gratale et al. (2005) found that the higher the level of privilege in a country (e.g., GDP or GDP/capita), the more favorable the coverage of United Nations (UN) efforts to fight AIDS. Similarly, a study by Eisenberg, Kester, Caputo, and Sierra (2006) found that the higher the level of privilege in a country, the more favorable the coverage of NGOs' efforts to fight AIDS. Therefore, the following hypotheses apply to coverage of HIV/AIDS:

H1: The higher the GDP in a country, the greater the media support for government responsibility to reduce HIV/AIDS (Central Intelligence Agency [CIA], 2011).

H2: The higher the GDP per capita, the greater the media support for government responsibility to reduce HIV/AIDS (CIA, 2011).

H3: The higher the literacy rate in a country, the greater the media support for government responsibility to reduce HIV/AIDS (CIA, 2011).

H4: The higher a nation's male life expectancy at birth, the greater the media support for government responsibility to reduce HIV/AIDS (CIA, 2011).

H5: The higher a nation's female life expectancy at birth, the greater the media support for government responsibility to reduce HIV/AIDS (CIA, 2011).

Healthcare access. According to Pollock (2007), the health care access of a city can be evaluated by "the proportion of the municipal budget that a city spends on health care, in addition to the availability of hospital beds and physicians" (p. 93). It is reasonable to expect that countries with high healthcare standards would have greater media support for government responsibility to reduce HIV/AIDS. Previous studies by Pollock (2007) found a positive correlation between the number of physicians per 100,000 residents and more favorable news coverage of stem cell research (pp. 89–100), along with a similar correlation between physicians per 100,000 residents and favorable coverage of physician-assisted suicide (pp. 75–88). In addition, in a more recent study by Pollock, Reda et al. (2010), the greater number of hospital beds per 100,000 and the greater the number of physicians per 100,000, the more cross-national media coverage emphasized "government responsibility" to address global warming. Accordingly:

H6: The greater the number of physicians per 100,000, the greater the media support for government responsibility to reduce HIV/AIDS (United Nations Development Programme, 2011).

H7: The greater the number of hospital beds per 10,000, the greater the media support for government responsibility to reduce HIV/AIDS (United Nations Statistics Division, 2011).

Disease prevention prevalence.   In any exploration of HIV/AIDS coverage and its association with social contexts, it is important to take into account awareness and prevalence of prevention strategies, such as knowledge of condom use and prevalence of condom use, both associated with relative "privilege." Therefore, the following is expected:

H8: The greater the percentage of women who know that consistent condom use prevents HIV/AIDS, the greater the media support for government responsibility to reduce HIV/AIDS (Joint United Nations Programme on HIV/AIDS [UNAIDS], 2010).

H9: The higher the prevalence of condom use among females, the greater the media support for government responsibility to reduce HIV/AIDS (UNAIDS, 2010).

H10: The greater the percentage of men who know that consistent condom use prevents HIV/AIDS, the greater the media support for government responsibility to reduce HIV/AIDS (UNAIDS, 2010).

H11: The higher the prevalence of condom use among males, the greater the media support for government responsibility to reduce HIV/AIDS (UNAIDS, 2010).

Vulnerability Hypothesis

Whereas newspapers often reflect the opinions of privileged groups, the vulnerability hypothesis urges that "media coverage [might] reflect the interests of a wide range of groups and concerns, including the least economically advantaged" (Pollock, 2007, p. 54). Explicitly, the vulnerability hypothesis suggests that newspapers mirror the interests of vulnerable groups, such as the poor, unemployed, and those living in higher crime areas (Pollock, 2007, p. 137). For example, a study after the *Roe v. Wade* decision found that coverage favored legalizing abortion in cities with higher poverty levels (Pollock & Robinson, 1977; Pollock, Robinson, & Murray, 1978). Moreover, in their study concerning widely reported New York City ethnic/religious group incidents, Pollock and Whitney (1997) showed that coverage of the incidents in cities with higher levels of poverty and unemployment was more appreciative of the claims of both Caribbean Americans and Hasidic Jews. A study on nationwide coverage of a Patients' Bill of Rights found higher poverty levels linked to more favorable coverage (Pollock, 2007, pp. 146–156). A study on coverage of universal health care found more media support in cities with higher percentages of Hispanics (Kiernicki, Pollock, & Lavery, 2013).

Specifically relevant to this study, a cross-national study regarding the UN's efforts to combat AIDS found infant mortality significantly linked with reporting emphasizing progress in UN efforts to fight AIDS (Gratale et al., 2005). Furthermore, a study by Kohn and Pollock (this issue) in regards to child labor found that the higher the percentage of a nation's population younger than 14, the greater the media emphasis on government responsibility to reduce child labor. Likewise, a cross-national study by Wissel et al. (this issue) found that the greater percentage of a nation's population without access to improved water services, the more coverage emphasized government responsibility for clean water access. Previous research suggests that various vulnerability variables may be associated with coverage emphasizing government responsibility for health-related issues. Therefore, the following can be expected:

H12: The higher a nation's poverty level, the greater the media support for government responsibility to reduce HIV/AIDS (United Nations Statistics Division, 2011).

H13: The higher a nation's fertility rate, the greater the media support for government responsibility to reduce HIV/AIDS (United Nations Statistics Division, 2011).

H14: The greater the percentage of undernourished, the greater the media support for government responsibility to reduce HIV/AIDS (United Nations Statistics Division, 2011).

H15: The higher the percentage of a nation's population younger than 14, the greater the media support for government responsibility to reduce HIV/AIDS (United Nations Statistics Division, 2011).

H16: The higher a nation's happiness score, the greater the media support for government responsibility to reduce HIV/AIDS (CIA, 2011).

Health vulnerability. In populations vulnerable to health crises such as HIV/AIDS, governments may have limited capacity to focus on the fight against the pandemic. The resources of international and local NGOs and social organizations are often sought to protect and adequately assist those in need of AIDS-related services. Indicators such as infant mortality rates and deaths per 100,000 due to diarrheal diseases or cholera can be used to identify populations with limited access to medical resources. Thus, the following can be hypothesized:

H17: The higher a nation's infant mortality rate, the less media support for government responsibility to reduce HIV/AIDS (United Nations Statistics Division, 2011).

H18: The greater the percentage of children younger than 5 with diarrhea receiving oral rehydration therapy with continued feeding, the less media support for government responsibility to reduce HIV/AIDS (CIA, 2011).

H19: The greater the number of cases of cholera per 100,000 in a nation, the less media support for government responsibility to reduce HIV/AIDS (CIA, 2011).

H20: The higher a nation's Gini inequality index, the greater the media support for government responsibility to reduce HIV/AIDS (CIA, 2011).

AIDS health vulnerability. For vulnerable populations, social organizations may be necessary for AIDS-related care, but preventative measures such as safe sex education fall to the government. According to a study by Gratale et al. (2005), the higher the level of privilege in a country, the more favorable the coverage of UN efforts to fight AIDS. A paper by Eisenberg et al. (2006) similarly found that the higher the level of privilege in a country, the more favorable the coverage of NGOs' efforts to fight AIDS. Thus, the following is expected:

H21: The higher the AIDS prevalence, the less media support for government responsibility to reduce HIV/AIDS (World Health Organization, 2007).

H22: The higher the AIDS incidence (rate of increase), the less media support for government responsibility to reduce HIV/AIDS (United Nations Statistics Division, 2011).

H23: The higher the percentage of HIV-infected orphans, the less media support for government responsibility to reduce HIV/AIDS (United Nations Statistics Division, 2011).

Access to resources. In areas that lack sufficient access to resources such as water, government efforts are crucial to the creation of a healthy living environment. A study by Pollock, Maltese-Nehrbass, Corbin, and Fascanella (2010) found that the higher the proportion of relatively disadvantaged groups, the greater the media support for disease-resistant, higher yield genetically modified food. Because most locations stricken by the AIDS epidemic have limited access to resources, the following can be expected:

H24: The greater percentage of a nation's population without access to improved water services, the greater the media support for government responsibility to reduce HIV/AIDS (CIA, 2011).

H25: The higher the percentage satisfied with water services, the less media support for government responsibility to reduce HIV/AIDS (United Nations Development Programme, 2010).

Stakeholder Hypothesis

Using the community structure approach, prior research has revealed that communities with higher percentages of "stakeholders" are more likely to exhibit newspaper coverage reporting favorably on issues of great concern to those stakeholders (McLeod & Hertog, 1999; Pollock, 2007, p. 172). Higher proportions of issue stakeholders can be linked to favorable coverage of their rights claims in mass media. In an investigation of sub-Saharan Anglophone African newspaper coverage of AIDS, Pollock, D'Angelo, et al. (2010) found that higher levels of AIDS prevalence in a nation correlated with greater media support for government activity to address/reduce the AIDS pandemic. The stakeholder categories in this study are female empowerment, energy production and infrastructure, and media access and penetration.

Female empowerment. The social trend toward gender equality has led to a more vocal and active female population. In cross-national research, Wissel et al. (this issue) found that the greater the evidence for female empowerment in a nation, the less media emphasis on government responsibility, and the more emphasis on "society" responsibility for water handling. Similarly, a cross-national paper by Kohn and Pollock (this issue) regarding child labor found that the greater the female school life expectancy, the more coverage supported societal responsibility to reduce child labor. As a result, it is reasonable to expect the following:

H26: The higher a nation's female literacy rate, the less media support for government responsibility to reduce HIV/AIDS (CIA, 2011).

H27: The greater the female school life expectancy, the less media support for government responsibility to reduce HIV/AIDS (CIA, 2011).

H28: The higher a nation's percentage of women in the workforce, the less media support for government responsibility to reduce HIV/AIDS (United Nations Statistics Division, 2011).

H29: The higher a nation's percentage of females who are satisfied with their freedom of choice, the less media support for government responsibility to reduce HIV/AIDS (United Nations Development Programme, 2008).

Energy production/consumption and infrastructure. Those who produce or consume the most energy tend to be among the most influential groups in a society. In a cross-national study, Wright et al. (2008) found that the greater terawatt hours of electricity production in a country, the less favorable the coverage of Muslim immigration. In addition, English, O'Conner, Smith, and Pollock (2012) found that the higher the rate of coal production in a country, the greater the cross-national newspaper support for intervention in Libya. Pollock, Reda et al. (2010), in a case study on climate change, found the greater oil production, natural gas production, and natural gas consumption in a nation, the greater the media support for government responsibility to address climate change. Therefore, it is reasonable to assume the following:

H30: The higher a nation's natural gas consumption, the greater the media support for government responsibility to reduce HIV/AIDS (CIA, 2011).

H31: The higher a nation's natural gas production, the greater the media support for government responsibility to reduce HIV/AIDS (CIA, 2011).

H32: The higher a nation's electricity consumption, the greater the media support for government responsibility to reduce HIV/AIDS (CIA, 2011).

H33: The higher a nation's electricity production, the greater the media support for government responsibility to reduce HIV/AIDS (CIA, 2011).

H34: The higher a nation's coal consumption, the greater the media support for government responsibility to reduce HIV/AIDS (CIA, 2011).

H35: The higher a nation's coal production, the greater the media support for government responsibility to reduce HIV/AIDS (CIA, 2011).

H36: The higher a nation's oil consumption, the greater the media support for government responsibility to reduce HIV/AIDS (CIA, 2011).

H37: The higher a nation's oil production, the greater the media support for government responsibility to reduce HIV/AIDS (CIA, 2011).

H38: The higher the total length of a nation's road network, the greater the media support for government responsibility to reduce HIV/AIDS (CIA, 2011).

H39: The higher a nation's industrial production growth rate, the greater the media support for government responsibility to reduce HIV/AIDS (CIA, 2011).

Stock of direct foreign investment at home. Stock of direct foreign investment at home is the total proportion of investments in a country made by nonresidents, including companies from other countries that have satellite sources in the home country. As much of the funding in the fight against HIV/AIDS relies on money from other country's companies and governments, it is reasonable to expect a nation's foreign stock investment would inversely correlate with media support for government responsibility:

H40: The greater a nation's foreign stock investment, the less media support for government responsibility to reduce HIV/AIDS (CIA, 2011).

Media access and penetration. Media access is another important stakeholder concern. A group of studies from Minnesota by Tichenor, Donohue, and Olien (1980) showed that larger cities and towns tended to have more diverse interests and perspectives than small communities due to the variety of demographics within the area. Consistently, Kohn and Pollock (this issue) found that the greater the number of broadband subscriptions per 100 citizens in a nation, the greater the media emphasis on government responsibility to reduce child labor. Similarly, Alexandre et al. (this issue) also found that the greater the number of broadband subscriptions per 100 citizens in a nation, the greater the media emphasis on government responsibility to end human trafficking. Finally, Wissel et al. (this issue) found that the more freedom of the press and the higher percentage of population covered by a mobile phone network, the more media emphasis on government responsibility for clean water access. Therefore, the following is predicted:

H41: The higher the Freedom of the Press Report score, the greater the media support for government responsibility to reduce HIV/AIDS (Organisation for Economic Co-operation and Development, 2011).

H42: The higher the number of daily newspapers per 1,000 citizens, the greater the media support for government responsibility to reduce HIV/AIDS (Organisation for Economic Co-operation and Development, 2011).

H43: The higher the percent of population covered by a mobile phone network, the greater the media support for government responsibility to reduce HIV/AIDS (Organisation for Economic Co-operation and Development, 2011).

H44: The higher the number of broadband subscriptions per 100 citizens in a nation, the greater the media support for government responsibility to reduce HIV/AIDS (Organisation for Economic Co-operation and Development, 2011).

By contrast,

H45: The higher the number of journalists imprisoned in a nation, the less the media support for government responsibility to reduce HIV/AIDS (Organisation for Economic Co-operation and Development, 2011).

METHODOLOGY

To investigate the topic of HIV/AIDS coverage, a cross-national sample of 18 major newspapers was selected from the NewsBank and All Africa databases, including all topic-relevant articles with 250 words or more, yielding 291 articles. The sample included the following publications: *New Vision*, the *Namibian*, the *Japan Times, China Daily, Turkish Daily News*, the *Sydney Morning Herald*, the *Herald*, the *New York Times*, the *Toronto Star*, the *Times, Times of Zambia, Daily Nation, Accra Mail, El Universal*, the *Times of India*, the *New Times*, the *Star*, and *This Day*.

The collection of data ranged from May 27, 2003, to September 13, 2013. On May 27, 2003, the first 5-year authorization of PEPFAR was ratified, with the second 5-year ratification issued on July 30, 2008. According to the PEPFAR website, "This program holds a place in the history of public health as the largest commitment by any nation to combat a single disease, establishing and expanding the infrastructure necessary to deliver prevention, care, and treatment services in low resource settings" ("PEPFAR's five-year strategy," n.d., para. 3). PEPFAR provides assistance dispersing medical information and acquiring and contributing health needs such as antiretroviral medication. PEPFAR's focus areas include those with HIV infection rates above 1%, "the accepted threshold for generalized epidemics" ("PEPFAR's five-year strategy," n.d., para. 3). The sample end date is the one-month anniversary of the release of Dolutegravir by the U.S. Food and Drug Administration, described as "the second approved antiretroviral (ARV) in the integrase strand transfer class after [raltegravir]" ("FDA approves," 2013, para. 1). A one-month buffer after the medication was released allowed for dispersal of information worldwide, opening access to articles on the release of this new, groundbreaking ARV.

Article Coding and Procedures

Each article was coded for prominence and direction, representing how prominently it was positioned in the newspaper and the way in which the HIV/AIDS issue was discussed (government responsibility, societal responsibility, balanced/neutral), respectively. Articles that portrayed HIV/AIDS primarily as a problem that should be confronted by domestic governments were coded as "government responsibility." An article in the *Japan Times* by Eric Johnston (2005) stated, "Confronting the AIDS virus in Asia must be a matter of political will. But for too many governments, it remains a matter of political won't" (para. 1). An article in the *Daily Nation* of Kenya discussed government approval for buying HIV testing kits:

> These supplies are critical and all must be done to ensure that judicial proceedings and litigation do not endanger or threaten the lives and health of the many Kenyans who require and depend on the said testing kits and other supplies ("Ministry Gets Go-Ahead," 2005, para. 8).

Articles that placed primary responsibility for HIV/AIDS in the hands of charities, non-governmental groups (such as the WHO or UN), agencies of foreign governments (such as USAID), or local groups (such as Drama in AIDS Education and Info4Africa, based in Durban, South Africa) were coded as "societal responsibility." These articles included information on how NGOs could educate the public on HIV/AIDS and assist victims. An article in the *Times of*

India stated, "The voluntary counseling and testing centre (VCTC) at Banaras Hindu University is [witnessing] trends with more people coming forward to seek counseling and testing" ("More Come Forward," 2009, para. 1). Another article from the *Turkish Daily News* stressed the importance of a health declaration made by the WHO: "The World Health Organisation (WHO) and the specialised agency UNAIDS declared that millions of lives could be saved if circumcision were widely and safely practised" ("UN Gives Green Light," 2007, para. 2).

Articles that ascribed both government responsibility and societal responsibility in the fight against AIDS, or assigned no responsibility at all, were coded as "balanced/neutral." A reporter in the *Times of Zambia* declared, "She [Community Development Deputy Minister Catherine Namugala] said Government would continue supporting women's organisations to ensure that families attained meaningful livelihoods" ("Include AIDS Lessons," 2003, para. 7). Similarly, an article by Celia W. Duggar (2009) in the *New York Times* primarily presented statistics: "Still, more than half the people with the disease [HIV] who need drug treatment still are not getting it. Two million died in 2007, according to the Joint United Nations Program on HIV/AIDS" (p. A10).

Half of all articles collected were double-coded for content direction, yielding a Scott's Pi coefficient of intercoder reliability of .857. The researchers utilized the prominence and direction scores for each article in the calculation of a Media Vector for each newspaper. Correlations between national characteristics and Media Vectors were analyzed by means of Pearson correlations and regression analysis. Strong associations were found between selected national characteristics and coverage of the fight against HIV/AIDS when utilizing these two research methods.

RESULTS

This study examined cross-national newspaper coverage of HIV/AIDS in 18 newspapers from May 17, 2003, through September 13, 2013. The *New Vision* from Uganda had the highest Media Vector, at 0.4974, whereas *This Day* from Nigeria had the lowest Media Vector, at −0.1465. The range of Media Vector results was .6439, demonstrating significant variation in coverage of HIV/AIDS. Of the 18 newspapers, nine (50%) reflected positive Media Vectors (emphasizing government responsibility), and the other nine revealed Media Vectors (emphasizing societal responsibility). Table 1 offers a complete list of Media Vectors. Results of Pearson correlations illustrated several significant relationships between national demographic indicators and Media Vectors. Table 2 provides a complete list of Pearson correlations.

DISCUSSION OF SIGNIFICANT FINDINGS

Violated Buffer and Vulnerability Significant

Percentage of women who know condom use prevents HIV (confirmed). Under the "violated buffer" hypothesis, it was expected that privilege would be associated with media support for government responsibility for HIV/AIDS because privileged groups would be averse to "biological threats" or "threats to a cherished way of life" (Pollock, 2007, p. 101). That

TABLE 1
Media Vector by Country

Country	Newspaper	Media Vector
Uganda	*New Vision*	0.4974
Namibia	*The Namibian*	0.1909
Japan	*The Japan Times*	0.1441
China	*China Daily*	0.1417
Turkey	*Turkish Daily News*	0.1153
Australia	*The Sydney Morning Herald*	0.0736
Zimbabwe	*The Herald*	0.0534
United States	*The New York Times*	0.0294
Canada	*The Toronto Star*	0.0084
United Kingdom	*The Times*	−0.0089
Zambia	*Times of Zambia*	−0.0277
Kenya	*Daily Nation*	−0.0364
Ghana	*Accra Mail*	−0.0423
Mexico	*El Universal*	−0.0429
India	*The Times of India*	−0.0551
Rwanda	*The New Times*	−0.0720
South Africa	*The Star*	−0.1359
Nigeria	*This Day*	−0.1465

hypothesis was confirmed in particular for countries with high levels of "disease prevention" knowledge. It was predicted that the greater the percentage of women who know that consistent condom use prevents HIV/AIDS, the greater the media support for government responsibility to reduce HIV/AIDS (UNAIDS, 2010). This hypothesis was confirmed ($r = .817, p = .004$). Educated females are often an indicator of more developed countries because their governments have more resources to advance social agendas and promote education about safe sex practices, especially condom use.

Percentage of men who know condom use prevents HIV (confirmed).   It was predicted that the higher the prevalence of condom use among males, the greater the media support for government responsibility to reduce HIV/AIDS. This hypothesis was also confirmed ($r = .710, p = .024$). Educated men are often an indicator of more developed countries because governments in these societies have more resources to direct toward education, and men informed about the efficacy of condoms may put more pressure on their governments in the fight against HIV/AIDS.

Percentage population undernourished (confirmed).   In accordance with the vulnerability hypothesis, it was predicted that the greater the percentage of the population that is undernourished, the greater the media support for government responsibility to reduce HIV/AIDS. This hypothesis was confirmed ($r = .488, p = .020$). It was expected that when more of the public suffers from "chronic" long-term conditions, the more it might rely on the government for help.

TABLE 2
Pearson Correlation Results

City Characteristics	Pearson Correlation	Significance
% of women who know condom use prevents HIV	.817	.004**
% of men who know condom use prevents HIV	.710	.024*
% of population undernourished	.488	.020*
Cases of cholera per 100,000	−.412	.045*
AIDS incidence rate	−.375	.062
% of women in workforce	.354	.089
% of HIV-infected orphans	−.300	.114
Poverty level	−.295	.125
Industrial growth rate	−.267	.142
Stock of direct foreign investment at home	.320	.143
Prevalence of male condom use	−.357	.156
Infant mortality rate	−.252	.157
Coal consumption	−.231	.186
Female choice	.211	.200
Prevalence of female condom use	−.345	.201
% satisfied with water services	.187	.229
Coal production	−.181	.236
Literacy rate	.168	.253
No. of journalists imprisoned	.682	.261
Female literacy rate	.144	.284
Freedom of the press	.137	.300
% of children <5 with diarrheal diseases	.126	.309
Electricity consumption	.121	.316
No. of broadband subscriptions	−.124	.323
Electricity production	.115	.325
Improved water services	−.102	.344
Newspapers per 1,000	−.149	.375
GDP	.079	.378
Physicians per 10,000	.075	.384
Female school life expectancy	−.069	.393
Fertility rate	.060	.406
Oil production	.056	.413
Oil consumption	.055	.414
Gini inequality index	−.055	.415
Happiness score	−.050	.422
Male life expectancy	.047	.427
Gas production	−.036	.444
Female life expectancy	.032	.449
AIDS prevalence	−.028	.456
GDP per capita	.025	.461
Population <14 years old	.018	.472
Gas consumption	.016	.475
Roads	−.010	.484
Hospital beds per 1,000	−.006	.491

Note. GDP = gross domestic product.
*Significant at .05 level, **significant at .01 level.

Cases of cholera per 100,000 (confirmed). In accordance with the vulnerability hypothesis, greater proportions of groups vulnerable to diseases or health-related emergencies would correlate with *less* media support for government responsibility to reduce HIV/AIDS, due to the perceived reliance on social organizations for relief and assistance. This hypothesis was confirmed ($r = -.412$, $p = .045$). The high incidence of cholera may be an indication of a government's inability to effectively manage critical or "emergency" medical issues, thus driving an emphasis on "society" (including NGOs and foreign aid) for assistance.

Regression Analysis

An initial regression analysis identified specific variables driving Media Vector scores, revealing that "Percentage of Women who Know Condom Use Prevents HIV" accounted for 63.7% of the variance, "Percentage of Men who Know Condom Use Prevents HIV" accounted for 10.6%, and "Percentage Population Undernourished" accounted for 10.5% (Table 3). Any single variable accounting for more than 50% of the variance in coverage is astonishing, and it reinforces the observation that knowledge about HIV/AIDS prevention plays a significant role in media coverage, particularly in relation to female education and empowerment. In turn, according to the data, these indicators emphasize media support for government action.

A second regression analysis was conducted that excluded "Percentage of Women who Know Condom Use Prevents HIV" and "Percentage of Men who Know Condom Use Prevents HIV," to ensure that only aggregate data were utilized, excluding data based on "opinion surveys." This regression analysis identified the three most significant "nonsurvey" independent variables with Media Vector scores and revealed that "Percentage of Population Undernourished" accounted for 25.0% of the variance, "Percentage of Females in the Workforce" accounted for 27.8%, and "AIDS Incidence" accounted for 13.6% collectively accounting for 66.4% of variance (Table 4).

Viewed together, the regression analyses reveal two important patterns. First, the "violated buffer" hypothesis is strongly confirmed, especially regarding female empowerment. In one regression model, "percentage of women who know condom use prevents HIV" was a powerful variable. In the second regression model, "percentage of females in the workforce" was also a strong driver of media coverage. Measures of female empowerment were therefore strongly connected to media coverage of responsibility for HIV/AIDS.

TABLE 3
Regression Analysis

Model	R (equation)	R^2 (cumulative)	R^2 Change	F Change	Significance of F Change
% of women who know condom use prevents HIV	.798	.637	.637	10.541	.018*
% of women who know condom use prevents HIV, % of men who know condom use prevents HIV	.743	.743	.106	2.069	.210
% of women who know condom use prevents HIV, % of men who know condom use prevents HIV, and % of population undernourished	.921	.849	.105	2.783	.171

*Significant at .05 level.

TABLE 4
Regression Analysis 2

Model	R (equation)	R^2 (cumulative)	R^2 Change	F Change	Significance of F Change
% of population undernourished	.500	.250	.250	4.659	.049*
% of population undernourished, % of females in the workforce	.726	.528	.278	7.644	.016*
% of population undernourished, % of females in the workforce, and AIDS incidence	.815	.664	.136	4.873	.047*

*Significant at .05 level.

Second, cross-national coverage of HIV/AIDS was curiously linked far more with broad social and political contexts than with specific patterns of AIDS vulnerability. AIDS incidence emerged only in the second regression model, and it accounted only for 13.6% of the variance. Far more robust as predictors of HIV/AIDS coverage variation were broader measures of vulnerability such as percentage undernourished (accounting for 10.5% of the variation in the first regression model, and 25% in the second), associated with media support for government responsibility for HIV/AIDS; and among the Pearson correlations, "cases of cholera per 100,000," significant at the .045 level, associated with support for "societal" rather than government responsibility. Further, the entire social context of "female empowerment" measures was more powerful in its association with variations in coverage of HIV/AIDS responsibility than were any measures linked directly to the proportions of those suffering from HIV/AIDS. Consistently, a recent multilevel study exploring the relation between different media systems or patterns of press-state relations and coverage of AIDS responsibility in sub-Saharan Africa found connections between a relatively "free" press at the media system level and coverage emphasizing government responsibility for HIV/AIDS (D'Angelo, Pollock, Kiernicki, & Shaw, 2013).

CONCLUSIONS AND IMPLICATIONS FOR FURTHER RESEARCH

Responsibility for the fight against HIV/AIDS is a critical issue, generating substantial discussion cross-nationally, as reflected in varied cross-national media coverage. Several important correlations were discovered, all related to "privilege" (violated buffer) and "vulnerability." Four contextual variables were confirmed significant: percentage of women who know condom use prevents HIV, percentage of men who know condom use prevents HIV, percentage population undernourished, and cases of cholera per 100,000.

A fascinating finding was that the greater the percentage of women who know condom use prevents HIV/AIDS, the greater the media support for government responsibility to reduce HIV/AIDS. In addition to the significant Pearson correlation generated, this variable also accounted for 63.7% of the regression variance in coverage. Women who are both educated and have choices in relationships are often indicators of greater national "development," thereby suggesting that developed countries are more likely to support government action against

TABLE 5
Selected Pearson Correlations Results for Percentage of Women
Who Know Condom Use Prevents HIV/AIDS and AIDS Incidence

City Characteristics	Pearson Correlation with % Women Who Know Condom Use Prevents HIV/AIDS	Significance
AIDS incidence	−.562	.058

HIV/AIDS. Furthermore, the statistical significance of the variable can suggest the necessity for public education on preventative measures against HIV/AIDS, highlighting the importance of various health communication campaigns already in place to educate the public on HIV/AIDS.

Curiously, a negative correlation between Media Vectors and AIDS incidence nearly approached significance ($p = .058$; Table 5); this negative correlation further implied an inverse relationship between the greater number of women educated in preventative measures against HIV/AIDS (which correlated positively with Media Vectors) and the incidence of HIV/AIDS in a country. This inverse correlation also highlighted the need for greater societal intervention in societies with fewer women who know condom use prevents HIV/AIDS. These societies are most likely those with less female empowerment, less female education, and fewer women in the workforce: developing countries.

In regard to further research, studies could specifically examine the favorable or unfavorable newspaper coverage of societal organizations such as NGOs and USAID combating HIV/AIDS in countries with high HIV/AIDS prevalence. It would be helpful to explore national characteristics linked to media portrayal of outside assistance to address an epidemic. In addition, it would be useful to investigate the prevention and remediation methods found effective in countries with high percentages of male and female knowledge of HIV/AIDS preventative measures, the degree to which those methods were implemented by societal or governmental organizations, and the media coverage they received. Finally, another recommendation would be to explore how coverage of responsibility for HIV/AIDS changes in the future, as medical advancements, legal changes, and other events could directly influence variations in coverage.

ACKNOWLEDGMENT

A previous version of this article was presented at the biannual University of Kentucky Conference on Health Communication, April 12, 2014.

REFERENCES

Allara, P. (2012). Diane Victor and Paul Emmanuel. *African Arts, 45,* 34–45.
Altheide, D. L. (2004). Media logic and political communication. *Theories and Principles, 21*(3), 3–6. Retrieved from http://www.sagepub.com/upm-data/19029_seib_vol_1_chap_01.pdf
Central Intelligence Agency (CIA). (2011). *The world factbook.* Retrieved from https://www.cia.gov/library/publica tions/the-world-factbook/

D'Angelo, P., Pollock, J. C., Kiernicki, K., & Shaw, D. (2013). Framing of AIDS in Africa: Press-state relations, HIV/AIDS news, and journalistic advocacy in four sub-Saharan Anglophone newspapers. *Politics and the Life Sciences, 33*, 100–125.

D'Silva, M. U., Leichty, G., & Agarwal, V. (2011). Cultural representations of HIV/AIDS in Indian print media. *Intercultural Communication Studies, 20*, 75–88.

Duggar, C. W. (2009, October 30). As donors focus on AIDS, child illnesses languish. *The New York Times*, p. A10. Retrieved from *The New York Times* database.

Eisenberg, D., Kester, A., Caputo, L. & Sierra, J. (2006, November). *International newspaper coverage of NGO efforts and HIV/AIDS: A community structure approach.* Paper presented at the annual conference of the National Communication Association, San Antonio, TX.

English, C., O'Conner, B., Smith, K., & Pollock, J. C. (2012, November). *Cross-national newspaper coverage of revolution in Libya: A community structure approach.* Paper presented at the annual conference of the National Communication Association, Orlando, FL.

FDA approves HIV drug Tivicay (Dolutegravir). (2013, August 13). *AIDSMEDS.* Retrieved from http://www.aidsmeds.com/articles/Tivicay_dolutegravir_1667_24371.shtml

Gao, J., Fu, H., Lin, L., Nehl, E. J., Wong, F. Y., & Zheng, P. (2013). Newspaper coverage of HIV/AIDS in China from 2000 to 2010. *AIDS Care, 25*, 1174–1178.

Gratale, S., Hagert, J., Dey, L., Pollock, J., D'Angelo, P., Braddock, P., . . . Montgomery, A. (2005, May). *International coverage of United Nations efforts to combat AIDS: A structural approach.* Paper presented at the annual conference of the International Communication Association, New York, NY.

Hallett, M. A., & Cannella, D. (1997). Gatekeeping through media format: Strategies of voice for the HIV-positive via human interest news formats and organizations. *Journal of Homosexuality, 32*(3–4), 17–36.

Higgins, C. (2010, March). Discursive enactments of the World Health Organization's policies: Competing cultural models in Tanzanian HIV/AIDS prevention. *Language Policy, 9*, 65–85.

Horvath, K. J., Harwood, E. M., Courtenay-Quirk, C., McFarlane, M., Fisher, H., Dickenson, T., . . . O'Leary, A. (2010). Online resources for persons recently diagnosed with HIV/AIDS: An analysis of HIV-related webpages. *Journal of Health Communication, 15*, 516–531.

Include AIDS lessons in club teachings. (2003, June 1). *Times of Zambia*, para. 7. Retrieved from NewsBank.

Johnston, E. (2005, July 3). Asia urged to confront AIDS before it's too late. *The Japan Times*, para. 1. Retrieved from NewsBank.

Joint United Nations Programme on HIV/AIDS (UNAIDS). (2010). *Global report: UNAIDS report on the global AIDS epidemic.* Retrieved from http://www.unaids.org/documents/20101123_globalreport_em.pdf

Jung, M. (2013). Framing, agenda setting, and disease phobia of AIDS-related coverage in the South Korean mass media. *Health Care Manager, 32*, 52–57.

Kiernicki, K., Pollock, J. C., & Lavery, P. (2013). Nationwide newspaper coverage of universal health care: A community structure approach. In J. C. Pollock (Ed.), *Media and social inequality: Innovations in community structure research* (pp. 116–134). New York, NY: Routledge.

Kingdon, M. J., Storholm, E. D., Halkitis, P. N., Jones, D. C., Moeller, R. W., Siconolfi, D., & Solomon, T. M. (2013). Targeting HIV prevention messaging to a new generation of gay, bisexual, and other young men who have sex with men. *Journal of Health Communication, 18*, 325–342.

McLeod, D. M., & Hertog, J. K. (1992). The manufacture of public opinion by reporters: Informal cues for public perceptions of protest groups. *Discourse and Society, 3*, 259–275.

McLeod, D. M., & Hertog, J. K. (1999). Social control, social change, and the mass media's role in the regulation of protest groups. In D. Demers & K. Viswanath (Eds.), *Mass media, social control, and social change: A macrosocial perspective* (pp. 305–331). Ames, IA: Iowa State University Press.

Ministry gets go-ahead to buy HIV/AIDS testing kits. (2005, July 7). *Daily Nation*, para. 8. Retrieved from NewsBank.

More come forward for testing. (2009, December 1). *The Times of India*, para. 1. Retrieved from NewsBank.

Muturi, N., & Mwangi, S. (2011). Older adults' perspectives on HIV/AIDS prevention strategies for rural Kenya. *Health Communication, 26*, 712–723.

Organisation for Economic Co-operation and Development. (2011). *Statistics from a to z.* Retrieved from http://www.oecd.org/statistics/

PEPFAR's five-year strategy. (n.d.). *The United States President's Emergency Plan for AIDS Relief.* Retrieved from http://www.pepfar.gov/about/strategy/document/133251.htm

Pollock, J. C. (2007). *Tilted mirrors: Media alignment with political and social change.* Cresskill, NJ: Hampton Press.

Pollock, J. C., D'Angelo, P., Shaw, D., Burd, A., Kiernicki, K., & Raudenbush, J. (2010, June). *African newspaper coverage of AIDS: Comparing new models of press-state relations and structural factors in sub-Saharan Anglophone Africa*. Paper presented at the annual conference of the International Communication Association, Singapore.

Pollock, J. C., Maltese-Nehrbass, M., Corbin, P., & Fascanella, P. B. (2010). Nationwide newspaper coverage of genetically-modified food in the United States: A community structure approach. *Ecos de la Comunicación, 3*(3), 51–75.

Pollock, J., Mink, M., Puma, J., Shuhala, S., & Ostrander, L. (2001, November). *Nationwide newspaper coverage of women in combat: A community structure approach*. Paper presented at the annual conference of the National Communication Association, Atlanta, GA.

Pollock, J. C., Reda, E., Bosland, A., Hindi, M., & Zhu, D. (2010, June). *Cross-national coverage of climate change: A community structure approach*. Paper presented at the annual conference of the International Communication Association, Singapore.

Pollock, J. C., & Robinson, J. L. (1977). Reporting rights conflicts. *Society, 13*, 44–47.

Pollock, J. C., Robinson, J. L., & Murray, M. C. (1978). Media agendas and human rights: The Supreme Court decision on abortion. *Journalism Quarterly, 53*(3), 545–548, 561.

Pollock, J. C., & Whitney, L. (1997, Fall). Newspapers and racial/ethnic conflict: Comparing city demographics and nationwide reporting on the Crown Heights (Brooklyn, NY) incidents. *Atlantic Journal of Communication, 5*, 127–149.

Pratt, C. B., Ha, L., & Pratt, C. A. (2002). Setting the public health agenda on major diseases in Sub-Saharan Africa: African popular magazines and medical journals. *Journal of Communication, 52*, 889–904.

Ren, C., Hust, S. J. T., & Zhang, P. (2010). Stigmatizing HIV/AIDS in the 21st century? Newspaper coverage of HIV/AIDS in China. *China Media Research, 6*, 3–14.

Rosario, V. (2013). Deep history of the AIDS virus. *Gay & Lesbian Review Worldwide, 20*, 32–34.

Sax, P. (2013, August 13). Dolutegravir: A new option in HIV therapy. *Medscape*. Retrieved from http://www.meds cape.com/viewarticle/808710

Tichenor, P. J., Donohue, G., & Olien, C. (1980). *Community conflict and the press*. Beverly Hills, CA: Sage.

Traquina, N. (2004). Theory consolidation in the study of journalism: A comparative analysis of the news coverage of the HIV/AIDS issue in four countries. *Journalism, 5*, 97–116.

Tubeza, P. (2012, October 24). *A first: Stem cell therapy cures HIV patient in Germany*. Retrieved from http://newsinfo. inquirer.net/294354/stem-cell-therapy-cured-man-of-hiv-in-germany-doh

UN gives green light to circumcision. (2007, March 29). *Turkish Daily News*, para. 2. Retrieved from NewsBank.

United Nations Development Programme. (2008). *2007/2008 human development report*. Retrieved from http://hdr stats.undp.org/indicators/58.html

United Nations Development Programme. (2010). *Human development report: The real wealth of nations, pathways to human development* (20th ed.). Retrieved from http://hdr.undp.org/en/reports/global/hdr2010/

United Nations Statistics Division. (2011). *UNSD statistical databases*. Retrieved from http://unstats.un.org/unsd/data bases.htm

University of California, San Francisco. (2009, March). President's Emergency Plan for AIDS Relief (PEPFAR): An overview. *HIV InSite*. Retrieved from http://hivinsite.ucsf.edu/InSite?page=pr-rr-10

World Health Organization. (2007). *World health statistics 2007*. Retrieved from http://www.who.int/en/

World Health Organization. (2011). *Global health observatory: HIV AIDS*. Retrieved from http://www.who.int/gho/ hiv/en/

Wright, J. B., Giovenco, D., DiMarco, G., Dato, A., Holmes, A. C., & Pollock, J. C. (2008). *International newspaper coverage of Muslim immigration since September 11, 2001: A community structure approach*. Paper presented at the annual conference of the National Communication Association, San Diego, CA.

Cross-National Coverage of Water Handling: A Community Structure Approach

Domenick Wissel, Kathleen Ward, John C. Pollock, Allura Hipper, Lauren Klein, and Stefanie Gratale

Department of Communication Studies
The College of New Jersey

A cross-national community structure survey examined the relationship between national characteristics and newspaper coverage of water handling. Sampling all relevant 250+ word articles from September 1, 2000 (the implementation of UN Millennium Development Goal target 7c) to September 1, 2010 in 21 newspapers worldwide in NewsBank and AllAfrica databases yielded 394 articles. Articles were coded for visual/editorial "prominence" and "direction" (framing of clean water access as primarily "government responsibility," "societal responsibility," or "balanced/neutral" coverage), then combined to produce composite "Media Vector" scores for each newspaper (+.5241 to −.3886, a range of .9127). Thirteen of 21 Media Vectors (60%) reflected coverage favoring government responsibility for water handling. Pearson correlations revealed the potency of 4 variable cluster scales (all $\alpha = .70+$) as major correlates of water handling coverage: "female empowerment," "vulnerability," "privilege," and "press freedom," with three clusters connected to "societal" responsibility. Regression analysis reinforced the strong role of female empowerment in coverage emphasizing societal responsibility. Overall, indicators of privilege and press freedom followed suit, also linked to coverage emphasizing "societal" responsibility for water handling, whereas indicators of vulnerability instead correlated with more media emphasis on government responsibility.

INTRODUCTION

Lack of access to clean drinking water is an international health crisis demanding global attention. According to the World Health Organization (WHO; 2012), at least 11% of the world's population, or about 753 million people, lack access to clean drinking water. Clean drinking water is critical for healthy living, as more than 3,000 children die each day due to diarrheal diseases caused by contaminated water. Due to the significance of this issue and the vast number of nations without clean water access, this issue has received extensive cross-national coverage.

In media coverage of water handling and other important issues, journalists utilize frames to "[organize] events into a coherent story, presenting some perspectives as more reasonable than others" (Pollock, 2007, p. 1). Media framing can significantly impact the way the public forms stances on an issue. Two primary frames in reporting of water handling are the "government responsibility" and "societal responsibility" frames. Coverage in the "government responsibility" frame exposes the inadequacies of current water handling policies and promotes government responsibility in increasing access to clean water. Conversely, coverage with a "societal responsibility" frame emphasizes the severity of the water handling crisis with an implicit or explicit responsibility placed among various societal actors, without a call for government action. These frames are analyzed by examining cross-national newspaper coverage of the water handling issue.

This study utilizes a community structure approach to analyze newspaper coverage of the water handling issue, exploring the relationship between national-level community characteristics and newspaper coverage of this pressing issue (Pollock, 2007, p. 23). Rather than asking how media affect society, community structure theory explores how the makeup of society influences media. To examine the influence of national demographics on media coverage of water handling, the following two research questions are explored:

RQ1: How much variation exists in cross-national coverage of water handling?
RQ2: How closely linked is that variation to differences in national characteristics?

Prior community structure theories have considered correlations between newspaper coverage and key demographic clusters, such as privilege (gross domestic product [GDP], literacy rates, life expectancy) and vulnerability (infant mortality, poverty, rates of undernourishment), which this study considers. Of particular interest to this study is the exploration of indicators of female empowerment. Women play a crucial role in addressing human rights crises at the community level, as shown by other community structure studies, and female empowerment is also tied to privilege, as more privileged populations have advocated the advancement of women. As a result, it is important to examine any connections between the authority of women and media emphasis on government or societal responsibility. This study tests several hypotheses to elucidate any connections between national demographics and coverage of water handling.

LITERATURE REVIEW

Although the global scope of the water handling issue has generated strong interest among disciplines such as engineering, biology, political science, and social science, the communication studies field has not significantly explored the relationship between mass media and water handling. Using the terms "water" with "access," "sanitation," and "supply" in the EBSCOhost Communication and Mass Media Complete and Communication Institute for Online Scholarship ComAbstracts databases returned few relevant results discussing mass media and water handling. Although newspapers themselves devote significant attention to the water handling issue, there has been little scholarly attention exploring the subject of media coverage of water handling.

Some communication studies articles addressed water handling but focused on interpersonal communication or attitude surveys. One article examined "water habits and attitudes" in Sydney to be considered when discussing solutions to a water crisis (Sofoulis, 2005, pp. 446–447). Another studied the impact of the water crisis on children in South Africa and how it affected their perceptions about health (Geere, Mokoena, Jagals, Poland, & Hartley, 2010). Still, these articles did not consider media coverage of the issue.

A few studies have analyzed aspects of media coverage of water handling, though they have not examined the relationship between such coverage and national demographics. One examined public resistance to a proposed water reclamation plant, in part because of the " 'professionally pathetic' local media" that focused on politics rather than facts, thereby confusing the public (van Vuuren, 2009, p. 34). In addition, another study examined newspaper headlines and lead paragraphs in Australia, determining the "crisis" label was more frequently associated with government responsibility for crises rather than corporate or business responsibility. Though the study did discuss the significance of media in important social issues, water handling represented just one of several topics under the "crisis" frame, with little specific attention (Power & McLean, 2007). Overall, only a scant number of articles discussed the frames media could take when covering water handling, and they typically focused on the interpersonal rather than mass media subfield of communication studies, or on the impact of media on society. In addition, none of the articles adopted a comparative, cross-national scope, revealing a gap in communication studies literature.

In contrast to the dearth of articles in the communication studies field, a search of the engineering field through the ScienceDirect database yielded 700 results. The biology database PubMed returned thousands of results, while 461 results were yielded in the World Wide Political Science Abstracts, a political science database. Finally, the Applied Social Sciences Index and Abstracts, a social science database, yielded 160 results. Therefore, it is clear that the communication studies field has given inadequate attention to the water handling issue, as media coverage of water handling has been consistently overlooked. By investigating connections between variations in national characteristics and media framing of an important human rights issue, this study intends to bridge the gap between the communication studies field and other fields that have given critical attention to this important topic,.

HYPOTHESES

The following 35 hypotheses were formulated using the community structure approach; they can be categorized into three subgroups: buffer, vulnerability, and stakeholder.

The Buffer Hypothesis

The buffer hypothesis states that in communities with greater levels of privilege, newspapers tend to more favorably cover human rights claims (Pollock, 2007). The reason for this pattern is that privileged groups may be "buffered" from economic and occupational uncertainty and have sympathy for those who are not. Privilege in cross-national research can be conceptualized by high GDP, GDP per capita, literacy rates, and life expectancy.

The buffer hypothesis has been supported through previous cross-national research. Pollock, Reda, Bosland, Hindi, and Zhu (2010) found the greater the proportion of privileged groups in a nation, the more media emphasis on government responsibility for addressing climate change. Pollock and Koerner (2010) found the higher the proportion of privileged groups in a nation, the greater media emphasis on government action to reduce human trafficking. A study on cross-national coverage of the United Nations' (UN's) efforts to combat AIDS showed that the higher the level of privilege in a nation, the more favorable the coverage of UN efforts to fight AIDS (Gratale et al., 2005). Another study on AIDS revealed a correlation between privilege and favorable coverage of nongovernmental organization (NGO) efforts to fight AIDS (Eisenberg, Kester, Caputo, Sierra, & Pollock, 2006). Access to clean water would be considered a basic human right of privileged groups in developed nations, so the following can be predicted:

H1: The higher a nation's GDP, the greater the media emphasis on government responsibility for clean water access (Central Intelligence Agency [CIA], 2011).

H2: The higher a nation's GDP per capita, the greater the media emphasis on government responsibility for clean water access (CIA, 2011).

H3: The higher a nation's literacy rate, the greater the media emphasis on government responsibility for clean water access (CIA, 2011).

H4: The higher a nation's male life expectancy at birth, the greater the media emphasis on government responsibility for clean water access (United Nations Statistics Division, 2011).

H5: The higher a nation's female life expectancy at birth, the greater the media emphasis on government responsibility for clean water access (United Nations Statistics Division, 2011).

H6: The higher percentage of a nation's citizens who are satisfied with the water quality, the greater the media emphasis on government responsibility for clean water access (United Nations Development Programme, 2010).

H7: The higher a nation's total percentage of citizens who are satisfied with their freedom of choice, the greater the media emphasis on government responsibility for clean water access (United Nations Development Programme, 2010).

Health care access. Another strong indicator of a privilege is access to health care services. Pollock and Yulis (2004) discovered the greater the number of physicians per 100,000 citizens in a city, the more favorable the newspaper coverage of physician-assisted suicide. A study on stem cell research found a positive relationship between physicians per 100,000 citizens and more favorable reporting on stem cell research (Pollock, 2007, pp. 89–100). A cross-national study on climate change revealed that the greater the number of hospital beds per 100,000 and the greater the number of physicians per 100,000, the greater the media support for government activity addressing climate change (Pollock, Reda et al., 2010). When a nation has increased access to health services, it is reasonable to assume that the privileged population will understand the importance of water sanitation as a public health issue warranting government action. Therefore, the following is expected:

H8: The greater number of physicians per 100,000 people in a nation, the greater the media emphasis on government responsibility for clean water access (United Nations Statistics Division, 2011).

H9: The greater number of hospital beds per 100,000 people in a nation, the greater the media emphasis on government responsibility for clean water access (United Nations Statistics Division, 2011).

The Vulnerability Hypothesis versus Guard Dog Hypothesis

In addition to the perspectives of the privileged, the interests of the vulnerable or "unbuffered" groups may also be represented in media coverage. According to the vulnerability hypothesis, media reflect the interests of vulnerable groups through coverage of issues critical to such groups. Furthermore, previous community structure studies have illustrated that media coverage may be indicative of the viewpoints of a range of publics, so "mirroring" of issues important to vulnerable groups can occur even though vulnerable groups are rarely associated "with maximum newspaper readership" (Pollock, 2007, p. 137).

Prior research confirms the vulnerability hypothesis. A study on capital punishment revealed that higher levels of poverty in U.S. cities correlated with less favorable coverage of the death penalty, because the impoverished "are more vulnerable to criminal legislation and are often underrepresented in the court system" (Pollock, 2007, p. 145). Another study found that the higher the proportions below the poverty level in a city, the more coverage supported a Patient's Bill of Rights, as the proposal benefited those without sufficient access to health care (Pollock, 2007, p. 154). In addition, Watson and Riffe (2011) analyzed public affairs place blogs in 232 U.S. cities and found a positive correlation between sophisticated measures of "community stress," including a city's per capita murder rate and percentage of households receiving government cash assistance and the presence of public affairs place blogs. In a cross-national study on human trafficking, Pollock and Koerner (2010) showed that higher numbers of thefts per 100,000 and higher proportions below the poverty level correlated with greater media emphasis on government responsibility in human trafficking.

In contrast, Donohue, Tichenor, and Olien's (1995) guard dog hypothesis directly contradicts the contentions of the vulnerability hypotheses, asserting that "media function to preserve the interests of city elites" (Pollock, 2007, p. 24). This "guard dog" perspective may be applicable to the global water handling issue as a nation's elites are likely to already have access to safe drinking water. According to WHO (2012), 753 million people do not have access to safe drinking water, and because water is a scarce resource in a multitude of nations, increased resource competition that comes with government support for increased water access could adversely impact the privileged. As a result, it could be expected that in cases of substantial vulnerability, coverage will support the status quo or ambiguous social efforts, rather than focusing on government responsibility. Thus, the following is expected:

H10: The higher a nation's infant mortality rate, the less media emphasis on government responsibility for clean water access (United Nations Statistics Division, 2011).

H11: The higher a nation's proportion of citizens living below the national poverty level, the less media emphasis on government responsibility for clean water access (United Nations Statistics Division, 2011).

H12: The higher a nation's fertility rate, the less media emphasis on government responsibility for clean water access (United Nations Statistics Division, 2011).

H13: The greater percentage of a nation's population that is undernourished, the less media emphasis on government responsibility for clean water access (United Nations Statistics Division, 2011).

H14: The greater percentage of a nation's population without access to improved water services, the less media emphasis on government responsibility for clean water access (United Nations Development Programme, 2010).

H15: The greater number of deaths due to diarrheal diseases per 100,000 in a nation, the less media emphasis on government responsibility for clean water access (CIA, 2011).

H16: The greater the number of cases of cholera/100,000 in a nation, the less media emphasis on government responsibility for clean water access (CIA, 2011).

H17: The higher a nation's Gini inequality index, the less media emphasis on government responsibility for clean water access. (CIA, 2011).

The Stakeholder Hypothesis

Female empowerment. Tichenor, Donohue, and Olien (1973, 1980) found that the larger a population within a city, the greater variety of viewpoints the media present. More significantly, Pollock (2007) showed that "the size of particular stakeholder groups may have a great deal to do with reporting on issues that affect those groups" (p. 171). In particular, higher proportions of specific stakeholders are linked to coverage emphasizing their concerns (McLeod & Hertog, 1999); in this case, government responsibility for issues affecting those stakeholders. Pollock, D'Angelo, et al. (2010) found, in an examination of African newspaper coverage of AIDS, that higher levels of AIDS prevalence or incidence in a nation correlated with greater media support for government activity to address/reduce the AIDS pandemic. Female empowerment is especially important in regards to the water handling issue because women are imperative for the success of water sanitation projects. The International Water and Sanitation Centre found that "projects designed and run with the full participation of women are more sustainable and effective than those [without it]," confirming an earlier study finding a correlation between female participation and the effectiveness of water projects (Task Force on Gender and Water, 2006, p. 2). Accordingly, when a nation's female population is empowered, media coverage is expected to favor government action to improve water handling, as women are critical stakeholders in the success of water sanitation improvements. As a result, the following is predicted:

H18: The higher a nation's female literacy rate, the greater the media emphasis on government responsibility for clean water access (CIA, 2011).

H19: The higher a nation's female school life expectancy, the greater the media emphasis on government responsibility for clean water access (CIA, 2011).

H20: The higher a nation's female labor force participation rate, the greater the media emphasis on government responsibility for clean water access (United Nations Statistics Division, 2011).

H21: The higher a nation's percentage of females who are satisfied with their freedom of choice, the greater the media emphasis on government responsibility for clean water access (United Nations Development Programme, 2010).

Energy production/consumption and infrastructure. Populations that produce or consume large quantities of different energy resources are particularly influential stakeholder groups. Previous case studies have linked these stakeholder groups with media coverage that supports maintaining the status quo. Wright et al. (2008) found the greater terawatt hours of electricity production, the less favorable the coverage of Muslim immigration, as media did not seek to change public perceptions about growing numbers of immigrants. Curiously, a case study on climate change by Pollock, Reda et al. (2010) found the greater oil/natural gas production and natural gas consumption is in a nation, the greater emphasis on government activity addressing climate change; yet in this case, "the status quo was best preserved by highlighting government efforts to mitigate the possible risks associated with climate change" (p. 12). Yet it is logical to assume that populations producing or consuming large amount of energy resources would seek to preserve the status quo through less emphasis on government intervention regarding water handling; nations with stronger infrastructure, which facilitates the production of resources, would likely adopt a similar viewpoint. Therefore, the following can be expected:

H22: The higher a nation's natural gas consumption, the less media emphasis on government responsibility for clean water access (CIA, 2011).

H23: The higher a nation's natural gas production, the less media emphasis on government responsibility for clean water access (CIA, 2011).

H24: The higher a nation's electricity consumption, the less media emphasis on government responsibility for clean water access (CIA, 2011).

H25: The higher a nation's electricity production, the less media emphasis on government responsibility for clean water access (CIA, 2011).

H26: The higher a nation's coal consumption, the less media emphasis on government responsibility for clean water access (CIA, 2011).

H27: The higher a nation's coal production, the less media emphasis on government responsibility for clean water access (CIA, 2011).

H28: The higher a nation's oil consumption, the less media emphasis on government responsibility for clean water access (CIA, 2011).

H29: The higher a nation's oil production, the less media emphasis on government responsibility for clean water access (CIA, 2011).

H30: The higher the total length of a nation's road network, the less media emphasis on government responsibility for clean water access (CIA, 2011).

H31: The higher a nation's industrial production growth rate, the less media emphasis on government responsibility for clean water access (CIA, 2011).

Communication penetration and press freedom. A nation's degree of freedom of expression is an indication of the manner in which critical issues will be presented to the public. Norris (2004) found that media systems must meet a number of conditions in order to positively affect democratic development: "The analyses substantiate that the normatively postulated positive relationship between democratic government and human development and media systems is manifest only in countries that meet both conditions of an independent free press and open pluralistic access for all citizens" (p. 13). In addition, case studies by Pollock, D'Angelo, et al. (2010) and D'Angelo, Pollock, Kiernicki, and Shaw (2013) revealed that higher levels of press freedom in a nation correlated with greater media support for government assistance to fight AIDS in sub-Saharan Africa. As a result, the following is predicted:

H32: The greater the number of daily newspapers per 1,000 people in a nation, the greater the media emphasis on government responsibility for clean water access (United Nations Development Programme, 2010).

H33: The greater percent of a population covered by a mobile phone network in a nation, the greater the media emphasis on government responsibility for clean water access (United Nations Development Programme, 2010).

H34: The greater number of broadband subscriptions per 100 people in a nation, the greater the media emphasis on government responsibility for clean water access (United Nations Development Programme, 2010).

H35: The greater a nation's freedom of the press, the greater the media emphasis on government responsibility for clean water access (Freedom House, 2011).

METHODOLOGY

To conduct a thorough analysis of water handling coverage, all relevant newspaper articles with a minimum of 250 words were selected from a cross-national representative sample of 21 prestige newspapers (or the most distinguished papers available on accessed databases) from various nations. This research yielded a total of 394 articles, all retrieved from the NewsBank and AllAfrica databases. The selection included the following publications: *Accra Mail, China Daily*, the *Daily Monitor, Daily Nation*, the *Herald*, the *Japan Times, El Mercurio, La Nación*, the *Namibian, New Strait Times*, the *New Times, New Vision*, the *New York Times*, the *Sydney Morning Herald, This Day*, the *Times*, the *Times of India, Times of Zambia*, the *Toronto Star, Turkish Daily News*, and *El Universal*.

The sample data collection ranged from September 1, 2000, to September 1, 2010. In September 2000, the United Nations developed and signed the Millennium Development Goals (MDGs), articulating eight international development goals that members of the United Nations and numerous international organizations have pledged to accomplish by 2015. The MDGs encourage global partnerships to improve social and economic conditions in less privileged countries. Under the environmental sustainability goal, target 7C strives to "halve, by 2015, the proportion of the population without sustainable access to safe drinking water and basic sanitation" (United Nations, 2010, para. 3). According to the World Health Organization (2012), 6.1 billion people, or 89% of the world's population, gained access to improved water services by the end of 2010, exceeding the MDG2015 target and representing a reasonable end date for data collection.

Article Coding and Procedures

Each article was assigned two scores that together convey its issue projection in a newspaper: "prominence" (representing editorial positioning of the article within the paper) and "direction" (framing of the issue as government or societal responsibility, or balanced/neutral). Articles were coded as "government responsibility" if they emphasized government accountability for clean water access and supported government action to improve water conditions. Articles that detailed government-related improvements to the water supply were also coded as "government responsibility." An article from *China Daily* stated, "China will secure safe drinking water for 267 million rural residents by 2012, three years ahead of the schedule required by the UN's Millennium Declaration. . . . [It] will also exceed requirement by helping 70 percent of people in need" ("Nation to Secure," 2006, para. 1–2). In general, articles in the government responsibility frame placed an emphasis on government as a primary actor in the water handling issue and/or advocated for government intervention in increasing clean water access.

In contrast, some articles detailed the severity of the water crisis without discussing a need for government action, instead presenting water handling as a concern of nongovernmental actors such as NGOs or international agencies. These articles were coded as "societal responsibility." An article from Kenya's *Daily Nation* stated, "The area is synonymous with severe and frequent water shortages, which also threaten to halt the operations of colleges, schools, hospitals and prisons" (Mutua, 2008, para. 2–3). This article described the bleak state of the water supplies without discussing any need or recommendation for government action. Overall, articles that emphasized more ambiguous societal responsibility on the part of any one of many nongovernmental actors that could bring about change represented the societal responsibility frame.

Articles were coded as "balanced/neutral" if both sides of the water handling issue were considered, either by discussing both challenges and progress or by attributing responsibility to both governmental and societal actors. Balanced/neutral articles did not assign sole responsibility to any one party but could reference both government and society or leave the issue open-ended. A balanced/neutral article in Uganda's *New Vision* discussed the UN MDG target 7C, establishing targets for improved water access and sanitation; yet the article also noted that "despite [the] significant investment in water, a large proportion of the population still has no access to safe and clean water" (Bazira, 2009, para. 3). This article explained both the goal of increasing clean water access and its lack of success. Generally, balanced/neutral articles simply described the water handling issue without taking a strong stance or assigning responsibility.

Two researchers coded 296 of the 394 articles, resulting in a Scott's Pi coefficient of intercoder reliability of .9025. Prominence and direction scores for each article were combined into a single Media Vector for each newspaper. Researchers used Pearson correlations and regression analysis to illustrate connections between Media Vectors and national demographics, and to identify the variables most significantly driving coverage.

RESULTS AND SCALE CONSTRUCTION

This study examined cross-national newspaper coverage of water handling by comparing media coverage and resulting Media Vectors from 21 nations from September 1, 2000, to

TABLE 1
Media Vectors by Nation

Nation	Newspaper	Media Vector
Ethiopia	The Daily Monitor	.5241
Japan	The Japan Times	.3859
Rwanda	The New Times	.3624
Nigeria	This Day	.2936
Ghana	Accra Mail	.2088
China	China Daily	.1750
Malaysia	New Strait Times	.0885
Zimbabwe	The Herald	.0653
Zambia	Times of Zambia	.0446
Mexico	El Universal	.0292
Turkey	Turkish Daily News	.0225
United States	The New York Times	.0198
Uganda	New Vision	.0176
United Kingdom	The Times	−.0173
Chile	El Mercurio	−.0182
India	The Times of India	−.0595
Namibia	The Namibian	−.1949
Australia	The Sydney Morning Herald	−.2413
Argentina	La Nación	−.2650
Canada	The Toronto Star	−.3466
Kenya	Daily Nation	−.3886

September 1, 2010. Thirteen of the 21 Media Vectors, or roughly 60%, ranged from .0176 to .5241 and emphasized government responsibility in their coverage of clean water access. Media coverage in eight nations yielded Media Vectors that reflected societal responsibility for clean water access, with scores from −.0173 to −.3886. The overall range of Media Vectors was .9127. Strikingly, African nations represented the majority of nations with newspaper coverage reflecting an emphasis on government responsibility, with the following Media Vector scores: Ethiopia (.5421), Rwanda (.3624), Nigeria (.2936), Ghana (.2088), Zimbabwe (.0653), Zambia (.0446), and Uganda (.0176) displaying positive Media Vectors. Table 1 lists all Media Vectors.

Pearson correlations demonstrated correlations between Media Vectors and several national characteristics. Significant relationships were discovered in stakeholder, vulnerability, and violated buffer categories, and Pearson correlation results are presented in Table 2.

Stakeholder Hypothesis Significant

Role of female empowerment. Regarding stakeholder hypotheses about female empowerment, it was hypothesized that the higher a nation's female literacy rate, female school life expectancy, female labor force participation rate, and percentage of females who are satisfied with their freedom of choice, the greater the media emphasis on government responsibility for clean water access. Indicators related to female empowerment were confirmed as significant correlates with coverage of water handling, yet not in the direction predicted. Higher female

TABLE 2
Pearson Correlation Results

National Characteristic	Pearson Correlation	Significance
Female literacy rate	−.491	.012*
Literacy rate	−.480	.014*
Female school life expectancy	−.479	.014*
Deaths due to diarrheal diseases/100,000	.457	.019*
Percentage satisfied with water quality	−.421	.029*
Percentage covered by a mobile phone network	−.418	.030*
Percentage without access to improved water services	.411	.032*
Freedom of the press	−.393	.039*
Infant mortality rate	.387	.042*
Percentage of females satisfied with freedom of choice	−.366	.052*
Overall population satisfied with freedom of choice	−.355	.057
Fertility rate	.336	.069
Physicians/100,000	−.329	.072
Male life expectancy	−.298	.094
Female life expectancy	−.274	.114
Industrial production growth rate	.273	.116
GDP per capita	−.273	.116
Percentage undernourished	.264	.124
Cases of cholera	.215	.196
Daily newspapers/1,000	.211	.235
Broadband subscriptions/100	−.202	.197
Percentage living below national poverty level	.193	.208
Coal production	.166	.278
Coal consumption	.147	.307
Natural gas production	−.118	.306
Gini Inequality Index	−.111	.315
Hospital beds/10,000	.090	.349
GDP	.083	.360
Electricity consumption	.079	.366
Electricity production	.069	.384
Oil production	−.061	.396
Female labor force participation rate	.056	.405
Oil consumption	.047	.420
Natural gas production	−.027	.454
Length of a nation's road network	−.012	.480

Note. GDP = gross domestic product.
*$p < .05$.

literacy rate ($r = -.491$, $p = .012$) and female school life expectancy ($r = -.479$, $p = .014$) were found to be significant at an almost .01 level, correlating with coverage emphasizing "societal" responsibility. In addition, percentage of females satisfied with their freedom of choice ($r = -.366$, $p = .052$) was found marginally significant and also correlated with the societal responsibility frame.

The female stakeholder indicators were powerful drivers of media coverage of water handling, perhaps because of the significance of women as stakeholders for this issue. An article in the *Japan Times* stated, "Experts argue that the gender issue holds great significance when discussing water issues, as women are often the most vulnerable, especially in rural areas where they sometimes have to walk long distances to access water for daily household needs" (Murakami, 2003, para. 3). Other articles described the role of women as gatekeepers for family health, responsible for collecting and providing clean water to their communities, and elaborated the tremendous difficulties women encounter in locating and transporting clean water.

Prior scholarly research has explored strong ties between women and access to clean water. Fisher (2008) examined the effect of implementation of clean water supplies, finding that in four communities in India, the addition of water access points was followed by an increase in girls' school attendance and women's literacy rates. Fisher also noted that a "rural supply and sanitation project of the World Bank in Morocco found a 20% increase in school attendance over four years, attributed in part to a reduction of between 50–90% in the time required for fetching water" (p. 225). These findings display the intricate connection between clean water access and female literacy rates and school attendance, two of this study's most significant indicators.

The established connection between women and water handling would seemingly predict a correlation between empowered women and a call for government action. Yet this study has elucidated precisely the opposite, as indicators of female empowerment were tied to a strong emphasis on societal responsibility. It is possible that coverage of water handling may reflect women's awareness of experiences and struggles regarding water handling, and the crucial role they are compelled to play. The prominent, well-documented role for women in water handling may negate any conceptualization of a corollary role for government. Perhaps this finding is not counterintuitive to the notion of female empowerment influencing media coverage of water handling in a proactive way but rather a reasonable offspring of the connection between empowered females and clean water access. As females become more literate and independent, they may legitimize this empowerment through an internalization of responsibility for change. Instead of calling for government reform, they see themselves as agents of change through vehicles of societal advocacy and action, emerging from the ground up rather than through top-down influences. Empowered females, therefore, might see a need for change as a call to change. This conceptualization may have influenced the correlation between female empowerment and coverage favoring societal responsibility.

Role of media access. Another significant stakeholder indicator was press freedom/access. Greater levels of communication freedom were predicted to correlate with coverage emphasizing government responsibility because, according to Norris (2004), a positive relationship exists between human development and "free" media systems. Yet Pearson correlations for percentage covered by a mobile phone network ($r = -.418$, $p = .030$) and freedom of the press ($r = -.393$, $p = .039$) correlated with the societal responsibility frame.

The disconfirmation of these hypotheses led to an analysis of Media Vector scores, which revealed a strong correlation between high ("government responsibility") Media Vectors and African nations with lower levels of Press Freedom, including Ethiopia (.5421), Rwanda (.3624), Zimbabwe (.0653), and Zambia (.0446). In many African nations, media systems are heavily restricted by government intervention, and journalists are coerced into self-censorship due to threats of prosecution (Freedom House, 2011). As a result, newspapers in these nations might inflate discussions of government efforts to address water handling. Alternatively, consensus opinion in these nations might consider government to be a critical actor in addressing the water handling crisis, due to the severity of the problem. Either of these circumstances could have played a role in the correlation between higher levels of press freedom/access and less support for the government responsibility frame.

Guard Dog Hypothesis Disconfirmed; Vulnerability Hypothesis Prevails

The guard dog hypothesis originally predicted higher proportions of vulnerable populations in a nation would correlate with less emphasis on government responsibility in the coverage of clean water access. Because water is such a scarce resource in many nations, it was hypothesized that elites would seek to prevent any increased competition for resources that results from government action to broaden access, and that media would promote the status quo rather than focus on social progress. After running Pearson correlations, the guard dog hypothesis was disconfirmed. Characteristics representing vulnerability, including deaths due to diarrheal disease per 100,000 ($r = .457, p = .019$), percentage without access to improved water services ($r = .411, p = .032$), and infant mortality rate ($r = .387, p = .042$), were found significant, with a higher prevalence of such conditions correlating with greater media emphasis on government responsibility. In this manner, media coverage of water handling seems to reflect the interests of vulnerable populations, thereby supporting the vulnerability rather than the guard dog hypothesis.

Indicators of vulnerability are especially pertinent to the water handling issue. Contaminated water increases the risk of contracting diarrheal disease, and access to clean drinking water aids in its prevention, so nations with greater numbers of deaths due to diarrheal diseases are in dire need of increased clean water access. According to the WHO, "diarrheal disease is the second leading cause of death in children under five years old," with children under two worldwide predominately being affected (WHO, 2009, para. 1). Therefore, lack of access to clean water may be a substantial contributor to a nation's infant mortality rate. As a result, nations with higher proportions of citizens without access to improved water services may find their interests reflected in media that call for government responsibility in water handling, thereby reinforcing the vulnerability hypothesis.

Violated Buffer Hypothesis Confirmed

Using the buffer hypotheses, it was expected that the greater proportion of privileged residents in a nation, the more likely media would report on human rights issues like water access emphasizing government responsibility (Pollock, 2007). Privileged groups are considered "buffered" from economic and occupational uncertainty and thus assumed to be more sympathetic to human rights claims. However, Pearson correlations revealed the opposite pattern. More specifically, two characteristics indicating privilege, literacy rate ($r = -.480, p = .014$) and percentage satisfied with water quality ($r = -.421, p = .029$), yielded significant correlations with coverage emphasizing societal over government responsibility.

These findings may actually be more aptly examined through the lens of the "violated buffer hypothesis," which links "levels of privilege in a [nation] and reporting on 'ominous' issues: those that contain biological threats or threats to a cherished way of life" (Pollock, 2007, p. 101). The empirical correlation between privilege and less emphasis on government responsibility suggests that restricted access to clean water and water sanitation can signify a biological danger and threat to a cherished way of life for privileged individuals. When this way of life is endangered or a threat is posed, privileged individuals in a nation may consider themselves at risk, leading to negative newspaper coverage of the perceived threat. In this case, a violated buffer hypothesis was seemingly reflected in newspaper reporting on water handling that deemphasized government responsibility and intervention; perhaps privileged groups had greater confidence that "societal" elements such as charities, NGOs, the United Nations, and foreign aid could be more efficacious in addressing the issue of clean water access.

Variable Reduction to Four Scales

Based on initial Pearson correlations, the most powerful variables were combined into four composite scales: "female empowerment" (Cronbach's $\alpha = .776$), consisting of female literacy rate, female school life expectancy, percentage of females satisfied with their freedom of choice, and female life expectancy indicators; "vulnerability" (Cronbach's $\alpha = .784$), consisting of the deaths due to diarrheal diseases, percentage without access to improved water services, infant mortality rate, and fertility rate indicators; "privilege" (Cronbach's $\alpha = .746$), consisting of literacy rate, percentage satisfied with water quality, overall population satisfied with their freedom of choice, and male life expectancy indicators; and "press freedom" (Cronbach's $\alpha = .710$), consisting of the percentage covered by a mobile phone network, freedom of the press, and broadband subscriptions indicators. Cronbach's reliability analysis was used to measure the strength of the scales, yielding significant results for "female empowerment," "vulnerability," and "privilege" scales. An "energy" scale was also considered, despite such indicators not reaching significance in the Pearson correlations, but discarded because it had a Cronbach's alpha of .563. The four other scales had Cronbach's alphas higher than .70. New Pearson correlations between the four reliable scales and Media Vectors are listed in Table 3.

Regression analysis linking the new indicator scales with the Media Vector scores revealed that "female empowerment" accounted for 9.9% of the variance. This finding reinforces the supposition that female empowerment plays a significant role in media coverage of water handling, perhaps because clean water access is associated, in particular, with greater female literacy rates and school life expectancies. Greater levels of female empowerment correlated with coverage emphasizing societal responsibility for water handling. Female empowerment may thus work in opposition to a perceived need or call for government intervention, as females may be seen as crucial actors in lieu of government or may not trust government to help them or their families. Table 4 displays the regression analysis.

TABLE 3
Pearson Correlations Between Indicator Scales and Media Vectors

Indicator Scale	Cronbach's α	Pearson Correlation	Significance
Female Empowerment	.776	−.466	.017*
Vulnerability	.784	.439	.023*
Privilege	.746	−.418	.03*
Press Freedom	.710	−.271	.124

*$p < .05$.

TABLE 4
Regression Analysis of Indicator Scales

Model	R (equation)	R^2 (cumulative)	R^2 Change	F Change	Significance of F Change
Female Empowerment	.315	.099	.099	1.981	.176

CONCLUSIONS AND IMPLICATIONS FOR FURTHER RESEARCH

Notwithstanding many areas of significant correlations, perhaps the most salient results pertain to female empowerment. Of interest, higher female literacy rate, female school life expectancy, and percentage of females satisfied with their freedom of choice were all associated with less emphasis on government responsibility for clean water access, disconfirming the original hypotheses. The importance of the female indicators was furthered confirmed through the creation of composite scales. A regression analysis of the composite scales found female empowerment to be by far the most significant scale associated with Media Vectors. These results emphasize the important role that women play as gatekeepers for family health and the complex association of empowered women with media coverage. Because women are crucial to the water handling issue, if they are more empowered, women in general may be regarded as more capable of addressing this issue and less reliant on government action.

This study also revealed several other significant correlations between national characteristics and media coverage of water handling. When analyzing such correlations in totality, a pattern emerges: Characteristics of more developed nations correlated with a media emphasis on societal responsibility, whereas indicators associated with developing nations correlated with media emphasis on government responsibility. In particular, higher deaths due to diarrheal diseases per 100,000, percentage without access to improved water services, and infant mortality rate were associated with greater media emphasis on government responsibility for clean water access. On the other hand, higher literacy rates and percentage satisfied with water quality were associated with less media emphasis on government responsibility for clean water access. These results support a violated buffer hypothesis, which expects that more privileged groups will be connected with media support for human rights claims linked to biological threats or threats to a cherished way of life. In this case, perhaps privileged groups favored the intervention of societal groups and saw them as more capable of addressing the problem than governments of nations struggling with water crises.

Further analysis found that African nations with coverage emphasizing government responsibility for clean water access often manifested government restrictions on press freedom. In addition, nations with a greater percentage covered by a mobile phone network and increased freedom of the press displayed coverage with less emphasis on government responsibility. These findings, in conjunction with the important role press freedom was found to play in coverage of the African AIDS epidemic (Pollock, D'Angelo et al., 2010), reveal the importance of considering nations' media systems, specifically levels of press freedom, in addition to other structural conditions when conducting cross-national studies of social justice issues (D'Angelo et al., 2013).

The observed connections between characteristics of more developed nations and a societal media frame, and corresponding characteristics of developing nations and a government frame, can be readily explained. More developed nations may have a more thriving social sector.

With basic needs met, the populations have a greater ability to devote time to social action. The public may consider itself more empowered in enacting change, with a stronger belief in individual efficacy. Moreover, more privileged nations might also contend that international organizations with more resources could make greater strides in improving water access than individual governments in crisis areas. These characteristics could logically correlate with media emphasis on societal responsibility for key human rights issues.

In contrast, developing nations struggling to meet more basic needs would likely have fewer resources to devote to the social sector. The populations may feel less empowered to effect change through social activism, and as a result, government may appear a necessary actor in mitigating social crises. With an issue such as water handling, affected populations might believe that true progress cannot be made without government support, particularly if the government is more controlling. Thus, fragile social conditions could result in a media emphasis on government responsibility for addressing social issues.

One avenue for further research on cross-national newspaper coverage of water handling would be to examine the effects of MDG target 7C and its aim to halve the population without clean water access by 2015 (United Nations, 2010). A new study could begin with coverage after September 1, 2010, the end of this study's date range. Another possibility for further research would be to conduct a similar study on a smaller scope. Focusing solely on African nations, for example, would allow for more in-depth regional study across more similar nations, particularly those with more restricted media systems. Future research could also focus on a smaller subset of national characteristics, such as those pertaining to female empowerment. Depending on the availability of data, additional indicators to consider in this analysis would be women in the workforce, women in government, and women in media.

Finally, future studies could utilize a different approach in the analysis of national indicators. With the emergence of the government versus societal responsibility frames, it could be useful to consider hypotheses grouped according to characteristics of developed nations versus developing nations. In this way, umbrella hypotheses such as stakeholder, vulnerability, and buffer could be analyzed in the aggregate as reflecting "macro" measures of level of development and press freedom (media system freedom; D'Angelo et al., 2013). Future community structure research could employ a new demographic dimension attempting to identify national indicators related to social sector activity. If relevant data are available, researchers could prepare a "social sector index" or "social capital index" to portray how active and prominent social sector efforts are in a nation and then test for correlations between media coverage and this index.

This community structure analysis of cross-national coverage of water handling confirms the validity of the stakeholder, violated buffer, and vulnerability hypotheses. It also demonstrates the utility of government and societal responsibility frames in relation to national indicators. Due to its success in identifying the association between national demographics and media coverage of water handling, community structure theory should be applied to further scholarly research on the water handling issue.

ACKNOWLEDGMENT

A previous version of this article was presented at the biannual conference of the University of Kentucky Conference on Health Communication, April 2012.

REFERENCES

Bazira, H. (2009, May 11). Harvest rain water to fight water scarcity. *New Vision*. Retrieved from NewsBank database.

Central Intelligence Agency (CIA). (2011). *The world factbook*. Retrieved from https://www.cia.gov/library/publica tions/the-world-factbook/

D'Angelo, P., Pollock, J. C., Kiernicki, K., & Shaw, D. (2013). Framing of AIDS in Africa: Press-state relations, HIV/AIDS news, and journalistic advocacy in four sub-Saharan Anglophone newspapers. *Politics and the Life Sciences, 33*, 100–125.

Donohue, G. A., Tichenor, P. J., & Olien, C. (1995). A guard dog perspective on the role of media. *Journal of Communication, 45*, 115–132.

Eisenberg, D., Kester, A., Caputo, L., Sierra, J., & Pollock, J. C. (2006, November). *Cross-national coverage of NGO's efforts to fight AIDS: A community structure approach.* Paper presented at the annual conference of the National Communication Association, San Antonio, TX.

Fisher, J. (2008). Women in water supply, sanitation and hygiene programmes. *Municipal Engineer, 161*, 223–229. doi:10.1680/muen.2008.161.4.223

Freedom House. (2011). *Freedom of the press*. Retrieved from http://www.freedomhouse.org/report-types/freedom-press

Geere, J. L., Mokoena, M. M., Jagals, P. P., Poland, F. F., & Hartley, S. S. (2010). How do children perceive health to be affected by domestic water carrying? Qualitative findings from a mixed methods study in rural South Africa. *Child: Care, Health & Development, 36*, 818–826. doi:10.1111/j.1365-2214.2010.01098.x

Gratale, S., Hagert, J., Dey, L., Pollock, J., D'Angelo, P., Braddock, P., . . . Montgomery, A. (2005, May). *International coverage of United Nations' efforts to combat AIDS: A structural approach.* Paper presented at the annual conference of the International Communication Association, New York, NY.

McLeod, D. M., & Hertog, J. K. (1999). Social control, social change, and the mass media's role in the regulation of protest groups. In D. Demers & K. Viswanath (Eds.), *Mass media, social control, and social change: A macrosocial perspective* (pp. 305–331). Ames, IA: Iowa State University Press.

Murakami, A. (2003, March 18). Water forum promotes role of women. *The Japan Times*. Retrieved from NewsBank database.

Mutua, K. (2008, June 10). Residents battle disease as taps remain dry for months. *Daily Nation*. Retrieved from NewsBank database.

Nation to secure safe drinking water. (2006, June 10). *China Daily*. Retrieved from NewsBank database.

Norris, P. (2004). Global political communication: Good governance, human development and mass communication. In F. Esser & B. Pfetsch (Eds.), *Comparing political communication: Theories, cases and challenges* (pp. 115–150). Cambridge, UK: Cambridge University Press.

Pollock, J. C. (2007). *Tilted mirrors: Media alignment with political and social change—A community structure approach*. Cresskill, NJ: Hampton Press.

Pollock, J. C., D'Angelo, P., Shaw, D., Burd, A., Kiernicki, K., & Raudenbush, J. (2010, June). *African newspaper coverage of AIDS: Comparing new models of press-state relations and structural factors in sub-Saharan Anglophone Africa*. Paper presented at the annual conference of the International Communication Association, Singapore.

Pollock, J. C., & Koerner, M. (2010). *Cross-national coverage of human trafficking: A community structure approach* (Documento de Trabajo # 2). Departamento de Derecho y Ciencia Política/Universidad Nacional de La Matanza, Buenos Aires, Argentina.

Pollock, J. C., Reda, E., Bosland, A., Hindi, M., & Zhu, D. (2010, June). *Cross-national coverage of climate change: A community structure approach*. Paper presented at the annual conference of the International Communication Association, Singapore.

Pollock, J. C., & Yulis, S. G. (2004). Nationwide newspaper coverage of physician-assisted suicide: A community structure approach. *Journal of Health Communication, 9*, 281–307.

Power, M., & McLean, H. (2007). The crisis frame in Australian newspaper reports in 2005. *Australian Journal of Communication, 34*, 39–57. Retrieved from EBSCOhost database.

Sofoulis, Z. (2005). Big water, everyday water: A sociotechnical perspective. *Continuum: Journal of Media & Cultural Studies, 19*, 445–463. doi:10.1080/10304310500322685

Task Force on Gender and Water. (2006). *Gender, water and sanitation: A policy brief*. Retrieved from http://www.unwater.org/downloads/unwpolbrief230606.pdf

Tichenor, P. J., Donohue, G., & Olien, C. (1973). Mass communication research: Evolution of a structural model. *Journalism Quarterly 50*, 419–425.

Tichenor, P. J., Donohue, G., & Olien, C. (1980). *Community conflict and the press.* Beverly Hills, CA: Sage.

United Nations. (2010). United Nations Millennium Development Goals. Retrieved from http://www.un.org/millen niumgoals/environ.shtml

United Nations Development Programme. (2010). *Human development report: The real wealth of nations, pathways to human development* (20th ed.). Retrieved from http://hdr.undp.org/en/reports/global/hdr2010/

United Nations Statistics Division. (2011). *UNSD statistical databases.* Retrieved from http://unstats.un.org/unsd/data bases.htm

van Vuuren, K. (2009). Water pressure: The crisis in Australia. *Media Development, 56*, 33–37. Retrieved from EBSCOhost database.

Watson, B., & Riffe, D. (2011). Structural determinants of local public affairs place blogging: Structural pluralism and community stress. *Mass Communication and Society, 14*, 879–904.

World Health Organization. (2009). *Diarrheal disease.* Retrieved from http://www.who.int/mediacentre/factsheets/ fs330/en/index.html

World Health Organization. (2012, March 6). *Millennium Development Goal drinking water target met* [Press release]. Retrieved from http://www.who.int/mediacentre/news/releases/2012/drinking_water_20120306/en/index.html

Wright, J. B., Giovenco, D., DiMarco, G., Dato, A., Holmes, A. C., & Pollock, J. C. (2008, November). *International newspaper coverage of Muslim immigration since September 11, 2001: A community structure approach.* Paper presented at the annual conference of the National Communication Association, San Diego, CA.

Comparing Coverage of Child Labor and National Characteristics: A Cross-National Exploration

Jordan Gauthier Kohn and John C. Pollock

Department of Communication Studies
The College of New Jersey

A community structure analysis compared cross-national coverage of child labor in 21 countries, sampling all 250+ word articles from November 19, 2000, to November 6, 2012. The resulting 244 articles were coded for "prominence" and "direction" ("government intervention," "society—including nongovernmental organizations—intervention," or "balanced/neutral" coverage), then combined into newspaper "Media Vector" scores (range = .317 to −.382). Fourteen of 21 newspapers supported government intervention in child labor issues. Contrary to expectation, Pearson correlations revealed four significant privilege indicators supported coverage less reliant on "government" and more on "society" (nonprofits, nongovernmental organizations, foreign aid): female school-life expectancy ($r = -.585$, $p = .003$), gross domestic product/capita ($r = -.557$, $p = .004$), male life expectancy ($r = -.379$, $p = .045$), and female life expectancy ($r = -.364$, $p = .052$). "Stakeholder/media" access was also linked with less support for government intervention (broadband subscriptions/100 people in a nation: $r = -.619$, $p = .001$). A regression of varimax rotated factors against Media Vectors yielded "privilege" (primarily male, female life expectancy) and "gendered communication" (primarily female literacy rate, use of mobile phones) collectively accounting for 25% of the variance, all connected to coverage supporting "society" action on child labor. Female empowerment matters.

INTRODUCTION

Child labor is a difficult issue to address; it may seem virtuous to eradicate immediately this ongoing and flourishing practice, but in some cases, doing so could cause as much damage as good. The majority of children involved are from exceedingly poor families and need this income, even though diminutive, to supplement family funds or pay for personal education.

Denying them this possible income can lead children to seek different, lower paid work, and, often enough, prostitution. In 2008 the International Labour Organization (ILO) reported that 14.1% of children or about 152,850,000 children ages 5 to 12 were employed in various jobs, many of them physically or mentally hazardous (Diallo, Hagemann, Etienne, Gurbuzer & Mehran, 2010, p. 8). Noticeably, poverty is the leading factor contributing to child labor. According to the United Kingdom Committee for UNICEF,

> debt, bloated military budgets and structural adjustment programmes imposed by the International Monetary Fund and the World Bank have eroded the capacity of many governments to provide education and services for children, and have also pushed up prices for basic necessities. (Shah, 2001, p. 1)

Despite immediate economic benefit for children or their families, there is little dispute about whether child labor is socially acceptable or immoral. Many would concur that it is immoral. The question this investigation raises is: Should domestic governments be strongly involved in addressing this unethical practice? Some believe it is vital for governments to act stalwartly to resolve the child labor issue that plagues many developing countries. They would argue that this responsibility is in line with the role of any government to protect its citizens, especially its vulnerable youth. Conversely, others reason that the issue of child labor should be left to society, either individuals or groups, to deal with the predicament. Within the communication and journalism fields, scholars often refer to divergent media perspectives as "frames;" a majority of media reporting on child labor almost certainly lies within one of these two frames, government or society responsibility, reflecting public debates.

This analysis investigates recent media reporting on the topic of global child labor, specifically in newspapers. This study utilizes the community structure approach to assess the manner in which society affects newspaper coverage of this issue. Using the framework of the community structure approach, this study explores how specific national indicators are linked to leading newspaper coverage of child labor. This study's analysis of framing variations in international newspaper coverage of child labor therefore addresses two major research questions:

RQ1: How much variation is there in newspaper coverage of child labor cross-nationally?

RQ2: To what extent do different national demographics correspond with variations in reporting on child labor?

Several demographic factors can influence media coverage regarding child labor. This study explores the precise relationship between national demographics and coverage of government involvement in child labor issues.

LITERATURE REVIEW

Child labor has become a prevalent topic of interest for several fields of study. Humanities, sociology, and business have all examined the controversy of child labor and have given it considerable attention. While the study of media coverage of child labor would appear relevant for communication studies research, the communication field has largely neglected to investigate child labor in the media. Communication databases such as Communication and Mass Media Complete (CMMC) and the Communication Institute for Online Scholarship were searched using terms including "child labor" and "Child labor AND media coverage." Only a few articles were relevant to the framing of child labor in the media.

Searches of "child labor and media coverage" as well as "child labor and newspaper coverage" yielded zero results in the Communication Institute for Online Scholarship ComAbstracts. Varying search terms were used in the CMMC database; each included the pairing of "child labor" with "media coverage" and "news coverage." Although "Child labor" yielded 41 hits and "child labor AND media coverage" yielded only one article, "Child labor AND news coverage" surfaced 743 hits. However, only approximately 30 actually dealt with media coverage of child labor. In large part these articles could be sorted into three major categories: news coverage of past labor strikes, news coverage of political controversy over labor unions, and news coverage of women's rights in the workforce. One article, "Child Labor And Photojournalism," provided a review of the photographic evidence of child labor and violation of human rights in Africa, South Asia, South America, and Northeastern Europe (Gianotti, 2011). A second article found in the CMMC database studied framing analysis and attribution theory for media coverage of CBS's reality series *Kid Nation* (Arganbright, Gehrke, & Ren, 2008), finding that newswriters framed *Kid Nation* as a child labor issue, attributing substantial blame to the children's parents and the CBS network for conceptualizing the television show. The third relevant article commented on past attempts to regulate child labor within the United States with both positive and negative, true and false, propaganda (Morgan, 1925). Although some articles were found regarding child labor within the communication studies field, ultimately, only one (Gianotti, 2011) focused on how the child labor issue was presented in the media.

Although communication studies research yielded minimal results, the humanities have given more serious attention to examining child labor. In one database alone, Humanities Full Text (H.W. Wilson), the search term "child labor AND global" yielded seven relevant results. In the sociology field, the Applied Social Sciences Index and Abstracts database yielded 1,353 results with the search term "child labor" and 32 results with the search term "child labor and media." Articles included such topics as national newspaper excerpts on work-related issues including child labor ("Media focus," 1997), child labor practices in the advertising and film industry (Garbas, 2009), and the impact of international standards on domestic attitudes regarding child labor (Doepke & Zilibotti, 2010). In the business database Business Source Premier, search terms including "child labor AND media coverage" yielded one related article hit, and "child labor" yielded 1,808 articles, many directly related to this study. The terms "child labor AND media coverage" unearthed 1,480 articles in Business Abstracts with Full Text (Wilson Web), covering such subjects as the economics of child labor, the history of antilabor movements (Bachman, 2000), and the promotion of international labor standards (Schrage & Ewing, 2005).

Clearly, the field of communication studies has not devoted sufficient attention to media framing of child labor or government involvement in child labor. In contrast, the disciplines of humanities, sociology, and business have offered extensive coverage of this important issue. This study intends to address the gap, comparing differences in national characteristics with variations in international media coverage of child labor.

HYPOTHESES

The following 36 hypotheses were developed using the community structure approach. They can be categorized into three subgroups: violated buffer, vulnerability, and stakeholder.

Violated Buffer Hypothesis

Before focusing on the violated buffer hypothesis, its counterpart, the buffer hypothesis, should be explained; the buffer hypothesis states that in communities with greater levels of privilege, newspaper coverage of human rights claims tends to be more favorable (Pollock, 2007, p. 61). In comparison, the violated buffer hypothesis suggests, "The greater the proportion of privileged citizens in a (community), the more unfavorable newspaper reporting is likely to be on issues framed as 'ominous,' hazardous to physical safety or a secure, predictable way of life" (Pollock, 2007, p. 53). Cross-national characteristics used to measure privilege include gross domestic product (GDP), GDP per capita, and literacy rates.

The violated buffer hypothesis has been supported through previous cross-national research. Pollock found higher levels of privilege in communities (measured by family income and education level) associated with media concerns about tobacco advertising to children, a practice that affected all children, whether from more or less privileged backgrounds (Pollock, 2007, p. 112). Also, Pollock, Mink, Puma, Shuhala, and Ostrander (2001) found that women's eligibility for roles in combat were seen as threats to resolute viewpoints that women should be protected from danger. Likewise Pollock and Koerner (2010) found that the higher the proportion of privileged groups in a nation, the greater media emphasis on government action to reduce human trafficking. Similarly, a study of media coverage relating to Magic Johnson's HIV announcement showed that coverage of the issue was less favorable in communities with high levels of privilege (Pollock, 2007, p. 217).

Typically, privileged groups function as though a "buffer" exists, protecting them from certain dangers, but these studies suggest that threats to an existing way of life cause this buffer to be "violated." Child labor is hazardous to the safety of children and violates any developed nation's cherished way of life. Based on previous research, it is reasonable to assume countries with a higher proportion of privileged citizens would similarly empathize with government involvement to regulate or end child labor. Therefore, the following hypotheses apply to coverage of child labor:

H1: The higher the GDP in a country, the greater the media emphasis on government responsibility to reduce child labor (Central Intelligence Agency [CIA], 2009).

H2: The higher the GDP per capita, the greater the media emphasis on government responsibility to reduce child labor (CIA, 2009).

H3: The higher the literacy rate, the greater the media emphasis on government responsibility to reduce child labor (CIA, 2009).

Female empowerment. Improving the rights and life chances of women is a measure of relative privilege. Feminists, both men and women alike, have fought for the rights and advancement of women and elimination of child labor. Therefore, empowered women are a crucial stakeholder in relation to child labor. For instance, from 1923 to 1925, the Chinese

Young Women's Christian Association (YWCA) led an international campaign to ban child labor (Littel-Lamb, 2011). Apart from protecting the welfare of children, these empowered women also represented a nation's willingness to treat both sexes equally. Therefore, the following is expected:

H4: The higher a nation's female literacy rate, the greater the media emphasis on government responsibility to reduce child labor (CIA, 2011).

H5: The greater the female school life expectancy, the greater the media emphasis on government responsibility to reduce child labor (CIA, 2011).

H6: The higher a nation's percentage of women in the workforce, the greater the media emphasis on government responsibility to reduce child labor (United Nations Statistics Division, 2011).

H7: The higher a nation's percentage of females who are satisfied with their freedom of choice, the greater the media emphasis on government responsibility to reduce child labor (United Nations Development Programme, 2008).

Healthcare access.   Healthcare access can be assessed by "the proportion of the municipal budget that a city spends on health care, in addition to the availability of hospital beds and physicians" (Pollock, 2007, p. 93). Research by Pollock (2007) shows a positive correlation between the number of physicians per 100,000 people in a city and coverage supporting increased stem cell research (p. 98). Another study regarding nationwide U.S. coverage of physician-assisted suicide showed a similar positive correlation between physicians/100,000 and supportive media (Pollock, 2007, p. 86). Therefore:

H8: The greater the number of physicians per 100,000, the greater the media emphasis on government responsibility to reduce child labor (United Nations Development Programme, 2008).

H9: The greater the number of hospital beds per 10,000, the greater the media emphasis on government responsibility to reduce child labor (United Nations Statistics Division, 2011).

Vulnerability Hypothesis

Whereas the violated buffer hypothesis expects a link between buffered or privileged populations and media coverage, the vulnerability hypothesis anticipates a link between "unbuffered" or vulnerable populations such as the poor, the underemployed, minorities, and those living in high crime areas and media coverage; it "expects media coverage to display some resonance with a wide range of publics," with particular attention to the claims of vulnerable populations in an area (Pollock, 2007, p. 137). The conviction that media can mirror the interests of the less fortunate contrasts with the "guard dog" hypothesis of Olien, Donohue, and Tichenor (1995), which suggests that media generally protect and reinforce the interests of social and economic elites, as opposed to advancing human rights claims. This media "mirroring" of the interests of the marginalized can occur despite the observation that vulnerable groups, such as the poor or unemployed, are rarely associated "with maximum newspaper readership" (Pollock, 2007, p. 137).

Olien et al.'s (1995) guard dog hypothesis directly opposes the vulnerability hypothesis, stating that "media function to preserve the interests of city elites" (Pollock, 2007, p. 24). This "guard dog" perspective is perhaps applicable to cross-national, comparative coverage of the child labor issue, as a nation's elites are unlikely to have children in the labor force. It may be reasonable to expect reporting in countries with high proportions of vulnerable groups to remain static, supporting the status quo rather than focusing on social progress.

By contrast, several previous community structure studies have supported the vulnerability hypothesis. One study on capital punishment found that areas in the United States with higher levels of poverty correlated with less favorable coverage of the death penalty because the impoverished "are more vulnerable to criminal legislation and are often underrepresented in the court system" (Pollock, 2007, p. 145). On a cross-national level, Pollock and Koerner (2010) found that the higher number of thefts per 100,000 and higher proportions below the poverty level, the more media emphasized government responsibility to take action against human trafficking. However, the same study found the higher a nation's infant mortality rate, the less the media emphasis on government action.

The vulnerability hypothesis has been confirmed through U.S. multicity media coverage of the *Roe v. Wade* Supreme Court decision to legalize abortion. In areas with higher percentages below the poverty line, media displayed more favorable coverage of the Supreme Court decision to legalize abortion (Pollock & Robinson, 1977; Pollock, Robinson, & Murray, 1978). An additional study found that higher poverty rates or unemployment levels corresponded with greater media support for genetically modified food (Pollock, Maltese-Nehrbass, Corbin, & Fascanella, 2010). Also, Pollock and Whitney (1997) found that higher rates of poverty or unemployment in an area corresponded with more "pluralistic" coverage of ethnic conflict in major U.S. newspapers, acknowledging the claims of both Caribbean Americans and Hasidic Jews.

In addition, other community structure studies also encountered positive correlations between higher vulnerability levels and support for human rights. For example, overall U.S. nationwide media coverage of a proposed Patient's Bill of Rights was found more favorable, "connected to the interests of those below the poverty level" (Pollock, 2007, p. 155). Overall, the higher percentage of disadvantaged populations in an area, the greater the chance that media perspectives may be more sympathetic toward selected social inequality issues, including universal health care (see Pollock, 2013, pp. 116–134). Therefore,

H10: The higher a nation's infant mortality rate, the greater the media emphasis on government responsibility to reduce child labor (United Nations Statistics Division, 2011).

H11: The higher a nation's poverty level, the greater the media emphasis on government responsibility to reduce child labor (United Nations Statistics Division, 2011).

H12: The higher a nation's fertility rate, the greater the media emphasis on government responsibility to reduce child labor (United Nations Statistics Division, 2011).

H13: The greater percentage of undernourished, the greater the media emphasis on government responsibility to reduce child labor (United Nations Statistics Division, 2011).

H14: The higher the percentage of a nation's population younger than 14, the greater the media emphasis on government responsibility to reduce child labor (United Nations Statistics Division, 2011).

H15: The higher a nation's happiness score, the less the media emphasis on government responsibility to reduce child labor (CIA, 2011).

H16: The higher the number of deaths in the workplace per 100,000 in a nation, the greater the media emphasis on government responsibility to reduce child labor (CIA, 2011).

H17: The greater a nation's foreign stock investment, the greater the media emphasis on government responsibility to reduce child labor (CIA, 2011).

H18: The higher a nation's Gini inequality index, the greater the media emphasis on government responsibility to reduce child labor (CIA, 2011).

H19: The greater percentage of a nation's population without access to improved water services, the greater the media emphasis on government responsibility to reduce child labor (United Nations Development Programme, 2008).

H20: The greater number of deaths due to diarrheal diseases per 100,000 in a nation, the greater the media emphasis on government responsibility to reduce child labor (CIA, 2011).

H21: The greater the cases of cholera/100,000 in a nation, the greater the media emphasis on government responsibility to reduce child labor (CIA, 2011).

H22: The higher the population percentage satisfied with water services, the less the media emphasis on government responsibility to reduce child labor (United Nations Development Programme, 2008).

Stakeholder Hypothesis

The larger the city size, the more varied the media viewpoints (Tichenor, Donohue, & Olien, 1973, 1980). It is expected that media will report and reflect issues that affect members of the largest stakeholder groups within a city or nation (Pollock, 2007, p. 171), generally representing the interests of the largest stakeholders. For instance, research has shown that the higher proportion of businesses or organizations marketing to the gay community in a city, the more favorable the coverage of same-sex marriage legalization (Pollock & Haake, 2010). In a study by Swisher and Reese (1992), it was concluded the media coverage in high tobacco-revenue regions was more favorable to tobacco interests as compared to other regions. McLeod and Hertog (1992) found an association between the size of protest groups and favorable coverage of their concerns.

Media access and penetration.   One stakeholder consideration is level of media access, which can be measured by the scope and reach of mediated channels of communication, and in turn, can reveal how citizens can use these channels to learn about public affairs and issues such as child labor (Norris, 2000). Countries with an abundance of media access also have the possibility of starting campaigns and movements to encourage social advancement and change due to the plethora of information and knowledge different media forms allow (Hindman, 1999). The greater the media access, the greater the capability of citizens to mobilize social groups to address public issues. Accordingly, the following hypotheses are expected:

H23: The higher the Freedom of the Press Report score, the less media emphasis on government responsibility to reduce child labor (Organisation for Economic Co-operation and Development, 2011).

80

H24: The higher the proportion of daily newspapers per 1,000 citizens, the less media emphasis on government responsibility to reduce child labor (Organisation for Economic Co-operation and Development, 2011).

H25: The higher the percentage of population covered by a mobile phone network, the less media emphasis on government responsibility to reduce child labor (Organisation for Economic Co-operation and Development, 2011).

H26: The higher the number of journalists imprisoned in a nation, the less media emphasis on government responsibility to reduce child labor (Organisation for Economic Co-operation and Development, 2011).

H27: The higher the number of broadband subscription per 100 citizens in a nation, the less media emphasis on government responsibility to reduce child labor (United Nations Development Programme, 2008).

Resource access: Energy production and consumption.   Nations with especially high energy production and consumption rates contain significant and influential stakeholder groups. Case studies have confirmed the link between these stakeholder groups and media coverage that supports current conditions, which in this circumstance supports "societal" rather than "government" responsibility and actions toward the issue of child labor. In a report by Oxfam America, it was confirmed that countries that depend on oil and mineral exports generally do worse than other nations at the same income level in regard to human development (Ross & Oxfam America, 2001). Such pressure and emphasis on energy production neglects the welfare of children as they are expected to contribute not only to their families' incomes but also to that of the nation. As discovered by Mankowski, Tronolone, and Miller (2012), the higher the rate of electricity consumption in a country, the less the media support for disaster/earthquake relief in Haiti. Energy-dependent countries that produce and consume high amounts of energy are expected to preserve the status quo. Therefore,

H28: The higher a nation's natural gas production rate, the less media emphasis on government responsibility to reduce child labor (CIA, 2011).

H29: The higher a nation's oil production rate, the less media emphasis on government responsibility to reduce child labor (CIA, 2011).

H30: The higher a nation's coal production rate, the less media emphasis on government responsibility to reduce child labor (CIA, 2011).

H31: The higher a nation's natural electricity production rate, the less media emphasis on government responsibility to reduce child labor (CIA, 2011).

H32: The higher a nation's natural gas consumption rate, the less media emphasis on government responsibility to reduce child labor (CIA, 2011).

H33: The higher a nation's natural electricity consumption rate, the less media emphasis on government responsibility to reduce child labor (CIA, 2011).

H34: The higher a nation's coal consumption rate, the less media emphasis on government responsibility to reduce child labor (CIA, 2011).

H35: The higher a nation's industrial growth rate, the less media emphasis on government responsibility to reduce child labor (CIA, 2011).

H36: The higher the total length of a nation's road network, the less media emphasis on the government responsibility to reduce child labor (CIA, 2011).

METHODOLOGY

To analyze cross-national coverage of the issue of international child labor, 21 prominent newspapers in as many countries across the globe were chosen, one newspaper per country. The selection included the following publications: *Accra Mail, China Daily, Daily Dispatch*, the *Daily Monitor, Daily Nation*, the *Herald*, the *Japan Times, Die Welt, La Nación*, the *Namibian, New Strait Times*, the *New Times, New Vision*, the *New York Times*, the *Sydney Morning Herald, This Day*, the *Times*, the *Times of India, Times of Zambia*, the *Toronto Star, Turkish Daily News*, and *El Universal*. Research from the NewsBank and AllAfrica databases yielded more than 744 articles. All relevant articles were then selected from sample time frame with a minimum of 250 words, yielding a total of 244 articles.

The data collected spanned a period of 12 years, dating from November 19, 2000, to November 6, 2012, the day before the 2012 U.S. presidential election. The initial date reflects a fundamental event in the history of child labor prevention. In November 2000, the Worst Forms of Child Labour Convention issued by the ILO was finally put into effect after being signed the previous year. As stated in Article 3, the objective of the Worst Forms of Child Labor Convention was to eliminate

> all forms of slavery or practices similar to slavery, such as the sale and trafficking of children, debt bondage and serfdom and forced or compulsory labour, including forced or compulsory recruitment of children for use in armed conflict; all forms of slavery or practices similar to slavery, such as the sale and trafficking of children, debt bondage and serfdom and forced or compulsory labour, including forced or compulsory recruitment of children for use in armed conflict; the use, procuring or offering of a child for illicit activities, in particular for the production and trafficking of drugs as defined in the relevant international treaties; work which, by its nature or the circumstances in which it is carried out, is likely to harm the health, safety or morals of children. (ILO, 1999)

Therefore, this date served as a crucial point, as it signaled the ratification of 175 members out of the 183 total members of the ILO. This research explores if the Worst Forms of Child Labor Convention had any effect on the media coverage of child labor.

Article Coding and Procedures

The researchers coded all articles for prominence (how significantly the article was displayed in the newspaper by editorial decisions) and direction (the dominant manner in which the issue of child labor was portrayed: government responsibility, societal responsibility, or balanced/neutral). Articles that highlighted domestic government support for eliminating, banning, fighting, or campaigning against child labor were labeled "government responsibility." The articles that emphasized governmental responsibility to reduce child labor accounted for 66% of the 235 articles sampled. An article in *The Times of India* explained the Indian government's goal to abolish child labor by the year 2012:

> A decision was taken in the seminar to run special child labourer schools in 23 districts of the state with financial resources provided by the state government. It was also decided to amend all laws related to child labour so that stern action could be taken against people employing children in hazardous industries. ("Govt to Abolish," 2006, p. 2)

Other articles that demonstrated stalwart action on behalf of the government and legislation shared similar messages, such as one from the *Daily Nation* (Kenya) that explained, "New laws to protect children from exploitation by employers are ready for implementation according to a senior official in the Ministry of Labour and Human Resources Development" ("New laws," 2012, p. 1). These examples clearly displayed media emphasis on governmental responsibility to reduce child labor.

Articles coded "societal responsibility" emphasized nongovernmental activity, on the part of NGOs or bodies like the United Nations, to eliminate child labor and provide children with adequate skills to seek a better future. An article published in the *Times of Zambia* in 2005 exemplified media coverage of a societal effect to reduce child labor through the arts:

> The International Labour Organisation in collaboration with the Child Labour unit of Zambia's Ministry of Labour and Social Security crowned musicians Sister D and St. Michael as Child labour ambassadors for Zambia. The appointment came as a recognition of the efforts exhibited by the duo in promoting the rights of children through their music and social work. (Kapatamoyo, 2005, p. 1)

Another article sampled from a Nigerian publication, *This Day*, demonstrated the role of NGOs versus the government: "Impact for Change and Development, a non-governmental organisation (NGO), took the campaign against child labour to the streets of Abuja recently to drum up support for the eradication of the menace" (Okenwa, 2004, p. 1).

Articles coded as "balanced/neutral" simply served to raise awareness of the issue of child labor, or called upon both government and societal entities to take action. An article published in the *Egyptian Gazette* declared, "The problem of child labour in Egypt should not remain unsolved. The Government, private sector, and civil societies should work together to combat this curse" ("Urgent Solution Needed," 2012, p. 1). Likewise, an article published in the *New Times* of Rwanda reported:

> Labour and Social Security Minister Austin Liato has described child labour as a social, human right and economic issue which should be addressed by all interest groups. Mr. Liato called on all parties dealing with child welfare-related issues to partner with the Government in addressing issues of child labour. ("Child Labour," 2011, p. 1)

All 235 articles were read by two coders, resulting in a Scott's Pi coefficient of intercoder reliability of .702. Article prominence and direction scores were factored into Media Vector scores for each newspaper, which, similar to a vector in physics, combined the two independent measures into a composite measure representing article "projection" for newspaper audiences. Connections between country/city characteristics and Media Vectors were calculated using Pearson correlations and regression analysis, then supplemented with factor analysis.

RESULTS

This study examined cross international newspaper coverage of child labor by comparing Media Vectors from 21 nations during the period of November 19, 2000, to November 6, 2012, the day before the 2012 U.S. presidential election. The *China Daily* had the highest

TABLE 1
Media Vector by Nation

Nation	Newspaper	Media Vector
China	China Daily	.317
Japan	The Japan Times	.276
Turkey	Turkish Daily News	.273
Rwanda	The New Times	.237
South Africa	The Daily Monitor	.159
Zambia	Times of Zambia	.140
Kenya	Daily Nation	.108
Ghana	Accra Mail	.106
Zimbabwe	The Herald	.091
United States	The New York Times	.076
Nigeria	This Day	.067
India	The Times of India	.057
Namibia	The Namibian	.043
Mexico	El Universal	.026
Malaysia	New Strait Times	−.040
Uganda	New Vision	−.040
Argentina	La Nación	−.043
Germany	Die Welt	−.259
Australia	The Sydney Morning Herald	−.272
United Kingdom	The Times	−.292
Canada	The Toronto Star	−.382

Media Vector at .317, whereas the *Toronto Star* had the lowest Media Vector at −.382, a range of .6999. Fourteen of the 21 Media Vectors, or about 66.6%, ranged from .317 to .026, emphasizing government's responsibility to reduce child labor. Seven nations yielded Media Vectors emphasizing societal responsibility to take action against child labor, ranging from −.040 to −.382. Curiously, African nations comprised the majority of nations displaying coverage emphasizing governmental action, with Rwanda (.237), South Africa (.159), Zambia (.140), Kenya (.108), Ghana (.106), Zimbabwe (.091), Namibia (.043), and Nigeria (.067) displaying positive Media Vectors. Table 1 displays the complete list of 21 Media Vectors. Pearson correlations connected national characteristics to variations in coverage. The degree of association between national characteristics and Media Vectors was matched to yield results specific to the global issue of child labor. The complete list of Pearson correlations is found in Table 2.

Violated Buffer Hypothesis Disconfirmed (Satisfaction With Water, GDP/Capita, Male Life Expectancy, Female Life Expectancy, Female School Life Expectancy All Linked to "Less" Support for Government Responsibility for Child Labor)

Using the violated buffer hypotheses, it was originally predicted that the higher the proportion of privileged groups in a nation, the more media emphasis on government action to address issues violating human rights, such as human trafficking (Pollock & Koerner, 2010). This

TABLE 2
Pearson Correlation Results

National Characteristic	Pearson Correlation	Significance
Broadband subscriptions/100	−.619	.001**
Percentage satisfied with water	−.590	.002**
Female school-life expectancy	−.585	.003**
GDP/capita	−.557	.004**
Freedom of the press	.548	.005**
Industrial production growth rate	.406	.034*
Infant mortality rate	.385	.042*
Male life expectancy	−.379	.045*
Female life expectancy	−.364	.052*
Percentage population <14 years	.364	.053*
Gini inequality index	.352	.059
Physicians/10,000	−.348	.061
Hospital beds/10,000	−.347	.061
Coal consumption	.347	.062
No. of journalists imprisoned	.347	.062
Percentage women satisfied w/freedom of choice	−.337	.067
Poverty level	.326	.074
Female literacy rate	−.326	.074
Literacy rate	−.314	.083
Percentage without access to improved water services	.307	.088
Coal production	.301	.092
Electricity consumption	.291	.100
Foreign stock investment	−.274	.115
Deaths due to diarrheal diseases/100,000	−.264	.123
Daily news/1000	−.248	.139
Percent undernourished	.244	.143
Electricity production	.237	.151
Fertility rate	.234	.154
GDP/million	.230	.158
Percentage of population covered by mobile phone network	−.217	.173
Length of nation's road network	.198	.195
Happiness score	−.146	.263
Oil consumption	.142	.270
Gas production	−.099	.334
Cases of cholera	.098	.337
Percentage of females in the workforce	−.096	.339
Percentage happy with freedom of choice	−.096	.340
Oil production	−.053	.410
Gas consumption	.020	.4465

Note. GDP = gross domestic product.
*Significant at .05 level, **significant at .01 level.

connection was assumed because those who are privileged are "buffered" from economic and occupational uncertainty and may believe that child labor poses a threat to their predictable way of life. However, after running Pearson correlations, the opposite result was confirmed.

Five characteristics indicating privilege—percentage satisfied with the quality of water ($r = -.590, p = .002$), GDP/capita ($r = -.557, p = .004$), female school life expectancy ($r = -.585$, $p = .03$), male life expectancy ($r = -.379, p = .045$), and female life expectancy ($r = -.364$, $p = .052$)—were found significant. All five indicators correlated with coverage emphasizing "societal" rather than "governmental" responsibility to reduce child labor. Although this finding is somewhat surprising, it might be attributed to the important role that NGOs play in developing countries. Relatively "privileged" developed countries may be motivated to support NGOs in their efforts to end child labor, rather than support domestic government organizations of questionable integrity.

The Vulnerability Hypothesis Partially Confirmed (Percentage of Population Younger Than 14 Years Old, Infant Mortality Rate)

The vulnerability hypothesis originally predicted higher proportions of vulnerable populations in a nation would correlate with greater media emphasis on government responsibility to reduce child labor. It was believed that there is also a link between "unbuffered" or vulnerable populations such as the poor, the underemployed, minorities, and those living in high crime areas and media coverage (Pollock, 2007, p. 137). After running Pearson correlations, the vulnerability hypothesis was confirmed for two indicators. Characteristics representing vulnerability, including infant mortality rate ($r = .385, p = .042$) and percentage population younger than 14 years old ($r = .364, p = .053$) were found significant. Higher infant mortality rate and higher proportions of the population younger than 14 correlated with more coverage supporting government responsibility to reduce child labor.

The Stakeholder Hypothesis Prevails: Media Access (Broadband Subscriptions/100, Level of Press Freedom, Industrial Production Growth Rate All Significant)

Regarding stakeholder hypotheses about media access, it was hypothesized that the higher a nation's broadband subscriptions per 100 people in a nation and the greater the freedom of the press in a nation, the greater the media emphasis on government responsibility to end child labor. The results are mixed. This study found that the higher a nation's broadband subscriptions are per 100 people in a nation, the "less" media support exists for government responsibility to reduce child labor ($r = -.619, p = .001$). Yet the greater the freedom of the press in a nation, the "more" media support for government efforts to reduce child labor ($r = .548, p = .005$). In parallel fashion, for another "stakeholder" variable, the higher the industrial production growth rate, the more support for government action to address child labor ($r = .406, p = .034$).

An analysis of Media Vector scores revealed a strong connection between African nations with lower levels of Press Freedom scores and high Media Vector scores, including Rwanda (.237), South Africa (.159), Zambia (.140), Kenya (.108), Ghana (.106), Zimbabwe (.091), Namibia (.043), and Nigeria (.067), all revealing media support for government action to reduce

TABLE 3
Regression Analysis of Indicator Scales

Model	R (equation)	R^2 (cumulative)	R^2 Change	F Change	Significance of F Change
Broadband subscription/100	.619	.384	.384	11.823	.003
Broadband subscription/100, % population <14	.696	.484	.100	3.505	.078
Broadband subscription/100, % population <14, female school-life expectancy	.728	.531	.047	1.689	.211
Broadband subscription/100, % population <14, female school-life expectancy, GDP/capita	.770	.593	.063	2.460	.136

Note. GDP = gross domestic product.

child labor. Surprisingly, these developing countries with heavily restrictive governments, and in some cases relatively low levels of press freedom, all expected to produce more media emphasis on societal action, instead yielded media support for government responsibility to reduce child labor.

Regression Analysis: Media Access and Privilege

Regression analysis revealed four variables were significantly associated with Media Vectors. "Broadband subscriptions/100" accounted for 38.4% of the variance, percentage of population younger than 14 years of age 10.0%, female school-life expectancy 4.7%, and GDP/capita 6.3%, combined to account for a total of 59.3% of the variance. Three of the four regression variables, all but percentage of population younger than 14 (10% of the variance), were linked with coverage supporting "less" government responsibility regarding child labor, for a total of 49.3% of the variance. This finding supports the assertion that nations with more privileged populations, whether measured in GDP/capita, female school life expectancy, or media access such as "broadband subscriptions/100," play significant roles in news coverage of child labor and emphasize support for societal responsibility. Table 3 displays the regression analysis.

Factor Analysis: Privilege and Gendered Communication Significant

To refine results further, a varimax rotated factor analysis was executed on the independent variables, yielding three significant factors, all with eigenvalues of 1.00 or more. Regarding factor variance alone, Factor 1 (Privilege, in particular male and female life expectancy) accounted for 41.7% of the variance; Factor 2 (Resource Access) accounted for 19% of the variance, and Factor 3 (Gendered Communication) accounted for 8.21% of the variance. The total factor variance accounted for was therefore 69%. Table 4 reveals the most significant components of each of the three factors, together with the factor loadings of each component.

After running a regression of the factors against the Media Vectors, privilege and gendered communication were found to be the two leading indicators, accounting for 25% of the variance (see Table 5). One reason that privilege accounted for 19.4% of the variance may be that those who are more privileged or more educated tend to be more sympathetic to human rights claims

TABLE 4

Descending Media Vectors of Significant Variables Within Privilege,
Resource Access, and Gendered Communication Factors

Factor	Component	Factor Loading
Privilege	Male life expectancy	0.894
	Female life expectancy	0.893
	% population <14	−0.835
	Gini inequality index	−0.814
	Poverty level	−0.795
	Broadband subs.	0.771
	Daily newspapers	0.738
	Infant mortality rate	−0.732
	GDP/capita	0.711
	Happiness score	0.693
	Female school life expectancy	0.679
	Undernourished	−0.667
	Improved water	−0.661
	Fertility rate	−0.635
Resource access	Gas consumption	0.961
	Oil consumption	0.951
	Gas production	0.950
	Oil production	0.923
	National road network	0.913
	GDP in millions	0.884
	Foreign stock investment	0.856
	Electricity production	0.854
	Electricity consumption	0.849
Gendered communication	Deaths due to DD	−0.892
	Female literacy rate	0.782
	Mobile phone	0.755
	Literacy rate	0.752

Note. GDP = gross domestic product; DD = diarrheal diseases.

TABLE 5

Regression Analysis of Significant Factors

Model	R (equation)	R^2 (cumulative)	R^2 Change	F Change	Significance of F Change
Privilege	0.441	0.194	0.194	4.582	0.046
Privilege + Gendered Communication	0.5	0.250	0.055	1.327	0.264

(see Pollock, 2007, pp. 61–100). In this case, privilege was linked with coverage showing little reliance or trust in domestic governments, far more in "society" (charities, foreign aid—whether directly from governments, such as USAID), NGOs, or intergovernmental organizations such as the United Nations.

This finding is consistent with the outcome of a cross-national study on national characteristics and variations in coverage of water handling (Wissel et al., this issue). In that case study, privilege, in particular female empowerment, was associated strongly with coverage placing trust and hope not in domestic governments but in "society:" charities, corporations, and foreign assistance. "Gendered communication" accounted for another 5.5% of the variance. This stakeholder group, linked strongly to female literacy rate and use of mobile phones, may be especially potent because it combines a measure of female empowerment with a digital means to express that empowerment: mobile phones.

CONCLUSIONS AND FURTHER RESEARCH

Child labor remains a vital issue, generating substantial debate cross-nationally, as reflected through varied media coverage across nations. Numerous significant correlations were discovered, found within all three umbrella hypothesis clusters: violated buffer, vulnerability, and stakeholder hypotheses. Overall, although two thirds of the leading newspapers supported some kind of government responsibility for addressing child labor concerns, most (six out of 10) of the significant correlations between national characteristics and Media Vectors were associated with coverage supporting "less" governmental responsibility, more societal action. Similarly, three out of the four initial regression variables, accounting for 49% of the variance, were associated with coverage supporting societal rather than governmental responsibility for child labor. Consistently, a varimax rotated factor analysis and regression analysis found that both significant factors, privilege and gendered communication, together accounting for 25% of the variance, were each associated with coverage emphasizing societal responsibility for child labor. A fascinating finding was that the greater broadband subscriptions per 100 people, the less media emphasis on government responsibility to reduce child labor. This negative correlation rejects initial assumptions that more broadband subscriptions would result in more media emphasis on government responsibility. Another notable result was that empowered women (high literacy rates, female school life expectancy) are associated with less media emphasis on government responsibility to reduce child labor. This finding suggests that relatively developed countries are more likely to support societal action.

Given the lack of news coverage within communication studies databases on the issue of child labor, two concrete recommendations can be made for further media research. First, a cross-national study might target only countries within a specific region, such as Africa and Asia, due to their substantial use of child labor, as well as the widely varied economic conditions within those nations. These areas may hold most of the child labor population, with the Asia-Pacific region accounting for 122 million child workers and sub-Saharan Africa accounting for 49.3 million child workers (International Trade Union Confederation, 2008, p. 3). Restricting newspaper coverage to one continent at a time would allow researchers to sample data from more countries in each region and to include papers from a wider range of cities in order to offer a more detailed grasp of media coverage of child labor in each geographic area. Another recommendation would be to examine more closely the influence of NGOs and their responsibility for reducing child labor. Eradicating child labor is associated strongly in the media with national characteristics pointing to society rather than governmental responsibility, and the role of NGOs is pivotal in that endeavor.

ACKNOWLEDGMENTS

A previous version of this article was presented at the International Communication Association Shanghai Regional Conference, "Communication and Social Transformation," November 8–10, 2013. The authors thank Christiana Nielsen and Dasia Stewart for their invaluable contributions to data collection, coding, and data analysis for an earlier version of this article.

REFERENCES

Arganbright, M., Gehrke, J., & Ren, C. (2008, November). *"40 kids. 40 days. No adults": Framing and blaming in the 'Lid Nation' controversy*. Paper presented at the annual conference of the National Communications Association, San Antonio, TX.

Bachman, S. L. (2000). A new economics of child labor: Searching for answers behind the headlines. *Journal of International Affairs, 53*, 545.

Central Intelligence Agency (CIA). (2009). *The world factbook*. Retrieved from https://www.cia.gov/library/publications/the-world-factbook/

Central Intelligence Agency (CIA). (2011). *The world factbook*. Retrieved from https://www.cia.gov/library/publications/the-world-factbook/

Child labour is everyone's business. (2011, June 14). *The New Times*. Retrieved from NewsBank database.

Diallo, Y., Hagemann, F., Etienne, A., Gurbuzer, Y., & Mehran, F. (2010, May). Global child labour developments: Measuring trends from 2004 to 2008. *The International Labour Organization*. Retrieved from http://www.ilo.org/dyn/clsurvey/lfsurvey.list?p_lang=en&p_country=XA

Doepke, M., & Zilibotti, F. (2010). Do international labor standards contribute to the persistence of the child-labor problem? *Journal of Economic Growth, 15*, 1–31. doi:.1007/s10887-009-9048-8

Garbas, M. (2009). Child labour in the media between pretense of protection, interest preservation and self-realization. *Diskurs Kindheits-Und Jugendforschung, 4*, 91–105. Retrieved from http://search.proquest.com/docview/60014551?accountid=10216

Gianotti, E. (2011). Child labor and photojournalism. In D. Papademas (Ed.), *Human rights and media (Studies in Communications*, Volume 6; pp. 139–160). Derby, UK: Emerald Group Publishing Limited.

Govt to abolish child labour in UP. (2006, August 4). *The Times of India*. Retrieved from NewsBank database.

Hindman, D. B. (1999). Social control, social change and local mass media. In D. Demers & K. Wiswanath (Eds.), *Mass media, social control, and social change: A macrosocial perspective* (pp. 99–116). Ames, IA: Iowa State University Press.

International Labour Organization (ILO). (1999, November). *C182-Worst Forms of Child Labour Convention, 1999 (no. 182)*. Retrieved from http://www.ilo.org/dyn/normlex/en/f?p=1000:12100:0::NO::P12100_INSTRUMENT_ID:312327

International Trade Union Confederation, (2008, June). Mini action guide—Child labour. Retrieved from http://www.ituc-csi.org/IMG/pdf/guide_CL_EN_Final.pdf

Kapatamoyo, M. (2005, January 25). Artistes in action against child labour. *Times of Zambia*. Retrieved from NewsBank online database.

Littell-Lamb, E. (2011). Caught in the crossfire. *Frontiers: A Journal of Women Studies, 32*, 134–166.

Mankowski, E., Tronolone, R., & Miller, M. (2012, November). *Cross-national newspaper coverage of disaster relief in Haiti: A community structure approach*. Paper presented at the annual conference of the National Communication Association, Orlando, FL.

McLeod, D. M., & Hertog, J. K. (1992). The manufacture of public opinion by reporters: Informal cues for public perceptions of protest groups. *Discourse and Society, 3*, 259–275.

Media focus: The ILO in the press. (1997). *World of Work, 20*, 30–31. Retrieved from http://search.proquest.com/doc view/57343425?accountid=10216

Morgan, J. (1925). Propaganda: Its relation to the child labor issues. *Education, 46*, 51–54.

New laws to protect child workers "ready." (2012, April 14). *The Daily Nation.* Retrieved from NewsBank database.

Norris, P. (2000). *A virtuous circle. Political communications in postindustrial societies.* New York, NY: Cambridge University Press.

Okenwa, L. (2004, July 20). Group takes anti-child labour campaign to streets. *This Day.* Retrieved from NewsBank onlinedatabase.

Olien, C. N., Donohue, G. A., & Tichenor, P. J. (1995). Conflict, consensus, and public opinion. In T. L. Glaser & C. T. Salmon (Eds.), *Public opinion and the communication of consent* (pp. 301–322). New York, NY: Guilford.

Organisation for Economic Co-operation and Development. (2011). *Statistics from a to z.* Retrieved from http://www.oecd.org/statistics/

Pollock, J., Mink, M., Puma, J., Shuhala, S., & Ostrander, L. (2001, November). *Nationwide newspaper coverage of women in combat: A community structure approach.* Paper presented at the annual conference of the National Communication Association, Atlanta, GA.

Pollock, J. C. (2007). *Titled mirrors: Media alignment with political and social change—A community structure approach.* Cresskill, NJ: Hampton Press.

Pollock, J. C. (Ed.). (2013). *Media and social inequality: Innovations in community structure research.* New York, NY: Routledge.

Pollock, J. C., & Haake, J. (2010). Nationwide US newspaper coverage of same-sex marriage: A community structure approach. *The Journal of PR, 1*, 13–40.

Pollock, J. C., & Koerner, M. (2010). *Cross-national coverage of human trafficking: A community structure approach* (Documento de Trabajo #2). Departamento de Derecho y Ciencia Política, Universidad Nacional de La Matanza (UNLaM), Buenos Aires, Argentina.

Pollock, J. C., Maltese-Nehrbass, M., Corbin, P., & Fascanella, P. B. (2010). Nationwide newspaper coverage of genetically-modified food in the United States: A community structure approach. *Ecos de la Comunicación, 3*, 51–75.

Pollock, J. C., & Robinson, J. L. (1977). Reporting rights conflicts. *Society, 13*, 44–47.

Pollock, J. C., Robinson, J. L., & Murray, M. C. (1978). Media agendas and human rights: The Supreme Court decision on abortion. *Journalism Quarterly, 53*, 545–548, 561.

Pollock, J. C., & Whitney, L. (1997, Fall). Newspapers and racial/ethnic conflict: Comparing city demographics and nationwide reporting on the Crown Heights (Brooklyn, NY) incidents. *Atlantic Journal of Communication, 5*, 127–149.

Ross, M., & Oxfam America. (2001). *Extractive sectors and the poor.* Retrieved from http://www.sscnet.ucla.edu/poli sci/faculty/ross/oxfam.pdf

Schrage, E. J., & Ewing, A. P. (2005). The cocoa industry and child labour. *Journal of Corporate Citizenship, 18*, 99–112.

Shah, A. (2001, January 1). Child labor. *Global Issues.* Retrieved from http://www.globalissues.org/article/62/child-labor

Swisher, C., & Reese, S. (1992). The smoking and health issue in newspapers: Influence of regional economics, the Tobacco Institute and news objectivity. *Journalism Quarterly, 69*, 987–1000.

Tichenor, P. J., Donohue, G., & Olien, C. (1973). Mass communication research: Evolution of a structural model. *Journalism Quarterly, 50*, 419–425.

Tichenor, P. J., Donohue, G., & Olien, C. (1980). *Community conflict and the press.* Beverly Hills, CA: Sage.

United Nations Development Programme. (2008). *2007/2008 human development report.* Retrieved from http://hdr stats.undp.org/indicators/58.html

United Nations Statistics Division. (2011). *UNSD statistical databases.* Retrieved from http://unstats.un.org/unsd/data bases.htm

Urgent solution needed. (2012, July 15). *The Egyptian Gazette.* Retrieved from NewsBank database.

Part II

Multi-City US Nationwide Coverage of Human Rights

Nationwide Newspaper Coverage of Same-Sex Marriage: A Community Structure Approach

Victoria Vales, John C. Pollock, Victoria Scarfone, Carly Koziol,
Amy Wilson, and Patrick Flanagan
Department of Communication Studies
The College of New Jersey

Using the community structure approach to compare coverage of same-sex marriage in leading U.S. newspapers in 35 major cities nationwide, all articles of 250+ words were sampled from a 5-year span of January 1, 2007, to June 23, 2011, for a total of 577 articles. Articles were coded for "prominence" and "direction," and then combined into a "Media Vector" score for each newspaper, ranging from .4523 to −.1067. Initial Pearson correlations revealed three clusters had significant relationships: stakeholder (stakeholder proportions correlating with favorable coverage of stakeholder concerns), buffer (privilege correlating with favorable coverage of human rights issues), and vulnerability (vulnerable populations correlating with coverage favoring their perspectives). The stakeholder cluster includes: (percentage 25–44: $r = .506$, $p = .001$; gay market index: $r = .432$, $p = .005$; percentage 65+: $r = −.397$, $p = .009$; percentage voting Democratic: $r = .335$, $p = .025$; percentage voting Republican: $r = −.330$, $p = .026$). The buffer hypothesis was also confirmed (percentage college educated: $r = .465$, $p = .002$; percentage family income of $100,000+: $r = .383$, $p = .012$; and percentage professional/technical occupations: $r = .300$, $p = .040$). One vulnerability indicator, percentage below the poverty line, was also confirmed ($r = −.297$, $p = .041$). A varimax rotated factor analysis and regression yielded 2 factors accounting for more than 29% of the variance: privilege/gay marketing/political identity, 24%, and Evangelicals, 5%.

INTRODUCTION

Considerable debate has been generated over whether same-sex couples should be granted the opportunity to marry legally. For some, a marriage, by definition, is between a man and a woman, whereas others believe a marriage can exist between same-sex partners. The argument over whether same-sex marriage enriches or detracts from the sanctity of marriage and family is a contentious issue on media and policy agendas in the United States.

95

Media can fulfill important social and political roles when they choose to "frame" critical events, thus influencing perceptions. Media framing is considered the "selection of some aspects [to] make them more salient in a communicating context, in such a way as to promote a particular problem, definition, causal interpretation, moral evaluation and/or treatment recommendation" (Entman, 1993, p. 53; see also D'Angelo, 2002; Scheufele, 1999). In the case of same-sex marriage, frames can be labeled generally as "favorable" or "unfavorable." The "favorable" frame suggests that there is no clear way in which same-sex marriage could be harmful, whereas the "unfavorable" frame suggests that there would be no positive outcomes from same-sex marriage (for a discussion of these and similar frames, see Pollock, 2007, pp. 48–57).

With more states voting on legalization of same-sex marriage, media coverage of the issue has increased accordingly. This study focuses specifically on newspaper coverage of same-sex marriage, applying a "community structure approach" to illuminate the relationship between community demographics and newspaper coverage. Utilizing the community structure framework, the study explores how community demographics are linked to media portrayals of same-sex marriage. Two primary research questions are addressed:

RQ1: How much variation exists in coverage of same-sex marriage among major U.S. cities?

RQ2: How closely is that variation linked to differences in community characteristics?

This study employs the use of several hypotheses to explore the relationship between city demographics and coverage of same-sex marriage.

LITERATURE REVIEW

Many different fields, including political science, sociology, and psychology, have attempted to examine the debate surrounding same-sex marriage. However, research on this issue is sparse in the communication studies field. Communication databases such as Communication and Mass Media Complete and Communication Institute for Online Scholarship ComAbstracts were searched, yielding few articles. Search terms included combinations of the following: "same-sex marriage," "gay marriage," "media," "news," "newspapers," and "coverage."

On the ComAbstracts database, "same-sex marriage and media" returned five results, one of which was relevant to newspaper coverage of the issue. Although several articles focused on the television medium, only one article discussed the effects of newspaper coverage on the debate of same-sex marriage. This community structure study explored links among different city characteristics and U.S. nationwide newspaper coverage from 2004 to 2007, finding connections between media coverage and both political affiliation and privilege (Pollock & Haake, 2010).

Although the communication studies field manifests relatively few articles on same-sex marriage, other disciplines produced considerably more research. Using the term "same-sex marriage," the political science database PIAS International yielded 48 articles. Similarly, a search utilizing the terms "same-sex marriage" and "media" in the sociology database Social Services Abstracts ILLUMINA yielded 49 results (without restricting publishing dates). The field of psychology was by far the most prolific, with the PsycINFO database yielding

239 articles. This article attempts to help bridge the gap between the communication studies field and other fields regarding same-sex marriage, particularly regarding media coverage.

HYPOTHESES

Twenty-six hypotheses regarding same-sex marriage were developed in accordance with the community structure approach. These hypotheses can be arranged in three umbrella categories: buffer, vulnerability, and stakeholder.

Buffer Hypothesis

The buffer hypothesis focuses on the notion of "relative privilege," suggesting that cities with a higher proportion of privileged groups "buffered" from economic uncertainty are more likely to report favorably on human rights claims (Pollock, 2007, p. 61). City characteristics used to measure privilege include levels of college education, family incomes of $100,000 or more, and professional or technical occupational status.

Several community structure approach studies have supported the buffer hypothesis. A study concerning Anita Hill's testimony in the Clarence Thomas–Anita Hill Supreme Court nomination hearings revealed media coverage reflecting a public outcry toward the insensitivity of policymakers on women's issues. The national event was framed to convey government responsibility for just conduct regarding women's issues, and injustice accorded Anita Hill was especially evident in media coverage in communities with high proportions of those with college degrees or professional/technical occupational status (Pollock, 2007, pp. 72–73). In the case of the legitimization of physician-assisted suicide, higher levels of privilege were found to have a direct correlation with positive media coverage (Pollock, 2007, pp. 75–88). In addition, stem cell research and the potential for resulting medical breakthroughs received more favorable media coverage in cities with greater proportions of educational privilege (Pollock, 2007, pp. 98–99). This study predicts that buffered groups will be associated with relatively favorable opinions toward same-sex marriage; accordingly:

H1: The higher percentage of college educated in a city, the more favorable the coverage of same-sex marriage (Lifestyle Market Analyst, 2008).
H2: The higher percentage of families in a city with incomes of $100,000 or more, the more favorable the coverage of same-sex marriage (Lifestyle Market Analyst, 2008).
H3: The higher percentage with professional or technical occupational status in a city, the more favorable the coverage of same-sex marriage (Lifestyle Market Analyst, 2008).

Healthcare access. Healthcare access, another indicator of privilege, can be measured by "the proportion of the municipal budget that a city spends on healthcare, in addition to the availability of hospital beds and physicians" (Pollock, 2007, p. 93). A study on embryonic stem cell research found a positive correlation between access to healthcare (physicians per 100,000 residents) and favorable news coverage (Pollock, 2007, pp. 98–99). The same was found in a study regarding the legalization of physician-assisted euthanasia, which revealed a positive correlation between physicians per 100,000 residents and favorable news coverage (Pollock,

2007, pp. 86–87; Pollock & Yulis, 2004). It is assumed that residents who live in areas with more healthcare access will be more informed and knowledgeable about health issues and other human rights issues. Therefore:

H4: The higher number of physicians per 100,000 citizens in a city, the more favorable the coverage on same-sex marriage (U.S. Census Bureau, 2010).

H5: The higher number of hospital beds per 100,000 citizens in a city, the more favorable the coverage on same-sex marriage (County and City Extra, 2010).

H6: The higher percentage of municipal spending on healthcare in a city, the more favorable coverage on same-sex marriage (County and City Extra, 2010).

Vulnerability Hypothesis

Unlike the buffer hypothesis, the vulnerability hypothesis, also known as the "guardian" or "unbuffered" hypothesis, states that "newspapers can reflect the interests of vulnerable populations" such as the poor, the underemployed, minorities, and those living in high crime areas (Pollock, 2007, p. 137). This hypothesis expects that the "higher the percent of these vulnerable populations in a city, the more likely the media will be sympathetic to human rights issues of importance to them" (Pollock & Haake, 2010, p. 20). This belief that media can mirror the interests of the less fortunate opposes the "guard dog" hypothesis of Olien, Donohue, and Tichenor (1995), which states that instead of acting as public advocates, the media often reinforce elite interests in a community. In addition, Watson and Riffe (2011), in an analysis of public affairs place blogs in 232 U.S. cities, found a connection between sophisticated measures of "community stress" and the presence of public affairs place blogs.

The vulnerability hypothesis has also been confirmed through media coverage before, during, and after the *Roe v. Wade* Supreme Court decision legalizing abortion, as higher proportions below the poverty line correlated with more favorable coverage of the decision to legalize abortion (Pollock & Robinson, 1977; Pollock, Robinson, & Murray, 1978). Pollock and Whitney (1997) found that the higher the poverty or unemployment levels in a city, the more "pluralistic" the newspaper coverage nationwide, appreciating claims of both Caribbean Americans and Hasidic Jews in coverage of ethnic conflict. Another study found that the higher the poverty rate or unemployment level, the greater the media support for genetically modified food (Pollock, Maltese-Nehrbass, Corbin, & Fascanella, 2010).

Yet some previous community structure research encountered negative correlations between higher vulnerability levels and support for human rights. For example, the greater the percent living below the poverty level in a city, the less favorable the coverage of gays in the Boy Scouts of America (Pollock, 2007). Another study found that the greater the percentage living below the poverty level, the less favorable the coverage of same-sex adoption (Pollock & Tobin, 2000). Thus, it can be assumed that minorities and those living under the poverty level may be less supportive of same-sex marriage. Accordingly:

H7: The greater the percentage living below the poverty line, the less favorable the coverage of same-sex marriage (County and City Extra, 2010).

H8: The higher percentage unemployed in a city, the less favorable the coverage of same-sex marriage (Lifestyle Market Analyst, 2008).

H9: The greater the crime rate, specifically hate crime in a city, the less favorable the coverage of same-sex marriage (County and City Extra, 2010).

Stakeholder Hypothesis

The stakeholder hypothesis states that the larger the presence of certain stakeholder groups in a city, the more favorable the coverage "on issues pertinent to these groups" (Pollock, 2007, p. 173). Studies by McLeod and Hertog (1992, 1999) found a correlation between the size of protest groups and favorable coverage of their concerns in mass media. McCluskey, Stein, Boyle, and McLeod (2009) found that compared to newspapers in more pluralistic communities, those in less pluralistic communities exhibited lower tolerance for social conflict. A study on the coverage of Islam one year after 9/11 revealed that the higher the percentage of foreign born or percentage speaking Arabic or Farsi at home, the less favorable the coverage of Islam (Pollock, Piccillo, Leopardi, Gratale, & Cabot, 2005). The stakeholder categories examined in this study include the gay, lesbian, bisexual, and transgender community; political identity; ethnic identity; generation; position in life cycle; and belief system.

Gay, lesbian, bisexual, and transgender community. When seeking a correlation between stakeholders in a city and coverage of gay rights issues, it seems reasonable that the number of gays and lesbians residing in a city should be taken into account (Pollock, 2007, pp. 234 235, 241–242). Pollock and Dantas (1998) found significant results by creating a Gay Market Index (an updated version of the Gay Market Index [Cronbach's $\alpha = .861$] can be found in Table 1); correlations revealed that the greater the proportion of businesses or organizations marketing to the gay community in a city, the more likely city newspapers were to report favorably on gays in the Boy Scouts (Pollock, 2007, pp. 241–242) and on efforts to legalize same-sex marriage in the 2004–2007 period in the United States (Pollock & Haake, 2010, p. 23). Therefore:

H10: The larger the number of businesses and organizations marketing primarily to gay and lesbian clientele in a city, the more favorable the expected coverage of same-sex marriage (Green, 2009).

Political identity. Another stakeholder category is affiliation with the two main political parties, Democrats and Republicans. Political identity was found to play a significant role in media coverage of oil drilling in the Arctic National Wildlife Refuge. Cities containing higher proportions of Democratic voters in the 1996 presidential election demonstrated less media support for drilling for oil in the Arctic National Wildlife Refuge, whereas the opposite was true of cities with higher proportions of Republican voters (Pollock, 2007, p. 192). In addition, in a case study of trying juveniles as adults, Democratic voters were found to be supportive of legislation that focused on rehabilitation rather than incarceration of juvenile offenders, whereas Republican voters favored "'get tough' measures against juvenile offenders" (Pollock, 2007, p. 204). These studies support the notion that the higher the proportion voting Democratic in a city, the greater the media support for legislation that protects the rights of the underprivileged. Thus, it can be expected:

TABLE 1
Updated Gay Market Index

City	Accommodations & Hotels	Archives, Libraries, Museums	Bars, Clubs, Discos	Bookstores	Religious Groups	Health Care & Counseling	Organizations & Resources	AIDS/HIV Health Care	Gay Publications	Broadcast Media	Sports & Outdoor	Total
San Francisco	32	4	62	6	20	24	85	12	8	0	23	276
Chicago	3	3	54	5	24	8	66	18	11	0	11	203
Seattle	7	0	24	5	16	21	58	10	1	0	17	159
Philadelphia	4	3	29	1	13	17	56	11	6	1	12	153
Portland	6	2	36	5	18	18	37	3	2	0	8	135
San Diego	9	1	23	1	5	3	46	9	3	0	25	125
Minneapolis	1	2	20	2	24	4	52	7	0	1	8	121
Atlanta	4	1	35	2	10	7	39	4	2	1	10	115
Dallas	0	0	28	2	9	5	45	6	3	3	14	115
Houston	2	0	23	1	11	10	34	4	4	2	17	108
Boston	8	1	15	2	2	5	40	3	3	0	16	95
Denver	1	1	23	2	6	5	27	1	3	0	18	86
St. Louis	2	1	19	1	11	2	27	4	3	0	4	74
New Orleans	21	0	24	1	4	0	17	4	0	0	2	73
Cleveland	2	1	17	1	6	3	29	3	3	0	2	67
Pittsburgh	1	0	15	2	7	4	26	3	1	0	6	65
San Antonio	7	1	19	1	6	3	15	4	0	0	1	57
Orlando	3	0	16	0	4	1	19	1	1	0	6	51
Sacramento	0	1	7	0	3	1	24	6	1	0	8	51
Las Vegas	0	0	20	1	3	5	15	2	0	0	2	50
Cincinnati	0	0	11	2	6	0	22	2	2	1	3	49
Buffalo	0	2	9	2	4	2	19	2	2	0	4	46
Charlotte	0	0	13	4	6	3	13	2	0	0	3	44
Madison	0	0	6	3	8	2	18	1	1	0	4	43
Salt Lake City	2	0	8	3	5	1	17	0	0	0	7	43
Detroit	1	0	20	0	1	0	9	4	0	0	5	40
Albany	1	1	7	0	3	3	16	5	0	1	2	39
Albuquerque	6	0	6	1	2	2	21	1	0	0	0	39
Memphis	0	0	10	2	6	0	11	1	0	0	4	34
Omaha	1	0	7	0	4	1	12	1	0	0	2	28
Wichita	0	0	10	1	4	0	9	2	0	0	1	27
Birmingham	0	0	5	0	4	0	9	3	0	0	1	22
Lexington	0	0	5	2	2	1	5	1	2	0	2	20
Mobile	0	0	6	0	2	0	9	1	0	0	1	19
Hartford	0	0	4	0	1	1	9	2	0	0	0	17
Columbia	0	0	5	0	2	0	6	1	0	2	0	16
Manchester	0	0	3	0	0	0	4	0	0	1	0	8
Biloxi	0	0	1	0	0	0	0	0	0	0	0	1

H11: The higher proportion of those voting Republican in the 2008 presidential election in a city, the less media support for same-sex marriage (County and City Extra, 2010).

H12: The higher proportion of those voting Democratic in the 2008 presidential election in a city, the greater media support for same-sex marriage (County and City Extra, 2010).

Ethnic identity. Ethnic identity also represents a stakeholder group. Although it may seem logical to assume that minority groups who suffer from oppression and prejudice would support gay rights, some evidence suggests otherwise. Some African Americans have expressed resentment toward gays and lesbians, arguing that ethnic identity is a cause for equal rights, unlike homosexuality, which in their eyes is a lifestyle choice (Pollock & Tobin, 2000). Similar perspectives could be held by the Hispanic community. Thus, it is reasonable to expect the following:

H13: The greater the percentage of African Americans in a city, the less favorable the coverage of gay marriage (Lifestyle Market Analyst, 2008).

H14: The greater the percentage of Hispanics in a city, the less favorable the coverage of gay marriage (Lifestyle Market Analyst, 2008).

Generation. Conventional wisdom suggests that different age groups will have differing opinions on particular topics. As the legalization of same-sex marriage has become more prominent over the past 10 years, it could be argued that older generations may not be as invested in the issue because they have seldom had to deal with it, and their children were not affected by it. In addition, older generations are typically more conservative, which is supported by Pollock and Yulis's (2004) study finding that the higher proportion of those 75 or older in a city, the less media support for the legalization of physician-assisted euthanasia. Yet a second case study also explored "traditional" expectations, finding that the higher proportion of those age 65 to 74, or those 75 or older in a city, the less media support for trying juveniles as adults. This is perhaps because people in those demographics view children as "grandchildren" and may be more compassionate to issues that affect young children (Pollock, 2007).

Meanwhile, higher proportions of 18- to 24-year-olds in cities have been found to correlate with less favorable views toward affirmative action in higher education (Brechman & Pollock, 2007) and toward government assistance for the less privileged such as the homeless, since the fall of the Lehman Brothers in September 2008 (Webb et al., 2010). Therefore, it would be reasonable to expect people 18- to 24-years-old to be unsupportive of, or at least apathetic toward, government regulation of an issue that does not affect them. Nevertheless, although previous research reveals mixed perspectives of young people on progressive issues, it is still reasonable to expect that younger people are more likely to favor progressive issues, with older generations more likely to disapprove. Consequently:

H15: The higher proportion of 18- to 24-year-olds in a city, the more favorable coverage of same-sex marriage (Lifestyle Market Analyst, 2008).

H16: The higher proportion of 25- to 44-year-olds in a city, the more favorable coverage of same-sex marriage (Lifestyle Market Analyst, 2008).

H17: The higher proportion of 45- to 64-year-olds in a city, the less favorable coverage of same-sex marriage coverage (Lifestyle Market Analyst, 2008).

H18: The higher proportion of those 65 and older in a city, the less favorable the coverage of same-sex marriage coverage (Lifestyle Market Analyst, 2008).

Position in life cycle. A study by Mink, Puma, and Pollock (2001) on the custody battle over Cuban refugee Elian Gonzalez found that nationwide newspaper coverage favoring the repatriation of Gonzalez to his biological father in Cuba was linked to the proportion of families in cities with children of similar age, 5 to 7. A study on gun control found that "certain groups are more likely to 'identify' with the fight for gun control," including parents with young children, as they would be more likely to empathize with the parents who lost children in the Columbine shooting and support greater gun control (Pollock, 2007, p. 175). Regarding gays in the Boy Scouts, it is reasonable to expect that families of elementary-age children might be more concerned about the safety and morality of the Boy Scouts, potentially leading media to mirror their concerns and oppose gays in the Boy Scouts. It is assumed that some traditional families may want to shield young children from gay lifestyles. Therefore:

H19: The higher proportion of families with children younger than age 5 in a city, the less the media support for same-sex marriage (Lifestyle Market Analyst, 2008).

H20: The higher proportion of families with children ages 5 to 10 in a city, the less the media support for same-sex marriage (Lifestyle Market Analyst, 2008).

H21: The higher proportion of families with children ages 11 to 15 in a city, the greater the media support for same-sex marriage (Lifestyle Market Analyst, 2008).

H22: The higher proportion of families with children ages 16 to 18 in a city, the greater media support for same-sex marriage coverage (Lifestyle Market Analyst, 2008).

Belief system. Some churches and other religious organizations have taken "strong stances" on the issue of same-sex marriage. Pollock et al. (1978) found a strong correlation between the percentage of Catholics within a city and negative coverage of *Roe v. Wade*. However, a study on the newspaper coverage of gays in the Boy Scouts found that "the higher percentages of Catholics in a city correlated positively with favorable coverage of gays in the Boy Scouts" (Pollock, 2007, p. 243). A previous study on nationwide coverage of same-sex marriage similarly found a higher percentage of Catholics in a city corresponded with more favorable newspaper coverage of same-sex marriage (Pollock & Haake, 2010). Moreover, some Mainline Protestant denominations (such as Episcopalians) do allow gay ministers and priests to be ordained in their religion. By contrast, higher proportions of devotional readers in a city have correlated with less favorable coverage of stem cell research (Pollock, 2007, p. 98) and of gays in the Boy Scouts (Pollock, 2007, p. 241), likely due to their literal interpretations of the Bible. Therefore:

H23: The higher percentage of Evangelicals in a city, the less favorable the coverage of same-sex marriage (Association of Religion Data Archives [ARDA], 2008).

H24: The higher percentage of devotional readers in a city, the less favorable the coverage of same-sex marriage (ARDA, 2008).

H25: The higher percentage of Catholics in a city, the more favorable the coverage of same-sex marriage (ARDA, 2008).

H26: The higher percentage of Mainline Protestants in a city, the more favorable the coverage of same-sex marriage (ARDA, 2008).

METHODOLOGY

A cross-national sample of 35 major newspapers yielded 577 articles on media coverage of same-sex marriage, all selected from the NewsBank database. The following newspapers were examined: the *Times Union, Albuquerque Journal*, the *Atlanta Journal-Constitution, Sun Herald*, the *Buffalo News, Charlotte Observer, Chicago Sun-Times*, the *Cincinnati Post*, the *Plain Dealer*, the *State*, the *Dallas Morning News*, the *Denver Post*, the *Detroit News*, the *Hartford Courant, Houston Chronicle, Lexington Herald-Leader, Wisconsin State Journal, New Hampshire Union Leader*, the *Commercial Appeal, Star Tribune: Newspaper of the Twin Cities, Press Register*, the *Times-Picayune, Omaha World-Herald*, the *Orlando Sentinel*, the *Philadelphia Inquirer*, the *Pittsburgh Post-Gazette*, the *Oregonian*, the *Sacramento Bee*, the *Deseret News, San Antonio Express-News*, the *San Diego Union-Tribune, San Francisco Chronicle, Seattle Post-Intelligencer, St. Louis Post-Dispatch*, and the *Wichita Eagle*. Publications such as the *New York Times*, the *Wall Street Journal*, the *Washington Post, USA Today*, and the *Los Angeles Times* were omitted because these papers have a nationwide audience rather than a local following.

The collection of data ranged from January 1, 2007, to June 23, 2011. On February 19, 2007, the Civil Union Act was passed, providing the same rights and benefits to same-sex couples as heterosexual couples united by marriage. The state of New York passed a bill to legalize same-sex marriage on June 24, 2011. The main focus of this study is on recent years up until the New York bill was passed, as it subsequently helped to redefine media framing of the issue (Pollock & Haake, 2010).

Article Coding and Procedures

All articles were coded for prominence (how significantly the article was positioned in the paper) and direction (whether the article covered the issue favorably, unfavorably, or in a balanced/neutral manner). Articles were coded as "favorable" if they supported same-sex couples' right to marry and/or promoted equality and acceptance for same-sex couples. For example, an article from the *San Francisco Chronicle* stated "[The Constitution] must properly be interpreted to guarantee this basic civil right to all Californians, whether gay or heterosexual, and to same-sex couples as well as opposite-sex couples" (Egelko, 2008, p. A1). This article was coded as "favorable" because it discussed how same-sex couples deserve equal rights and should be able to marry.

Articles that emphasized the immoral and unethical implications of same-sex marriage were coded as "unfavorable." This included instances where same-sex marriage was viewed as unlawful or harmful to the sanctity of marriage. For example, an article in the *Desert News* stated, "Legalizing same-sex marriage or civil unions endangers not only marriage as an institution but will endanger the civil rights of those who don't approve of it" (Moore, 2008, p. B04). In this case, same-sex marriage was portrayed as something that threatens the sanctity of marriage, leading to its coding as "unfavorable."

Articles were coded "balanced/neutral" if both sides of the issue were considered or given equal weight. In addition, any article in which no side was taken was coded in this category. In one article, the president of New Jersey's Family Policy Counsel was quoted as saying, "New Jerseyans said same-sex couples have a right to live as they choose, but they do not have a right to redefine marriage for the rest of society" (Henry, 2009, p. A1). In this article, both sides of the issue were addressed and given equal weight.

Eighty percent of the 577 articles were read by two coders, resulting in a Scott's Pi coefficient of intercoder reliability of .7467. The prominence and direction scores for the articles were combined to calculate a Media Vector score for each newspaper. Pearson correlations and regression analysis were subsequently used to assess the connection between community demographics and Media Vector scores.

RESULTS

Through Pearson correlations and regression analysis, several relationships were examined between city characteristics and Media Vectors. Overall, newspaper coverage during the period of January 1, 2007, through June 23, 2011, showed that the *Seattle Post Intelligencer* had the highest Media Vector, at 0.4523, whereas the *Plain Dealer* had the lowest Media Vector, at −0.1067, a range of .5590. Of the 35 sampled cities, 26 (74%) demonstrated favorable Media Vectors, whereas only nine demonstrated unfavorable Media Vectors. Table 2 offers a list of all Media Vector scores.

To examine regional variations in coverage, Media Vector scores were aggregated by region. The overall regional scores reflected favorable coverage of same-sex marriage with the South having the highest score. This finding is noteworthy due to traditional conservative political orientations and religious affiliations in the South. Pollock and Haake's (2010) previous study of 2004–2007 coverage in "Nationwide U.S. Newspaper Coverage of Same-Sex Marriage: A Community Structure Approach" found more traditional regional results confirming the South's predicted unfavorable view; however, the current study's more recent (2007–2011) results contradict those findings and suggest evolving viewpoints in the South (see Table 3). Pearson correlation results (see Table 4) revealed strong associations between city characteristics and Media Vectors.

DISCUSSION OF SIGNIFICANT FINDINGS

Stakeholders Significant: Ages 25 to 44, Gay Market Index, 65+, Political Partisanship

Percentage of 25- to 44-year-olds. Using the stakeholder hypothesis, it was expected that the higher proportion of 25- to 44-year-olds in a city, the more favorable the coverage of same-sex marriage, as this age group born after the civil rights movement would likely display more support of rights claims. In addition, the issue of marriage directly affects those who are of marrying age, a characteristic germane to this demographic. Not only was this hypothesis confirmed, but it also had the most significant results ($r = .506, p = .001$).

Gay market index. It was predicted that that the more businesses or organizations in a city marketing to the gay community, the more favorable that city's newspaper coverage of same-sex marriage. This relationship was confirmed ($r = .432, p = .005$) but was not as

TABLE 2
Media Vector by City

City	Newspaper	Media Vector
Seattle, WA	*Seattle Post Intelligencer*	0.4523
Chicago, IL	*Chicago Sun-Times*	0.3249
Charlotte, NC	*Charlotte Observer*	0.2856
Atlanta, GA	*The Atlanta Journal-Constitution*	0.2222
Houston, TX	*Houston Chronicle*	0.2027
Philadelphia, PA	*The Philadelphia Inquirer*	0.1838
Portland, OR	*The Oregonian*	0.1651
Omaha, NE	*Omaha World-Herald*	0.1571
Denver, CO	*The Denver Post*	0.1530
San Francisco, CA	*San Francisco Chronicle*	0.1360
Madison, WI	*Wisconsin State Journal*	0.1274
Lexington, KY	*Lexington Herald-Leader*	0.1259
Detroit, MI	*The Detroit News*	0.1117
Manchester, NH	*New Hampshire Union Leader*	0.0949
Columbia, SC	*The State*	0.0916
Albany, NY	*The Times Union*	0.0816
San Antonio, CA	*San Antonio Express-News*	0.0612
Mobile, AL	*Press Register*	0.0598
Wichita, KS	*The Wichita Eagle*	0.0577
San Diego, CA	*The San Diego Union-Tribune*	0.0500
Memphis, TN	*The Commercial Appeal*	0.0463
Salt Lake City, UT	*The Deseret News*	0.0415
Pittsburgh, PA	*The Pittsburgh Post-Gazette*	0.0406
Hartford, CT	*The Hartford Courant*	0.0392
Albuquerque, NM	*Albuquerque Journal*	0.0226
Buffalo, NY	*The Buffalo News*	0.0182
Dallas, TX	*The Dallas Morning News*	−0.0039
Minneapolis, MN	*Star Tribune: Newspaper of Two Cities*	−0.0090
St. Louis, MO	*St. Louis Post-Dispatch*	−0.0123
Biloxi, MS	*Sun Herald*	−0.0305
Cincinnati, OH	*The Cincinnati Post*	−0.0447
Sacramento, CA	*The Sacramento Bee*	−0.0531
New Orleans, LA	*The Times-Picayune*	−0.0583
Orlando, FL	*The Orlando Sentinel*	−0.0842
Cleveland, OH	*The Plain Dealer*	−0.1067

TABLE 3
Media Vector Scores by Region

Region	Pollock & Haake Media Vector 2004–2007	Vales et al. Media Vector 2007–2011	Difference
South	−.0234	.1525	+.1759
West	.0294	.1143	+.0849
Northeast	.0598	.0764	+.0166
Midwest	.1070	.0673	−.0397

TABLE 4
Pearson Correlation Results

City Characteristic	Pearson Correlation	Significance
Generation 25–44	.506	.001**
Proportion college educated	.465	.002**
Gay Market Index	.432	.005**
Generation 65+	−.397	.009**
Families with income $100,000+	.383	.012*
Proportion voting Democratic	.335	.025*
Proportion voting Republican	−.330	.026*
Proportion professional	.300	.040*
Proportion below poverty level	−.297	.041*
Mainline Protestant	.170	.164
Catholic	−.164	.173
Generation 45–64	−.143	.206
Hospital beds/100,000	−.137	.216
Hate crime	.125	.236
Municipal spending on healthcare	.090	.304
Proportion unemployed	.072	.340
Children 5 & younger	.064	.357
Evangelical	.065	.355
Generation 18–24	−.058	.370
Proportion African Americans	−.042	.405
Devotional readers	−.034	.422
Children 16–18	−.027	.439
Proportion Hispanic	.022	.449
Physicians/100,000	.015	.467
Children 5–10	.003	.494
Children 11–15	−.003	.493

*Significant at .05 level, **significant at .01 level.

significant as in Pollock and Haake's previous (2010) study on newspaper coverage of same-sex marriage in which the Gay Market Index yielded the most significant results. Since the passing of the Civil Union Act in February 2007, there may have been increased national acceptance of same-sex marriage beyond the cities and regions known to market to gay communities.

Percentage 65 years and older. For the percentage 65 years and older, the hypothesis was that the higher the proportion of 65-year-olds and older in a city, the less favorable coverage of same-sex marriage. This hypothesis was confirmed ($r = -.397$, $p = .009$). The finding is consistent with a case study that confirmed "traditional" expectations, revealing that the higher the proportion of retirees, residents ages 65 to 74, or those 75 or older in a city, the less media support for trying juveniles as adults.

Political partisanship. It was hypothesized that the higher percentage voting Republican would correlate with less favorable coverage of same-sex marriage, and the higher percentage voting Democratic would correlate with more favorable coverage. Democrats have traditionally been more supportive of gay rights, whereas Republicans have more conservative views on the issue. Both hypotheses were confirmed, with percentage voting Democratic correlating with favorable coverage ($r = .335, p = .025$) and percentage voting Republican correlating with unfavorable coverage ($r = -0.330, p = 0.026$), further confirming previous research in a study on coverage of gays in the Boy Scouts (Pollock, 2007, pp. 241–242).

Buffer Significant: College Educated, Family Income 100,000+, Professional/Technical Occupational Status

Percentage college educated. The buffer hypothesis for percentage college educated expected that the higher the percentage of college educated in a city, the more favorable the coverage of same-sex marriage. This relationship was confirmed ($r = .465, p = .002$). These results are consistent with the findings in the study conducted by Higgins, Dudich, and Pollock (2003) on same-sex adoption with significant results for the percentage of college educated in a city, supporting a strong connection between buffered groups and favorable newspaper coverage of human rights issues (Pollock & Haake, 2010, p. 19).

Percentage with family income of $100,000 or more. The hypothesis for the percentage with family income more than $100,000 was confirmed ($r = .383, p = .012$), as greater percentages of families with an income of more than $100,000 in a city correlated with more favorable coverage of same-sex marriage. It is reasonable to infer that buffered groups are more informed about the issues of homosexual rights and equality, making them more open-minded about the subject. This finding aligns with previous research on same-sex marriage (Pollock & Haake, 2010).

Percentage with professional or technical occupational status. Greater percentages with professional/technical occupational status correlated with more favorable coverage, confirming the original hypothesis ($r = .300, p = .040$) and reinforcing aforementioned findings regarding other indicators of privilege.

Vulnerability Significant: Poverty Level

Percentage living below the poverty line. Following the vulnerability hypothesis, it was predicted that the greater the percentage living below the poverty line, the less favorable the coverage of same-sex marriage. This hypothesis was confirmed ($r = -.297, p = .041$) and is consistent with previous community structure research revealing correlations between higher vulnerability levels and less favorable coverage of gays in the Boy Scouts (Pollock, 2007).

Factor Analysis

To refine results further, a varimax rotated factor analysis was executed on the independent variables, yielding five significant factors, all with eigenvalues of 1.00 or more. Regarding factor variance alone, Factor 1 (Lifecycle Position/Generation) accounted for 28% of the variance, Factor 2 (Privilege/Marketing/Politics) accounted for 20% of the variance, Factor 3 (Evangelical) accounted for 11% of the variance, Factor 4 (Hispanics) accounted for 8% of the

TABLE 5
Factor Analysis of National Characteristics

Varimax Rotated Component Matrix

Factor	Component	Factor Loading
Factor 1: Lifecycle Position/Generation	Families with children 5–10	.955
	Families with children 5 and younger	.950
	Families with children 11–15	.907
	Families with children 16–17	.824
	Generation 65+	−.785
	Generation 45–64	−.745
Factor 2: Privilege/Gay Marketing/Politics	College educated	.890
	Families with incomes of $100,000 or more	.866
	Gay Market Index	.839
	Voting Republican	−.772
	Voting Democratic	.760
Factor 3: Evangelical	Evangelical	.847
Factor 4: Hispanics	Hispanics	−.797
Factor 5: Health Care Access/Employment	Physicians per 100,000	.726
	Unemployed	−.726

variance, and Factor 5 (Health Care Access/Employment) accounted for 7% of the variance. The total factor variance accounted for was 74% (see Table 5).

After running a regression of the factors against the Media Vectors, it was revealed that privilege/marketing/politics and Evangelical were the two leading indicators, together accounting for 29.2% of the variance (see Table 6). One reason for privilege/marketing/generation accounting for 24% of the variance may be that those who are more privileged or more educated tend to be more aware of and thus sympathetic toward human rights issues, such as same-sex marriage. Similar to the findings of Pollock and Haake, percentage voting Democratic and percentage voting Republican were found significant, likely due, at least in part, to the ongoing debates in both parties. The combination of privilege, marketing to gays, and Democratic political identity, all positively associated with media support for same-sex marriage, is broadly consistent with prior research by Pollock and Haake (2010). Finally, percentage Evangelical accounted for 5.2% of the variance. This stakeholder group may be more invested in the debate over same-sex marriage because of its strong religious ties and traditional social views.

TABLE 6
Regression of Factors Linked to Coverage of Same-Sex Marriage

Model	R (equation)	R^2 (cumulative)	R^2 Change	F Change	Significance of F Change
Privilege/Gay Marketing/Politics	.490	.240	.240	181.578	.000
Privilege/Gay Marketing/Politics, Evangelical	.540	.292	.052	42.188	.000

CONCLUSIONS AND IMPLICATIONS FOR FURTHER RESEARCH

The controversial debate over same-sex marriage results in notable variations in newspaper coverage throughout the nation. Several significant correlations were revealed, all consistent with their original hypotheses. The most significant findings included the importance of the stakeholder indicators, including "generation" (ages 25–44), Gay Market Index, and political affiliation. Regarding the buffer hypothesis, favorable coverage of the topic correlated with high percentages of privileged groups in a city, particularly college educated, but also those with family incomes of $100,000 or more and those with professional or technical occupational status.

Future research on same-sex marriage could analyze cross-national coverage, to compare media coverage in other nations with that of the United States. In addition, coverage in smaller cities within the United States could be explored. Public opinion data, perhaps at the regional level, could be useful for further research as well. Public opinion polls would offer researchers the opportunity to analyze attitudes toward the issue and associations among city characteristics, media coverage, and public opinion. It would also be interesting to compare results of this study with future research about coverage after the passage of the New York bill, as well as coverage surrounding future presidential elections. Due to the many significant findings of this study, further community structure studies of media coverage of same-sex marriage in newspapers or other media outlets are warranted.

ACKNOWLEDGMENT

A previous version of this article was presented at the annual conference of the National Communication Association, November, 2012, in Orlando, Florida.

REFERENCES

Association of Religion Data Archives [ARDA]. (2008). Retrieved from http://www.thearda.com

Brechman, J. M., & Pollock, J. C. (2007). Nationwide newspaper coverage of affirmative action: A community structure approach. In A. R. Narro & A. C. Ferguson (Eds.), *Diversity and mass communication: The evidence of impact* (pp. 113–134). Southlake, TX: Fountainhead Press.

County and city extra: Annual metro, city, and county data book. (2007). Lanham, MD: Bernan Press.

County and city extra: Annual metro, city, and county data book. (2010). Lanham, MD: Bernan Press.

D'Angelo, P. (2002). News framing as a multi-paradigmatic research program: A response to Entman. *Journal of Communication, 52,* 890–918.

Egelko, B. (2008, May 16). Making history California Supreme Court, in 4–3 decision, strikes down law that bans marriage of same-sex couples. *San Francisco Chronicle,* p. A1. Retrieved from NewsBank database.

Entman, R. M. (1993). Framing: Toward clarification of a fractured paradigm. *Journal of Communication, 43*(4), 51–58.

Green, F. (Ed.). (2009). *Gayellow pages: The national edition, USA and Canada* (Book 33). New York, NY: Renaissance House.

Henry, C. (2009, November 18). Push for same-sex marriage in N.J. faces uncertain future. *The Philadelphia Inquirer,* p. A01. Retrieved from NewsBank database.

Higgins, K., Dudich, T., & Pollock, J. C. (2003, April). *Nationwide newspaper coverage of same-sex adoption: A community structure approach.* New Jersey Communication Association, The College of New Jersey, Ewing, New Jersey.

Lifestyle market analyst: A reference guide for consumer market analysis. (2008). Des Plaines, IL: Standard Rate and Data Service.

McCluskey, M., Stein, S. E., Boyle, M. P., & McLeod, D. M. (2009). Community structure and social protest: Influences on newspaper coverage. *Mass Communication and Society, 12,* 353–371.

McLeod, D. M., & Hertog, J. K. (1992). The manufacture of public opinion by reporters: Informal cues for public perceptions of protest groups. *Discourse and Society, 3,* 259–275.

McLeod, D. M., & Hertog, J. K. (1999). Social control, social change and the mass media's role in the regulation of protest groups. In D. Demers & K. Viswanath (Eds.), *Mass media, social control, and social change: A macrosocial perspective* (pp. 305–331). Ames, IA: Iowa State University Press.

Mink, M., Puma, J., & Pollock, J. C. (2001, May). *Nationwide newspaper coverage of the repatriation of Elian Gonzalez: A community structure approach.* Paper presented at the annual conference of the International Communication Association, Washington, DC.

Moore, C. A. (2008, August 23). Gay marriage criticized. *Deseret News,* p. B04.

Olien, C. N., Donohue, G. A., & Tichenor, P. J. (1995). Conflict, consensus, and public opinion. In T. L. Glaser & C. T. Salmon (Eds.), *Public opinion and the communication of consent* (pp. 301–322). New York, NY: Guilford

Pollock, J. C. (2007). *Titled mirrors: Media alignment with political and social change—A community structure approach.* Cresskill, NJ: Hampton Press.

Pollock, J. C., & Dantas, G. (1998, July). *Nationwide newspaper coverage of same-sex marriage: A community structure approach.* Paper presented to the Mass Communication Division at the annual meeting of the International Communication Association, Jerusalem, Israel.

Pollock, J. C., & Haake, J. (2010). Nationwide US newspaper coverage of same-sex marriage: A community structure approach. *The Journal of PR, 1,* 13–40.

Pollock, J. C., Maltese-Nehrbass, M., Corbin, P., & Fascanella, P. B. (2010). Nationwide newspaper coverage of genetically-modified food in the United States: A community structure approach. *Ecos de la Comunicación, 3,* 51–75.

Pollock, J. C., Piccillo, C., Leopardi, D., Gratale, S., & Cabot, K. (2005, February). Nationwide newspaper coverage of Islam Post-9/11: A community structure approach. *Communication Research Reports, 22,* 12–24.

Pollock, J. C., & Robinson, J. L. (1977). Reporting rights conflicts. *Society, 13,* 44–47.

Pollock, J. C., Robinson, J. L., & Murray, M. C. (1978). Media agendas and human rights: The Supreme Court decision on abortion. *Journalism Quarterly, 53,* 545–548, 561.

Pollock, J. C., & Tobin, B. (2000, April). *Nationwide newspaper coverage of same-sex adoption: A community structure approach.* Paper presented at the annual conference of the New Jersey Communication Association, Monmouth University, Long Branch, NJ.

Pollock, J. C., & Whitney, L. (1997). Newspapers and racial/ethnic conflict: Comparing city demographics and nationwide reporting on the Crown Heights (Brooklyn, NY) incidents. *Atlantic Journal of Communication, 5,* 127–149.

Pollock, J. C., & Yulis, S. G. (2004). Nationwide newspaper coverage of physician-assisted suicide: A community structure approach. *Journal of Health Communication, 9,* 281–307.

Scheufele, D. A. (1999). Framing as a theory of media effects. *Journal of Communication, 49,* 203–222.

U.S. Census Bureau. (2010). *State and metropolitan area data book 2010: A statistical abstract supplement* (7th ed.). Washington, DC: Author.

Watson, B., & Riffe, D. (2011). Structural determinants of local public affairs place blogging: Structural pluralism and community stress. *Mass Communication and Society, 14,* 879–904.

Webb, J., Novick, F., Pagan, H., Villanueva, M., O'Gorman, E., & Pollock, J. C. (2010, November). *Nationwide coverage of the homeless: A community structure approach.* Paper presented at the annual conference of the National Communication Association, San Francisco, CA.

Nationwide Newspaper Coverage of Detainee Rights at Guantanamo Bay: A Community Structure Approach

Kelsey Zinck, Maggie Rogers, John C. Pollock, and Matthew Salvatore
Department of Communication Studies
The College of New Jersey

A community structure analysis compared community characteristics and coverage of detainee rights and Guantanamo Bay in leading newspapers in 28 major cities nationwide, sampling all relevant 250+ word articles from September 12, 2001, to September 11, 2012. The resulting 359 articles were coded for "prominence" and "direction," then combined into a "Media Vector" score for each newspaper (range = .6034 to −.2500). About four out of five (82%) newspapers supported detainee rights. Stakeholder and buffer clusters were important. Pearson correlations revealed that stakeholders (the proportions and concerns of which are expected to be reflected in media coverage) were significant, with percentage of Mainline Protestant ($r - .550$, $p = .001$) linked to favorable media coverage of detainee rights and percentage of age 65 and older ($r = -.321$, $p = .048$) linked to unfavorable coverage. The buffer hypothesis (associating higher proportions of privileged groups with coverage receptive to human rights claims) was also confirmed, with percentage of college educated correlating with favorable coverage ($r = .409$, $p = .015$). Regression analysis yielded two significant variables—percentage Mainline Protestant, 33%, and percentage professional/technical occupational status (another "buffer" measure), 27%, totaling 59.9%, both linked to favorable coverage. Unexpectedly, the Midwest displayed more media support for detainee rights than any other region of the United States.

INTRODUCTION

After the September 11 terrorist attacks and the start of the Afghani War, the United States constructed camps to detain suspected terrorists. These camps, the most visible of which was Guantanamo Bay Naval Base in Cuba, came under scrutiny for their treatment of inmates. The crux of this controversy was whether detainees might be protected under U.S. judicial laws or the Geneva Conventions.

Detainee rights can be framed in two contexts by national media. One frame portrays a comprehensive "inclusive" or "favorable" approach to detainee rights, indicating detainees warrant protection under the Geneva Convention and U.S. judicial laws. Such protection would include the right to a fair and speedy trial and protections from inhumane treatment. An alternative "exclusive" or "unfavorable" frame denies such rights to detainees, asserting that they are a threat to homeland security and should be punished for their potential crimes against humanity.

This study examines newspaper coverage of detainee rights by utilizing the community structure approach to explore how community characteristics shape coverage of this issue. Through the framework of this approach, the study employs two research questions to examine the connection between specific community indicators and media reporting on detainee rights.

RQ1: How much variation exists in news coverage of detainee rights among U.S. cities?
RQ2: How closely linked is that variation to differences in community characteristics?

This study tests several hypotheses to explore the relation between differences in demographics in a community and variations in newspaper coverage.

LITERATURE REVIEW

A literature review revealed that the field of communication studies has devoted relatively little scholarly study to detainee rights. Utilizing the databases Communication and Mass Media Complete, ComAbstracts, and Communication Institute for Online Scholarship (CIOS) returned few articles directly addressing media coverage of detainee rights. By contrast, far more research on the issue was encountered in the fields of political science, criminology, and history.

Several key terms were used in the communication studies databases, including "detainee rights" and "Guantanamo Bay," producing minimal results. Communication and Mass Media returned 29 results for "Guantanamo Bay," eight of which were relevant, as they referenced Guantanamo Bay through the lens of media access to evaluate detainees' rights or lack thereof. In particular, an article in *Quill* ("Guantanamo Press," 2002) analyzed media access to detainees at Guantanamo: "When detainees began arriving at the base in January [2002] journalists could roam freely interviewing people.... Journalists now have no access to detainees and are separated from them at all times by a green screen, a measure that has been taken to protect detainees" (p. 35). Another article described the lack of availability and openness of Guantanamo Bay to the media (Upano, 2002). One study discussed in-depth the disparities in news coverage allowed from Guantanamo Bay, especially surrounding the trial of Abd al-Rahim al-Nashiri, a suspected terrorist (Berg, 2011).

Similarly, a different article covered the hardships reporters faced to get even a glimpse into the courtroom trials of detainees from Guantanamo Bay (Skallman, 2010). Worthington (2011) mapped a timeline of the facility's history, from early deprivations of basic rights, through improvements during the Obama presidency. Lain (2008) articulated the legal battle surrounding detainees:

> Both sides [heralded it as a victory]: the Bush Administration noted that the Court recognized their ability to charge citizens as enemy combatants as long as they are afforded due process in that determination, while the ACLU noted it as a victory for constitutional rights because it limited Presidential power. (pp. 9–10)

An article in *News Media & the Law* (Upano, 2002) discussed information leaked to the media, quoting Donald Rumsfeld: "'I think that anyone who has a position where they touch a war plan has an obligation to not leak it to the press or anybody else … Because it kills people'" (p. 23). The last relevant article by Hobbs (2007) analyzed the 2004 *Rasul v. Bush* case, which found that the government could not deny a detainee a trial because they were seen as enemy combatants.

Only one result was found for "detainee rights" in Communication and Mass Media Complete, a study by Meehan, Philbin, Wilson, and Pollock (2003) using a community structure approach to discuss nationwide newspaper coverage of detainee rights in the first year of coverage after 9/11. The study "revealed significant, favorable relationships between voting Republicans and detainee rights coverage. Catholics, Democrats, and Hispanics, however, were found to be significantly related to negative coverage of detainee rights" (p. 2). CIOS–ComAbstracts produced zero results for "Guantanamo Bay" and "detainee rights."

Although the communication studies field produced few relevant results on detainee rights, explorations in the fields of political science, criminology, and history yielded much more extensive scholarly examination pertinent to those fields. The political science database Westlaw produced 100 results when searching "detainee rights," "Guantanamo Bay," and "media coverage" with roughly 20 articles specifically relating to this study's topic. The criminology field, specifically in the Social Sciences Full Text database, yielded even more articles than political science, covering such topics as the injustices faced by detainees and considerations of closing Guantanamo (Smith, 2009). In the history field, the JSTOR database produced 126 articles discussing media coverage and detainee rights. It is evident that the political science, criminology, and history fields have examined detainee rights extensively, but the communication studies field has paid relatively little attention to media coverage of detainee rights and Guantanamo Bay. As a result, this study will attempt to help bridge this gap in the communication studies literature.

HYPOTHESES

This study utilized the community structure approach and previous research to develop 27 hypotheses to examine coverage of detainee rights. These hypotheses can be clustered in three umbrella groups: buffer, vulnerability, and stakeholder.

Buffer Hypotheses

The buffer hypothesis states that the greater the percentage of "privileged" families in a community, the more favorable the media coverage of those making human rights claims (Pollock, 2007, pp. 52, 62). Privilege can be measured in terms of the percentage of college educated, family income of $100,000 or more, and professional occupational status.

The buffer hypothesis has been examined in many case studies. In a nationwide study of newspapers and the "Open Door" policy toward Cuba, Pollock, Shier, and Slattery (1995) found "the higher the proportion of 'privileged' groups in a city, the more favorable the reporting of Cubans seeking asylum in the US, confirming … a 'buffer' hypothesis: Those buffered from economic uncertainty are relatively likely to respond to those making human rights claims with generosity and compassion" (pp. 67–86). Another study found that the higher the proportion of privileged groups in a city, the more favorable the coverage of same-sex marriage (Pollock & Haake, 2010). In the example of the Clarence Thomas–Anita Hill hearings in regards to gender discrimination in the workplace, favorable coverage of Hill's testimony correlated with the proportion of those with professional/technical occupational status in a city (Pollock, 2007, p. 66). Consequently, it is reasonable to assume that more "privileged" groups would be more informed and favorable toward human rights claims such as detainee rights. Therefore the following can be expected:

H1: The higher the percentage of college educated in a city, the more favorable the coverage of detainee rights (Lifestyle Market Analyst, 2008).

H2: The higher the percentage of families with incomes of $100,000 or more, the more favorable the coverage of detainee rights (Lifestyle Market Analyst, 2008).

H3: The higher the percentage of those with professional/technical occupational status, the more favorable the coverage of detainee rights (Lifestyle Market Analyst, 2008).

Healthcare access.   One attribute that signifies the level of privilege in a city is healthcare access. Pollock (2007) suggested that healthcare access can be measured by "the proportion of the municipal budget that a city spends on healthcare, in addition to the availability of hospital beds and physicians" (p. 93). A study on embryonic stem cell research found a positive correlation between access to healthcare (physicians per 100,000 residents) and favorable coverage of the issue (Pollock, 2007, p. 99). A cross-national study by Pollock, Reda et al. (2010) in regards to climate change showed that both the greater number of hospital beds per 100,000 as well as the greater number of physicians per 100,000, the greater the media support for government activity addressing climate change. Thus, better healthcare access may correlate with more support for human rights claims. Consequently, the following can be predicted:

H4: The higher the number of physicians per 100,000 people in a city, the more favorable the coverage of detainee rights (State and Metropolitan Area Data Book, 2010).

H5: The higher the number of hospital beds per 100,000 people in a city, the more favorable the coverage of detainee rights (County and City Extra, 2010).

H6: The higher the percentage of municipal spending on healthcare in a city, the more favorable the coverage of detainee rights (County and City Extra, 2010).

Vulnerability

The vulnerability hypothesis, as opposed to the buffer hypothesis, suggests that newspapers mirror the interests of vulnerable groups, such as the poor, unemployed, and those living in higher crime areas (Pollock, 2007, p. 137). Previous community structure studies have supported the vulnerability hypothesis. One study comparing coverage of racial/ethnic conflict showed "the higher the poverty or unemployment levels in a city, the more 'pluralistic' the coverage in newspapers nationwide, appreciating the claims of both Caribbean Americans and Hasidic Jews" (Pollock & Whitney, 1997). In a study by Pollock, Maltese-Nehrbass, Corbin, and Fascanella (2010), it was found that the higher the proportion of relatively disadvantaged groups (unemployed or below the poverty level), the greater the media support for disease-resistant, higher-yield genetically modified food (pp. 51–75). After the *Roe v. Wade* decision, it was found that coverage favored legalizing abortion in cities with higher poverty levels (Pollock & Robinson, 1977; Pollock, Robinson, & Murray, 1978).

In addition, it was found that the higher the percentage below the poverty level, the more favorable the coverage of a Patients' Bill of Rights (Pollock, 2007, p. 150). Moreover, another study showed that in communities with higher poverty, there is less favorable coverage of capital punishment (Pollock, 2007, pp. 138–146). In a study by Pollock, Davies, Effingham, and Heisler (2012), the higher the homicide rate, the more favorable the coverage of same-sex marriage. It is reasonable to expect that the individuals who fit into the vulnerable group will be in favor of rights for the detainees at Guantanamo Bay. Thus,

H7: The higher the percentage of people living below the poverty line, the more favorable the coverage of detainee rights (American Fact Finder, 2010).

H8: The higher the percentage unemployed in a city, the more favorable the coverage of detainee rights (American Fact Finder, 2010).

H9: The higher the crime rate in a city, the more favorable the coverage of detainee rights (County and City Extra, 2010).

Stakeholder Hypothesis

Tichenor, Donohue, and Olien (1980) have found, after several years of study, that "the larger the city size, the greater the plurality of viewpoints presented by the media" (Pollock, 2007, p. 171). In addition, the community structure approach has explored links between city demographics and reporting on stakeholder issues, expecting a "link between stakeholder size and relatively favorable coverage of stakeholder concerns" (Pollock, 2007, p. 172). Stakeholder categories included in this study are ethnic identity, political partisanship, belief system, generation, and position in lifecycle.

Ethnic identity. Certain ethnic groups have a more vested interest in the topic of detainee rights because they are more likely to have been affected by social injustice. According to Hughes (2009), Hispanics are substantially uninsured and would be more likely to favor universal healthcare. Kiernicki, Pollock, and Lavery (2012) found that the higher the percentage of Hispanics in a community, the more favorable the coverage of universal healthcare. A study by Pollock et al. (1978) discovered that the higher the poverty level in a city, the more favorable the coverage of *Roe v. Wade* during the time of the Supreme Court decision, and the higher the numbers of abortions performed in cities after legalization took effect. Strikingly, a study on nationwide newspaper coverage of Islam post-9/11 revealed that the higher the proportion of foreign born or Farsi or Arabic speakers in a city, the less favorable the coverage of Islam in the first year after 9/11 (Pollock, Piccillo, Leopardi, Gratale, & Cabot, 2005, pp. 15–24). Minority groups are therefore expected to have high stakes in the reporting of detainee rights. As a result, the following is predicted:

H10: The higher the percentage of African Americans in a city, the more favorable the coverage of detainee rights (County and City Extra, 2010).

H11: The higher the percentage of Hispanics in a city, the more favorable the coverage of detainee rights (County and City Extra, 2010).

H12: The higher percentage of those speaking Arabic or Farsi at home, the more favorable the coverage of detainee rights (County and City Extra, 2010).

H13: The higher percentage of foreign-born in a city, the more favorable the coverage of detainee rights (County and City Extra, 2010).

Belief system.   It seems plausible that certain religious beliefs, in conjunction with human rights issues, might contribute to selected coverage in newspapers. Pollock et al. (1978) found that the higher the percentage of Catholics in a city, the less favorable media coverage of elective abortion during the time of *Roe v. Wade*. Subsequent research found that the higher percentage of Bible/devotional reading in a city, the less favorable the coverage of gays in the Boy Scouts (Pollock, 2007, p. 243). Devotional reading has also been associated with media opposition to stem cell research (Pollock, 2007, p. 98).

However, more recent analysis of progressive issues such as same-sex marriage and same-sex adoption found that higher percentages of Catholics in a city are consistently associated with "favorable" coverage of the issue (Pollock & Haake, 2010) and more favorable coverage of gays in the Boy Scouts (Pollock, 2007, p. 243). Finally, a study by Pollock (2013) found that the higher the percentage of Mainline Protestants in a city, the more favorable the coverage of the "Occupy" movement in fall 2011, prior to the removal of protestors from Zuccotti Park. In line with certain belief systems, media coverage of controversial topics may emphasize some perspectives over others. Therefore, regarding detainee rights it is reasonable to expect the following:

H14: The higher the percentage of Evangelicals in a city, the less favorable the coverage of detainee rights (Association of Religion Data Archives, 2006).

H15: The higher the percentage of devotional readers in a city, the less favorable the coverage of detainee rights (Lifestyle Market Analyst, 2008).

H16: The higher the percentage of Mainline Protestants in a city, the more favorable the coverage of detainee rights (Association of Religion Data Archives, 2006).

H17: The higher the percentage of Catholics in a city, the more favorable the coverage of detainee rights (Association of Religion Data Archives, 2006).

Political identity.   Citizens of major cities can be categorized into two major political parties: Republican and Democratic. Coverage by media sources can reflect different political positions (Pollock, 2007, p. 177). In a study by Pollock (2007) regarding oil drilling in the Arctic, it was found that the percentage voting Republican was generally associated with favorable coverage of drilling, whereas the percentage voting Democratic was linked to coverage opposing drilling (p. 187). In a case study about trying juveniles as adults, it was found that the higher the percentage voting Democratic in the 1996 presidential election, the less favorable the coverage of the issue (Pollock, 2007, p. 198). Since Republicans opened Guantanamo Bay, and Republicans have previously been associated with less media support for human rights claims, the following is expected:

H18: The higher the percentage voting Republican in the last presidential election, the less favorable the coverage of detainee rights (Lifestyle Market Analyst, 2008).

H19: The higher the percentage voting Democratic in the last presidential election, the more favorable the coverage of detainee rights (Lifestyle Market Analyst, 2008).

Generation. Each generation has its own viewpoints on current issues based on prior life experiences. Younger generations tend to be more liberal and supportive of social movements. In contrast, older generations tend to be more conservative and reliant on traditional ideals. Webb et al. (2010) found that the higher the proportion of the population between the ages of 18 and 25, the less favorable the coverage of the less privileged, in particular the homeless. Similarly, Brechman and Pollock (2007) found that the higher the proportion of the population from 18 to 24, the less favorable the coverage of affirmative action (pp. 113–141). Yet older generations tend to support the status quo. Pollock and Yulis (2004) found that the larger the proportion of citizens older than 75, the less favorable the coverage of legalization of physician-assisted euthanasia (pp. 281–307). Another study by Pollock (2007) found that the higher proportion of people aged 65 and older, the less media support for trying juveniles as adults (pp. 195–207). Still, younger generations are generally considered more socially liberal in their viewpoints, whereas older generations are more likely to be conservative. Therefore, it is reasonable to expect the following:

H20: The higher the percentage of 18- to 24-year-olds in a city, the more favorable the coverage of detainee rights (Lifestyle Market Analyst, 2008).

H21: The higher the percentage of 25- to 44-year-olds in a city, the more favorable the coverage of detainee rights (Lifestyle Market Analyst, 2008).

H22: The higher the percentage of 45- to 64-year-olds in a city, the less favorable the coverage of detainee rights (Lifestyle Market Analyst, 2008).

H23: The higher the percentage of 65 year olds and older in a city, the less favorable the coverage of detainee rights (Lifestyle Market Analyst, 2008).

Position in lifecycle. It is reasonable to assume that families with children would be associated with more favorable coverage of detainee rights because it is a human rights issue. Mink, Puma, and Pollock (2001) examined the custody battle over Cuban immigrant Elian Gonzalez, a young boy. It was found that nationwide U.S. newspaper coverage favoring the repatriation of Gonzalez to his biological father in Cuba was directly associated with the proportion of families in cities with children of similar ages, 5 to 7. Pollock (2013) found that the higher the percentage of families with young children (younger than 5) in a city, the more support for the "Occupy" movement after the protestors were removed from Zuccotti Park. Yet a study of trying juveniles as adults found higher proportions of families with young children were associated with coverage supporting trying juveniles as adults, limiting teenage human rights claims, presumably to protect young children from dangerous teens (Pollock, 2007, pp. 195–207). Based on this research, it can be assumed that parents of children 18 and younger would be likely to support detainee rights due to their wish to preserve rights for their children in the future. Therefore, the following is predicted:

H24: The higher the percentage of families with children younger than age 5 in a city, the more favorable the coverage of detainee rights (Lifestyle Market Analyst, 2008).

H25: The higher the percentage of families with children ages 5 to 10 in a city, the more favorable the coverage of detainee rights (Lifestyle Market Analyst, 2008).

H26: The higher the percentage of families with children ages 11 to 15 in a city, the more favorable the coverage of detainee rights (Lifestyle Market Analyst, 2008).

H27: The higher the percentage of families with children ages 16 to 18 in a city, the more favorable the coverage of detainee rights (Lifestyle Market Analyst, 2008).

METHODOLOGY

To investigate the topic of detainee rights at Guantanamo Bay, a nationwide cross-section sample of 28 major U.S. newspapers was selected from the NewsBank database, including all relevant articles with 250 words or more in the sample period, yielding 359 articles. The collection of articles was selected from the following publications: the *Times Union*, the *Atlanta Journal-Constitution, Sun Herald, Boston Herald*, the *Buffalo News, Charlotte Observer, Chicago Sun-Times*, the *Cincinnati Post*, the *Plain Dealer*, the *State*, the *Dallas Morning News*, the *Hartford Courant, Houston Chronicle, Las Vegas Sun, Lexington Herald-Leader, Star Tribune: Newspaper of the Twin Cities, Press Register*, the *Times-Picayune*, the *Orlando Sentinel*, the *Philadelphia Inquirer*, the *Pittsburgh Post-Gazette*, the *Oregonian*, the *Deseret News, San Antonio Express-News, San Francisco Chronicle*, the *Seattle Times, St. Louis Post-Dispatch*, and the *Wichita Eagle*. Publications such as the *Washington Post, USA Today*, the *New York Times*, the *Wall Street Journal*, and the *Los Angeles Times* were omitted, as these papers target nationwide rather than local audiences.

The sample frame ranged from September 12, 2001, to September 11, 2012, an 11-year span. September 11, 2001, marked the terrorists' attacks on the World Trade Center; the Pentagon; and Shanksville, Pennsylvania, using commercial airplanes. On September 20, 2001, President George W. Bush declared a "War on Terror" that first included Afghanistan, followed by Iraq on March 19, 2003. The focus of this study is media framing of detainee rights in the period following the attacks and throughout the war.

Article Coding and Procedures

Each article was assigned two scores: prominence (identifying how significantly the article was positioned by editors in the paper) and direction (representing whether the issue was portrayed favorably, unfavorably, or in a balanced/neutral manner). Articles coded as favorable supported detainees gaining legal rights, often claiming that the detainees were being held against their will and denied formal legal rights. For example, an article in the *Hartford Courant* quoted the inspector general Glenn Fine as saying,

> Detainees were kept under a hold-until-cleared standard, 'based on the belief, which turned out to be erroneous, that the FBI's clearance process would proceed quickly.' The process took an average of 80 days per detainee, and detention was about as pleasant as it sounds; one prison officer said in an affidavit that detainees were regularly slammed against walls. (Caplan, 2003, p. C3)

Another article in the *Deseret News* shed new light on the status of trials of the detainees at Guantanamo Bay, stating, "bringing such detainees to trial on prior charges is one of many possibilities being considered" (Barrett, 2009, p. A03). These articles declared that, even though those being held at Guantanamo Bay may be terror suspects, they still deserved legal rights.

Articles coded as "unfavorable" opposed detainees being given formal legal rights and emphasized their terrorist aspects. An article in the *Dallas Morning News* declared that the detainees at Guantanamo Bay were not reserved legal rights: "President Bush has decided that the Geneva Convention applies to Taliban detainees but that they fail the treaty's tests for prisoner of war status" (Whittle, 2002, p. 1A). Another article in the *Seattle Times* stated, "The military spends $2.5 million a year to ensure that meals served to Muslim prisoners at Guantánamo were 'proper Muslim-approved food,' and [the military] had distributed 1,300 Qurans to detainees" (Curtius, 2005, p. A8). In these examples, the government asserted its treatment of detainees was humane and that they should not be afforded the same legal rights as other war detainees.

Articles were coded as balanced/neutral if both sides were displayed equally or if they simply provided information on detainee status at Guantanamo Bay. An article in the *Atlanta Journal-Constitution* discussed both sides, stating that the Pentagon assured "treatment is humane for the prisoners, who have not yet been charged with a crime" (Nelson, 2002, p. A6). On the other hand, a spokesman of the International Committee of the Red Cross was quoted saying that the U.S. government "breached the 1949 Geneva Convention" (Nelson, 2002, p. A6). In addition, an article in the *Cincinnati Post* portrayed alternative points of view and stated, "Information on the purported missing detainees was, in some cases, incomplete, the report acknowledged. Some detainees had been added to the list" (Satter, 2007, p. A13). Both of these examples depicted a balanced point of view.

Of 359 articles, 216 (60%) were read by two coders, resulting in a Scott's Pi coefficient of intercoder reliability of .8132. Media Vectors for all newspapers were measured by combining article prominence and direction scores. Pearson correlations and regression analysis were used to reveal connections between city demographics and Media Vectors.

RESULTS

This study examined newspaper coverage of detainee rights and Guantanamo Bay by comparing Media Vectors from 28 large cities during the period of September 12, 2001, through September 11, 2012. The *Star Tribune: Newspaper of the Twin Cities* had the highest Media Vector, at 0.6034, whereas the *Plain Dealer* had the lowest Media Vector, at −0.2500. The range of Media Vector results was .8534. Of the 28 sample papers, 23, or 82.1%, yielded favorable Media Vectors, whereas five, or 17.86%, demonstrated unfavorable Media Vectors. Table 1 offers a complete list of the Media Vectors scores found in this study.

To examine regional variations in coverage, Media Vector scores were averaged for each region's newspapers. Regional results, found in Table 2, all reflected favorable coverage. The Midwest displayed wide variation in scores, yet had the highest average regional Media Vector. The region manifesting the least favorable coverage was the West.

Pearson correlations were calculated using SPSS to explore connections between city characteristics and newspaper coverage. These calculations are shown in Table 3.

TABLE 1
Media Vector by City

City	Newspaper	Media Vector
Minneapolis, MN	*Star Tribune: Newspaper of the Twin Cities*	.6034
Atlanta, GA	*The Atlanta Journal-Constitution*	.4522
Charlotte, NC	*Charlotte Observer*	.3315
Buffalo, NY	*The Buffalo News*	.1991
Wichita, KS	*The Wichita Eagle*	.1863
Albany, NY	*The Times Union*	.1397
St. Louis, MO	*St. Louis Post-Dispatch*	.1241
San Antonio, TX	*San Antonio Express-News*	.1129
Mobile, AL	*Press Register*	.1111
Houston, TX	*Houston Chronicle*	.1066
Lexington, KY	*Lexington Herald-Leader*	.1058
Cincinnati, OH	*The Cincinnati Post*	.1040
Columbia, SC	*The State*	.0898
Seattle, WA	*The Seattle Times*	.0884
Chicago, IL	*Chicago Sun-Times*	.0600
New Orleans, LA	*The Times-Picayune*	.0575
Portland, OR	*The Oregonian*	.0560
Las Vegas, NV	*Las Vegas Sun*	.0545
Salt Lake City, UT	*The Deseret News*	.0485
Pittsburgh, PA	*The Pittsburgh Post-Gazette*	.0232
San Francisco, CA	*San Francisco Chronicle*	.0229
Philadelphia, PA	*The Philadelphia Inquirer*	.0029
Hartford, CT	*The Hartford Courant*	.0027
Boston, MA	*Boston Herald*	−.0193
Orlando, FL	*The Orlando Sentinel*	−.0309
Biloxi, MS	*Sun Herald*	−.0688
Dallas, TX	*The Dallas Morning News*	−.1106
Cleveland, OH	*The Plain Dealer*	−.2500

TABLE 2
Media Vector Scores by Region

Region	Media Vector
Midwest	0.1448
South	0.1051
Northeast	0.0735
West	0.0541

DISCUSSION OF SIGNIFICANT FINDINGS

Stakeholder Significant: Mainline Protestant, Age 65 and Older

Percent of Mainline Protestants (confirmed). It was predicted that the greater percentage of Mainline Protestants in a city, the more favorable the coverage of detainee rights.

120

TABLE 3
Pearson Correlation Results

City Characteristic	Pearson Correlation	Significance
Percentage Mainline Protestant	.550	.001**
Percent college educated	.409	.015*
Age 65+	−.321	.048*
Percentage Farsi speakers	−.331	.057
Percentage professional/technical occupations	.294	.064
Percentage physicians/100,000	−.256	.094
Percentage Hispanic	−.254	.096
Percentage income 100,000+	.232	.117
Percentage devotional readers	.216	.135
Percentage Evangelical	.215	.136
Ages 25 to 44	.205	.148
Ages 45 to 64	.192	.164
Percentage foreign born	−.188	.169
Children 5 to 10	.182	.177
Percentage Catholic	−.180	.180
Children 11 to 15	.164	.201
Children 16 to 18	.160	.209
Children younger than 5	.157	.213
Percentage below poverty	−.146	.230
Percentage hospital beds per 1,000	−.136	.245
Homicide	−.097	.318
Percentage voting Republican	.093	.318
Crime rate	.094	.324
Percentage voting Democrat	−.090	.325
Percentage exercise/fitness	.088	.328
Percentage unemployed	.086	.332
Hate crime	.083	.343
Percentage eating healthy/natural foods	−.066	.370
Percentage self-improvement	.053	.394
Violent crimes known to law enforcement	−.055	.395
Percentage African American	.044	.413
Percentage dieting/weight control	−.043	.415
Age 18 to 24	−.030	.439
Gay Market Index	.026	.448
Percentage single-parent households	−.022	.455
Percentage municipal spending on healthcare	−.006	.487

*Significant at .05 level, **significant at .01 level.

This hypothesis was confirmed with the study's most significant positive correlation ($r =$ .550, $p = $ .001). This result could potentially be related to the Protestant ideals of "optimism and self-reliance in the face of adversity" (Pollock, 2013, p. 23) articulated by Max Weber (2010) in his classic *The Protestant Ethic and the Spirit of Capitalism*. Therefore, from the perspective of robust self-reliance, detainees deserve legal rights to overcome the adversity of being imprisoned in Guantanamo Bay, affirming the hypothesis.

TABLE 4
Regression Analysis

Model	R (equation)	R² (cumulative)	R² Change	F Change	Significance of F Change
Percentage Mainline Protestant	.574	.330	.330	14.106	.001**
Percentage Mainline Protestant & professional/ technical occupational status	.774	.599	.270	10.922	.003**

**Significant at .01 level.

Percentage of 65 year olds and older in a city (confirmed). It was predicted that the greater the percentage of people age 65 and older in a city, the less favorable the coverage of detainee rights. It was expected that those age 65 and older would espouse more conservative perspectives and be less favorable to detainee rights. This hypothesis was also confirmed ($r = -.321, p = .048$).

Buffer Significant: Percentage College Educated

Percentage of college educated in a city (confirmed). The buffer hypothesis stated the higher the percentage of college educated in a city, the more favorable the coverage of detainee rights. It was predicted that cities with more college-educated people would manifest favorable coverage toward detainee rights as they would be more informed about legal rights, more likely to be up-to-date on world news, and better able to understand the situation. The hypothesis was confirmed ($r = .409, p = .015$).

Regression Analysis

Regression analysis revealed that the percentage of Mainline Protestants in a city was the most significant variable, accounting for 33% of the variance. The second most significant variable was the percentage with professional/technical occupational status, accounting for 27% of the variance. These variables, one under the stakeholder hypothesis and one under the buffer hypothesis, were both linked to favorable coverage of detainee rights, together accounting for 59.9% of the variance. The remaining results are displayed in more detail in Table 4.

CONCLUSIONS AND IMPLICATIONS FOR FURTHER RESEARCH

The debate as to whether detainees housed at the Guantanamo Bay Naval Base deserve legal rights has been vigorously discussed in the media since the September 11 terrorist attacks. This study found correlations between community characteristics and media coverage of detainee rights, the most significant of which was percentage of Mainline Protestants in a city tied to favorable coverage.

Additional significant correlations were found in the proportion of 65 year olds and older in a city, another stakeholder hypothesis (linked to unfavorable coverage), as well as percentage of college educated in a city, a buffer hypothesis (linked to favorable coverage). A curious finding was the lack of significant associations between those voting Democratic or Republican in the last presidential election and variations in coverage of detainee rights. These nonpartisan findings suggest that community support for detainee rights may be more related to belief systems than political affiliation. Another surprising finding disconfirmed hypotheses linked to the percentage of Arabic/Farsi speakers in a city as well as the percentage of foreign-born in a city, both of which are stakeholder hypotheses. These nonsignificant findings suggested that varied levels of exposure to relatively new U.S. residents from other countries did not play a role in media coverage of detainee rights at Guantanamo.

In regard to future research, additional studies could sample newspapers cross-nationally to examine how papers published elsewhere cover detainee rights and Guantanamo Bay. Because many detainees are still housed at Guantanamo Bay, even after President Obama declared his intention to shut it down in 2008, it would be useful to explore whether coverage changed after the 2012 presidential election. Further, the results from prior to the 2012 election and after the 2012 election could then be compared.

ACKNOWLEDGMENT

A previous version of this article was presented at the annual conference of the New Jersey Communication Association in April 2013.

REFERENCES

American Fact Finder. (2010). Retrieved from http://factfinder2.census.gov/faces/nav/jsf/pages/index.xhtml

Association of Religion Data Archives. (2006). Retrieved from http://www.thearda.com

Barrett, D. (2009, March 17). Gitmo detainees may get new trials. *The Deseret News*, p. A03. Retrieved from NewsBank database.

Berg, K. (2011). Reform comes slowly to Guantanamo Bay. *News Media & the Law, 35,* 27–29.

Brechman, J. M., & Pollock, J. C. (2007). Nationwide newspaper coverage of affirmative action: A community structure approach. In A. R. Narro & A. C. Ferguson (Eds.), *Diversity and mass communication: The evidence of impact* (pp. 113–141). Southlake, TX: Fountainhead Press.

Caplan, L. (2003, August 3). Government's in-house watchdogs. *The Hartford Courant*, p. C3. Retrieved from NewsBank database.

County and City Extra: Annual metro, city, and county data book. (2010). Lanham, MD: Bernan Press.

Curtius, M. (2005, May 30). Guantanamo Bay is no "gulag," general says. *The Seattle Times*, p. A8. Retrieved from NewsBank database.

Guantanamo press restrictions increase. (2002, October). *The Quill, 90*(8), p. 35.

Hobbs, P. (2007). Extraterritoriality and extralegality: The United States Supreme Court and Guantanamo Bay. *Text & Talk, 27,* 171–200.

Hughes, M. (2009, June 10). *Quality: More likely to get sick, less likely to have access to care* [Web blog post]. Retrieved from http://www.newamerica.net/blog/new-health-dialogue/2009/quality-more-likely-get-sick-less-likely-have-access-care-12387

Kiernicki, K., Pollock, J. C., & Lavery, P. (2012). Nationwide newspaper coverage of universal healthcare: A community structure approach. In J. C. Pollock (Ed.), *Media and social inequality: Innovations in community structure research* (pp. 116–134). Mahwah, NJ: Routledge.

Lain, B. (2008, November). *Citizenship and detention: How Bush learned the lessons of internment and applied them in Guantanamo.* Paper presented at the annual meeting of the National Communication Association, San Diego, CA.

Lifestyle market analyst: A reference guide for consumer market analysis. (2008). Des Plaines, IL: Standard Rate and Data Service.

Meehan, S., Philbin, B., Wilson, S., & Pollock, J. C. (2003, May). *Nationwide newspaper coverage of detainee rights.* Paper presented at the annual meeting of the International Communication Association, San Diego, CA.

Mink, M., Puma, J., & Pollock, J. C. (2001, May). *Nationwide newspaper coverage of the reparation of Elian Gonzalez: A community structure approach.* Paper presented at the annual conference of the International Communication Association, Washington, DC.

Nelson, C. (2002, January 16). War on terrorism: Rights groups skeptical of detainees' treatment. *The Atlanta Journal-Constitution*, p. A6. Retrieved from NewsBank database.

Pollock, J. C. (2007). *Tilted mirrors: Media alignment with political and social change—a community structure approach.* Cresskill, NJ: Hampton Press.

Pollock, J. C. (2013). Introduction: Social media and inequality. In J. C. Pollock (Ed.), *Media and social inequality: Innovations in community structure research* (pp. 1–30). Mahwah, NJ: Routledge.

Pollock, J. C., Davies, M., Effingham, A., & Heisler, B. (2012, November). *Nationwide coverage of same-sex marriage after New York legalization: A community structure approach.* Paper presented at the annual conference of the National Communication Association, Orlando, FL.

Pollock, J. C., & Haake, J. (2010). Nationwide newspaper coverage of same-sex marriage: A community structure approach. *Journal of PR, 1*, 13–40.

Pollock, J. C., Maltese-Nehrbass, M., Corbin, P., & Fascanella, P. B. (2010). Nationwide newspaper coverage of genetically-modified food in the United States: A community structure approach. *Ecos de la Comunicacion, 3*, 51–75.

Pollock, J. C., Piccillo, C., Leopardi, D., Gratale, S., & Cabot, K. (2005). Nationwide newspaper coverage of Islam Post-9/11: A community structure approach. *Communication Research Reports, 22*, 15–24.

Pollock, J. C., Reda, E., Bosland, A., Hindi, M., & Zhu, D. (2010, June). *Cross-national coverage of climate change: A community structure approach.* Paper presented at the annual conference of the International Communication Association, Singapore.

Pollock, J. C., & Robinson, J. L. (1977). Reporting rights conflicts. *Society, 13*, 44–47.

Pollock, J. C., Robinson, J. L., & Murray, M. C. (1978). Media agendas and human rights: The Supreme Court decision on abortion. *Journalism Quarterly, 53*, 545–548, 561.

Pollock, J. C., Shier, L., & Slattery, P. (1995). Newspapers and the "Open Door" policy towards Cuba: A sample of major cities—community structure approach. *Journal of International Communication, 2*, 67–86.

Pollock, J. C., & Whitney, L. (1997). Newspapers and racial/ethnic conflict: Comparing city demographics and nationwide reporting on the Crown Heights (Brooklyn, NY) incidents. *Atlantic Journal of Communication, 5*, 127–149.

Pollock, J., & Yulis, S. (2004). Nationwide newspaper coverage of physician-assisted suicide: A community structure approach. *Journal of Health Communication, 9*, 281–307.

Satter, R. G. (2007, June 7). Rights groups identify detainees they believe secretly held by U.S. *The Cincinnati Post*, p. A13. Retrieved from NewsBank database.

Skallman, D. (2010). The Pentagon's culture of secrecy. *News Media & the Law, 34*, 4–9.

Smith, C. S. (2009). Closing Guantanamo. *New Statesman, 138*, 26–31. Retrieved from http://www.ebscohost.com/public/social-sciences-full-text

State and Metropolitan Area Data Book. (2010). Retrieved from http://www.census.gov/prod/2010pubs/10smadb/2010 smadb.pdf

Tichenor, P. J., Donohue, G., & Olien, C. (1980). *Community conflict and the press.* Beverly Hills, CA: Sage.

Upano, A. (2002). U.S. military in Cuba keeps journalists at bay. *News Media & the Law, 26*, 43.

Webb, J., Novick, F., Pagan, H., Villanueva, M., O'Gorman, E., & Pollock, J. C. (2010, November). *Nationwide coverage of the homeless: A community structure approach.* Paper presented at the annual conference of the National Communication Association, San Francisco, CA.

Weber, M. (2010). *The Protestant ethic and the spirit of capitalism.* New York, NY: CreateSpace.

Whittle, R. (2002, February 8). Bush says Geneva rights apply to Taliban but not al-Qaeda detainees still denied POW status. Treatment will remain the same. *The Dallas Morning News*, p. 1A. Retrieved from NewsBank database.

Worthington, A. (2011). The 'worst of the worst'? *Extra!, 24*, 11–12.

Nationwide Newspaper Coverage of Immigration Reform: A Community Structure Approach

John C. Pollock, Stefanie Gratale, Kevin Teta, Kyle Bauer, and
Elyse Hoekstra

Department of Communication Studies
The College of New Jersey

A community structure analysis compared community characteristics and nationwide coverage of immigration reform in newspapers in 21 major U.S. cities, sampling all 250+ word articles April 23, 2010 to November 12, 2013. The resulting 262 articles were coded for "prominence" and "direction" ("favorable," "unfavorable," or "balanced/neutral" coverage), then combined into each newspaper's composite "Media Vector" (range = .632 to −.4800). Nineteen of 21 newspapers showed favorable coverage of immigration reform. Pearson correlations yielded 4 significant results, the most powerful of which supported immigration reform. The "vulnerability" hypothesis (media "mirror" the interests of marginal/disadvantaged groups) was essentially confirmed. Higher percentages below the poverty line ($r = .607$, $p = .003$) and higher crime rates ($r = .490$, $p = .017$) correlated with more favorable coverage of immigration reform. By contrast, higher percentages of women in the workforce ($r = −.543$, $p = .008$) and higher proportions of hate crimes ($r = −.403$, $p = .048$) were linked with less favorable coverage. Regression analysis yielded the percentage living below the poverty line accounting for 37.2% of the variance, and proportion of hate crimes yielded an additional 19.1% of the variance. The Midwest had by far the most favorable coverage of immigration reform, more than any other region.

INTRODUCTION

The United States is considered to be a nation of opportunity and freedom, the motivation for which 800,000 immigrants migrate to the United States every year. Not all of these immigrants enter the country following United States' laws and regulations. Approximately 11 million people residing in the Unites States are working and living here illegally. Immigration is an issue of particular significance to the United States, considering the nation's early roots with founding immigrants from various areas of the world, and its representation as a land of opportunity and justice for all. As a result, immigration reform has been a complex, politicized issue that has been debated for years. Comprehensive immigration reform legislation has been proposed and debated in Congress, but decisive legislation has not yet been passed.

Immigration and the path to citizenship have been highly contentious issues in the past, dividing Republicans and Democrats; yet recently, immigration reform has garnered more bipartisan support, largely because of the rise of Hispanic and Asian populations in the United States (Rodriguez, 2013). Curiously, current political conversations reveal that both Democrats and Republicans see the issue of immigration reform as a potential avenue for expanding voting blocks. Among the public, a primary concern in the discussion about immigration reform is whether it will satisfy complex societal goals: providing a fair pathway to citizenship for current illegal immigrants but reducing further illegal immigration, while balancing the need for economic growth with the need for national security.

In this study, immigration reform is explored through two contrasting frames in media coverage: favorable or unfavorable. Examining media framing helps illustrate how information about the issue is organized by journalists and how it can be interpreted by audiences (Pollock, 2007, p. 17). With multifaceted, often polarizing social issues like immigration reform, journalists can select which components of the issue to highlight in order to portray the issue in a sympathetic or a negative light. These editorial decisions serve to create narratives that appeal to certain demographics or groups over others, and thus the way journalists put together stories for certain events can have a major impact on public opinion (Pollock, 2007).

Favorable media framing of immigration reform discusses the benefits of reform. Specifically, it explores the economic benefits of having highly skilled immigrants in the country, which can help create jobs and promote productivity. Favorable coverage also emphasizes the desire to legitimize the 11 million undocumented workers currently in the United States, improving working conditions for all workers, and creating a more even playing field for all prospective employees ("Fixing Our Broken Immigration System," 2013). Further, legalizing current illegal immigrants could serve to increase tax revenue and add to the tax base needed to support social programs such as Social Security, Medicare, and Medicaid. A streamlined, updated immigration system could also simplify understanding of the path to citizenship and promote support for the legal naturalization process while reducing the incentive for illegal immigration.

In contrast, the unfavorable media frame for immigration highlights current problems with border security. It focuses on such issues as violent conflicts between illegal immigrants and border security agents and crimes perpetrated by illegal immigrants. It also perpetrates opposition to citizenship pathways for illegal immigrants because they have already broken the law (Mishak, 2013). This oppositional media frame reinforces current policy stands or increased restrictions on immigration and presents illegal immigrants as a drain on the economy and on law-abiding Americans from whom they may be taking jobs.

Although many media outlets have extensively covered the issue of immigration reform, this study focuses on newspaper coverage. It examines the media frames for immigration reform by utilizing a community structure approach exploring the influence that society has on media coverage of important issues. Through the lens of the community structure approach, this study examines how community demographic indicators correlate with newspaper reporting on immigration reform. This study poses two research questions:

RQ1: How much variation is there in nationwide coverage of immigration reform among U.S. cities?

RQ2: How closely is that variation linked to differences in community characteristics?

The research questions are explored through several in-depth hypotheses regarding community demographics and newspaper coverage of immigration reform.

LITERATURE REVIEW

Scholars in certain fields of research, including sociology, have thoroughly examined the issue of immigration reform in the United States. Other fields such as political science and economics have devoted less attention to the topic of media coverage and immigration reform. Examinations of scholarly research in the communication studies field reveal that scant attention has been paid to media coverage of immigration reform, particularly significant for the communication studies discipline.

The communication studies databases searched included Access World News, Communication Institute for Online Scholarship, ComAbstracts, and Communication and Mass Media Complete, combining terms such as "immigration reform," "media," "deportation," and "pathway to citizenship" to yield 10 results. When the search was broadened to just "immigration," 586 results emerged. However, many of these articles were irrelevant, lacking information on the reform process or the path to U.S. citizenship. One article (Brayton, 2011) discussed how media portray immigrants in popular culture and the exploitative nature of cinema, but not the policies behind immigration reform. Another article reviewed gendered differences in rhetorical styles and moral arguments during the 2007 debate over immigration reform (Levasseur, Sawyer, & Kopacz, 2011). Still, most articles found did not focus on the policies or key points of the debate about immigration reform.

One communication studies article discussed a more relevant study conducted by the periodical *Extra!*; it analyzed 2013 immigration reform media coverage in the Nexis news media database for news programs of seven television networks including American Broadcasting Company, Cable News Network, and Fox News. The study found that immigrants' opinions were noticeably missing from coverage in all seven networks (Kim, 2013, p. 10). A similar study by Gil de Zúñiga, Correa, and Valenzuela (2012) found that viewers of Fox News tend to have more negative perceptions toward immigration of Mexicans than Cable News Network viewers. Another communication studies article analyzed how President George W. Bush constructed the immigration issue as he pushed for comprehensive reform and discussed how his conflicted rhetoric could inform how future presidents will construct this issue (Edwards & Herder, 2012, p. 43). An article by Grimm and Andsager (2011) examined California-proposed legislation H.R. 4437 that threatened to treat illegal immigrants as felons, including a content analysis of news coverage of the bill that revealed that frames of the legislation varied based on race and geography of the surrounding communities. Although some articles were relevant to media coverage of immigration reform, for the most part, the communication studies discipline neglected to delve into the topic thoroughly.

Similar to the field of communication studies, political science produced relatively few results related to immigration reform issues in the United States. Searching the Worldwide

Political Science Abstracts database using the terms "immigration reform" and "media" yielded 33 results. Topics included negative media depictions of Mexican immigrants and the resulting governmental response (Aguirre, 2008) and the emerging prevalence of immigration issues involving Latinos after a referendum to block illegal aliens from using state-run systems, which gathered massive amounts of attention. The economic database EconLit produced more articles than political science, returning 61 results in searches of "immigration and media," "border security and media," and "immigration reform and media"; including articles covering topics on increased media attention to immigration in border states (Branton & Abrajano, 2010, p. 359) and "slanted" news coverage of immigration reform (Branton & Dunaway, 2009).

Strikingly, results were prolific in sociology databases such as Applied Social Sciences Index and Abstracts, Social Sciences Full Text (H.W. Wilson), and Journal Storage: The Scholarly Journal Archive, which returned hundreds of articles using the keywords "immigration," "immigration reform," "border security," "citizenship," and "media." Studies covered subjects such as Congress's postponement of reform efforts (Shear & Preston, 2013), advocacy efforts to expedite reform (Jeong, 2013), congressional attitudes on remedying past failures in immigration reform (Marquez & Schraufnagel, 2013), and differences in media coverage on immigration in Spanish-language newspapers (Abrajano & Singh, 2009). Overall, the sociology field produced an overwhelming amount of scholarly research on the topic. Yet, clearly, the communication studies field has devoted little scholarly attention to immigration reform, particularly as it relates to media analysis. Because the communications studies discipline has not robustly explored the immigration issue, this article attempts to address this gap.

HYPOTHESES

Several hypotheses can be applied to media coverage immigration reform utilizing the framework of the community structure approach. These hypotheses can be categorized into three umbrella groups: buffer, vulnerability, and stakeholder.

Buffer Hypothesis

The buffer hypothesis focuses on the way that levels of privilege in cities can be linked to the direction of media coverage (Pollock, 2007). This hypothesis expects that the greater the percentage of "privileged" individuals in a community, "the more favorable the media coverage of those making human rights claims" (Pollock, 2007, pp. 52, 62). In this case, privilege is measured in terms of the percentage of college educated, families with incomes of $100,000 or more, and the percentage with professional occupational status.

The buffer hypothesis has been confirmed in many case studies. For example, a study of the Anita Hill–Clarence Thomas hearings illustrated that higher percentages of people with professional/technical occupational status in a community were linked to reporting more favorable to Anita Hill (Pollock, 2007, p. 72). Similarly, a nationwide study of newspapers and the "Open Door" policy toward Cuba found that

> the higher the proportion of 'privileged' groups in a city, the more favorable the reporting on
> Cubans seeking asylum in the US, confirming ... a "buffer" hypothesis: Those buffered from

economic uncertainty are relatively likely to respond to those making human rights claims with generosity and compassion. (Pollock, Shier, & Slattery, 1995, pp. 67–86)

Consistently, a cross-national study by Pollock and Koerner (2010) suggested that the higher proportions of privileged groups in a nation, the greater the emphasis on government action to reduce human trafficking. In addition, a study found that the higher the proportion of privileged groups in a city, the more favorable the coverage of same-sex marriage (Pollock & Haake, 2010). Another revealed that higher percentages of family incomes of $100,000 or more correlated with favorable coverage of homosexuals in the Boy Scouts (Pollock, 2007, pp. 231–248). Consequently, there is often a link between privilege and media coverage favorable toward human rights claims. Thus, the following is expected:

H1: The higher the percentage of college educated in a city, the more favorable the coverage of immigration reform (Lifestyle Market Analyst, 2008).

H2: The higher the percentage of families with incomes of $100,000 or more, the more favorable the coverage of immigration reform (Lifestyle Market Analyst, 2008).

H3: The higher the percentage of those with professional/technical occupational status, the more favorable the coverage of immigration reform (Lifestyle Market Analyst, 2008).

Healthcare access. Healthcare access is a significant indicator of privilege in a city. Pollock (2007) suggested that health care access can be measured by "the proportion of the municipal budget that a city spends on health care, in addition to the availability of hospital beds and physicians" (p. 93). In a study of legalization of embryonic stem cell research, a positive correlation was found between access to health care (physicians per 100,000) and more favorable newspaper coverage of legalization (Pollock, 2007, p. 93). A cross-national study on climate change by Pollock, Reda, Bosland, Hindi, and Zhu (2010) showed greater numbers of hospital beds per 100,000 as well as greater numbers of physicians per 100,000 correlated with increased media support for government activity in addressing climate change. An earlier study by Pollock and Yulis (2004) also found healthcare access correlated positively with coverage of physician-assisted suicide. Media in areas with greater healthcare access and municipal spending on healthcare seem to be more sympathetic to human rights claims. Therefore, the following is predicted:

H4: The higher the number of physicians per 100,000 people in a city, the more favorable the coverage of immigration reform (State and Metropolitan Area Data Book, 2010).

H5: The higher the number of hospital beds per 100,000 people in a city, the more favorable the coverage of immigration reform (County and City Extra, 2010).

H6: The higher the percentage of municipal spending on healthcare in a city, the more favorable the coverage of immigration reform (County and City Extra, 2010).

Vulnerability

The vulnerability hypothesis diverges from the buffer counterpart by suggesting that newspapers can mirror the interests of vulnerable groups, such as the poor, unemployed, and those living in high crime areas (Pollock, 2007, p. 137). Previous community structure studies have confirmed the vulnerability hypothesis. One study of newspaper coverage of racial and ethnic conflicts showed "the higher the poverty or unemployment levels in a city, the more 'pluralistic' the coverage in newspapers nationwide, appreciating the claims of both Caribbean Americans and Hasidic Jews" (Pollock & Whitney, 1997). Furthermore, a study on coverage of capital punishment revealed a "clearly significant relationship [between] negative reporting on capital punishment and percent below the poverty level" (Pollock, 2007, pp. 143, 145). Another study found that the higher the percentage below the poverty level, the more favorable the coverage of a Patients' Bill of Rights (Pollock, 2007, p. 150).

Regarding the U.S. Supreme Court decision *Roe v. Wade*, coverage was more favorable toward legalizing abortion in cities with higher poverty levels (Pollock & Robinson, 1977; Pollock, Robinson, & Murray, 1978). Pollock, Maltese-Nehrbass, Corbin, and Fascanella (2010) also found that the higher the proportion of relatively disadvantaged groups, the greater the media coverage supporting higher yield genetically modified foods (pp. 51–75). Based on previous studies, it is reasonable to expect that vulnerable groups will be more supportive of immigration reform, as they may empathize with issues faced by those on the path toward legal citizenship. Thus, the following is expected:

H7: The higher the percentage of people living below the poverty line, the more favorable the coverage of immigration reform (American Fact Finder, 2010).

H8: The higher the percentage of people who are unemployed in a city, the more favorable the coverage of immigration reform (American Fact Finder, 2010).

H9: The higher the crime rate in a city, the more favorable the coverage of immigration reform (County and City Extra, 2010).

H10: The higher the homicide rate in a city, the more favorable the coverage of immigration reform (County and City Extra, 2010).

Stakeholder Hypothesis

The stakeholder hypothesis expects a link between stakeholder size and relatively favorable coverage of stakeholder concerns (Pollock, 2007, p. 172; McLeod & Hertog, 1999). Tichenor, Donohue, and Olien asserted that the larger the city size, the greater the plurality of viewpoints presented by the media (as cited in Pollock, 2007, p. 171). Stakeholder categories in this study are female empowerment, ethnic identity, political identity, belief system, generation, and position in lifecycle.

Female empowerment. Females in the workforce can be considered an important stakeholder group for many prominent social issues. Having dealt historically with inequities in pay and certain rights, females may be more sympathetic toward human rights claims. Specifically, empowered women may display empathic opinions toward groups that may have experienced discrimination or other social challenges. Thus, "females in the workforce" will be assumed to display sympathetic opinions toward immigration reform.

H11: The higher percentage of females in the workforce in a city, the more favorable the coverage of immigration reform (County and City Extra, 2010).

Ethnic identity. Ethnic identity is particularly relevant to the topic of immigration reform. Hispanics are generally the minority group most affected by discussions of immigration reform. Kiernicki, Pollock, and Lavery (2012) found that the higher the percentage of Hispanics in a community, the more favorable the coverage of their interests regarding universal healthcare. Pollock and Branca (2011) discovered that higher proportions of Hispanics in communities were linked to coverage emphasizing government responsibility for clean water.

A study by Pollock, Robinson, and Murray (1978) discovered that the higher the percentage of African Americans, the more favorable the coverage of *Roe v. Wade* during the time of the Supreme Court decision legalizing abortion in 1973. Higher city poverty levels, especially among African Americans, also corresponded with higher levels of abortions performed in cities after legalization took effect. A study on nationwide newspaper coverage of Islam post-9/11 revealed that the higher proportion of foreign-born or Farsi or Arabic speakers in a city, the less favorable the coverage of Islam in the first year after 9/11 (Pollock, Piccillo, Leopardi, Gratale, & Cabot, 2005, pp. 15–24). Following previous findings, it is expected that stakeholder categories of immigration reform will be linked to more favorable coverage, as stated in the following hypotheses:

H12: The higher the percentage of African Americans in a city, the more favorable the coverage of immigration reform (County and City Extra, 2010).

H13: The higher the percentage of Hispanics in a city, the more favorable the coverage of immigration reform (County and City Extra, 2010).

H14: The higher the percentage of foreign-born in a city, the more favorable the coverage of immigration reform (County and City Extra, 2010).

Belief system. Religious belief systems may play a significant role in stakeholder positions. Pollock et al. (1978) found that the higher percentage of Catholics in a city, the less favorable the media support for elective abortion in coverage of the *Roe v. Wade* U.S. Supreme Court decision. A study of newspaper coverage of gays in the Boy Scouts also found that the higher percentage of Bible/devotional reading in a city, the less favorable the coverage on that topic (Pollock, 2007, p. 243). Higher proportions of devotional readers were further associated with less favorable coverage of stem cell research (Pollock, 2007, p. 98).

Yet when analyzing more recent issues such as same-sex marriage and same-sex adoption, it was found that higher percentages of Catholics were associated with favorable coverage (Pollock & Haake, 2010), as well as with favorable coverage of gays in the Boy Scouts (Pollock, 2007, p. 243). Furthermore, a study by Pollock (2013, pp. 1–30) confirmed that the higher the percentage of Mainline Protestants in a city, the more favorable the coverage of the "Occupy" movement in the fall of 2011, prior to the removal of protestors from Zuccotti Park. Higher proportions of Mainline Protestants were also linked with more favorable coverage of detainee rights at Guantanamo Bay (Zinck, Rogers, Pollock, & Salvatore, this issue). Clearly, belief systems represent complex stakeholder positions that can affect media coverage of social issues. Therefore, it is reasonable to expect the following:

H15: The higher the percentage of Evangelicals in a city, the less favorable the coverage of immigration reform (Association of Religion Data Archives, 2006).

H16: The higher the percentage of devotional readers in a city, the less favorable the coverage of immigration reform (Lifestyle Market Analyst, 2008).

H17: The higher the percentage of Catholics in a city, the more favorable the coverage of immigration reform (Association of Religion Data Archives, 2006).

H18: The higher the percentage of Mainline Protestants in a city, the more favorable the coverage of immigration reform (Association of Religion Data Archives, 2006).

Political identity. Citizens of major cities can often be categorized into two main political parties, Republicans and Democrats. A study by Pollock (2007) regarding Arctic drilling found that higher proportions of Republicans were linked to favorable coverage of drilling, whereas higher percentages of Democrats were linked to coverage opposing Arctic drilling (p. 192). Another study discovered that the higher the percentage voting Democratic in the 1996 presidential election, the less favorable the coverage of trying juveniles as adults (Pollock, 2007, p. 204). Thus, because Democratic voters are often affiliated with liberal viewpoints and support of human rights claims, the following is expected:

H19: The higher the percentage voting Democratic in the last presidential election, the more favorable the coverage of immigration reform (Lifestyle Market Analyst, 2008).

H20: The higher the percentage voting Republican in the last presidential election, the less favorable the coverage of immigration reform (Lifestyle Market Analyst, 2008).

Generation. Different generations may have divergent viewpoints on critical public issues. Typically, younger generations tend to be more liberal and supportive of social movements. In contrast, older generations tend to be more conservative and reliant on traditional ideals, and more likely to support the status quo regarding public issues. Pollock and Yulis (2004) found that the larger the proportion of citizens older than 75, the less favorable the coverage on legalization of physician-assisted euthanasia. Yet a study by Webb, Novick, Pagan, Villanueva, O'Gorman, and Pollock (2010) found that the higher the proportion of the population between the ages of 18 and 25, the less favorable the coverage of housing for the less privileged, in particular the impoverished. Still, older generations are typically more likely to be socially conservative, so it is reasonable to expect younger generations to be more favorable toward immigration reform. Therefore, the following is predicted:

H21: The higher the percentage of 18- to 24-year-olds in a city, the more favorable the coverage of immigration reform (Lifestyle Market Analyst, 2008).

H22: The higher the percentage of 25- to 44-year-olds in a city, the more favorable the coverage of immigration reform (Lifestyle Market Analyst, 2008).

H23: The higher the percentage of 45- to 64-year-olds in a city, the less favorable the coverage of immigration reform (Lifestyle Market Analyst, 2008).

H24: The higher the percentage of 65-year-olds and older in a city, the less favorable the coverage of immigration reform (Lifestyle Market Analyst, 2008).

Position in life cycle. It is reasonable to expect that those with a specific "position in the life cycle," in particular families with children, are more likely to favor immigration reform because it is a human rights issue. Mink, Puma, and Pollock (2001) examined the custody battle over Cuban immigrant Elian Gonzalez, concluding that U.S. newspaper coverage favoring the repatriation of Gonzalez to his biological father in Cuba was directly associated with the proportion of families in cities with children of a similar age, 5 to 7. Another study found significant relationships specifically between households with higher percentages of children 8 to 10, 11 to 12, and 13 to 15 and unfavorable coverage of gun control (Pollock, 2007, p. 183). Pollock (2013) found that the higher the percentage of families with young children (younger than 5) in a city, the more support for the "Occupy" movement after the protestors were removed from Zuccotti Park (pp. 1–30). Based on this research, it can be assumed that families with children 18 and younger would likely be associated with coverage supporting immigration reform because they would want to preserve rights for children in the future. Therefore the following is predicted:

H25: The higher the percentage of families with children younger than age 5 in a city, the more favorable the coverage of immigration reform (Lifestyle Market Analyst, 2008).

H26: The higher the percentage of families with children ages 5 to 10 in a city, the more favorable the coverage of immigration reform (Lifestyle Market Analyst, 2008).

H27: The higher the percentage of families with children ages 11 to 15 in a city, the more favorable the coverage of immigration reform (Lifestyle Market Analyst, 2008).

H28: The higher the percentage of families with children ages 16 to 18 in a city, the more favorable the coverage of immigration reform (Lifestyle Market Analyst, 2008).

METHODOLOGY

For this study, researchers selected a sample of newspaper articles of 250 words or more from 21 major metropolitan newspapers, yielding a total of 262 articles. All newspaper articles were retrieved from The NewsBank database. The selection included the following publications: the *Atlanta Journal Constitution*, the *Boston Herald*, the *Buffalo News*, the *Charlotte Observer*, the *Chicago Sun-Times*, the *Commercial Appeal*, the *Las Vegas Sun, New Hampshire Union Leader*, the *Oregonian*, the *Philadelphia Inquirer*, the *Pittsburgh Post-Gazette*, the *Plain Dealer*, the *Post Register*, the *Sacramento Bee, San Antonio Express News*, the *Salt Lake City Tribune*, the *Seattle Times*, the *Star Tribune: Newspaper of the Twin Cities*, the *State, St Louis Post Dispatch*, and *Wisconsin State Journal*. The newspapers *USA Today*, the *New York Times, Wall Street Journal*, and the *Los Angeles Times* were not included in this study because they focus on national rather than local readership. The sample data collection ranged from April 23, 2010, to November 12, 2013, to cover the period including the proposal of the Arizona "Show Me Your Papers Law" up to the day after Veteran's Day 2013, when immigrant veterans created a campaign to show the contributions of immigrants in the armed forces.

Article Coding and Procedures

Researchers assigned each article two scores, the prominence (representing how editors positioned the article in the paper) and direction (representing framing as favorable, unfavorable or balanced/neutral), that together depict the article's issue projection. Articles that demonstrated community interest in passing immigration reform legislation were coded as "favorable."

Favorable articles also emphasized the positive effects of immigration and conveyed support for legislation such as The Dream Act. For example, an article in the *Philadelphia Inquirer* quoted Pennsylvania senator Jeffrey S. Chisea as saying immigration reform was one of the most important bills he would vote on in his Senate career and that supporting the measure was "the right thing for me to do" (Tamari, 2013, p. B01). Another article in the *Buffalo News* explained that senator Charles E. Schumer's greatest legislative triumph was passing the immigration bill through the Senate, which offered a "pathway to citizenship for 11 million undocumented aliens while drastically boosting border security" (Zremski, 2013, p. 1).

Articles that emphasized negative aspects of immigration reform or expressed disapproval of reform legislation or efforts for an accelerated pathway to citizenship were coded as "unfavorable." For example, an article in the *Plain Dealer* quoted an individual saying that "by making the environment for illegal aliens so inhospitable, especially in economic terms—if you can't get a job, can't pay rent—then maybe it's not the good deal it's cracked up to be" (Caniglia, 2012, p. B2). In the *Pittsburgh Post-Gazette*, an article explained that the Supreme Court allowed Arizona to revoke the business licenses of companies that knowingly employed illegal immigrants, rejecting the contention that state law intruded on the federal government's power to control immigration (Barnes, 2011).

Finally, coverage of immigration reform was coded "balanced/neutral" if it displayed an equal discussion of both sides of the issue or took no position at all. This coding category included any articles that debated the advantages as well as the disadvantages of immigration reform or assigned no positive or negative judgments about the issue. For example, the *Star Tribune: Newspaper of the Twin Cities* discussed a study on the economic effects of immigration. The article offered findings that "immigrants may have adverse wage effects of taking away jobs from U.S. born workers, but that is offset by economic benefits such as the more efficient use of labor, lower prices and increased economic activity" (Brunswick, 2013, p. 03B). An article in the *Salt Lake City Tribune* discussed a study that would look into the cost-benefit analysis of illegal immigration in Utah and mainly focused on the issue of understanding pros and cons before considering legislative measures (Montero, 2012).

A total of 142 of 262 articles were independently read by two coders, resulting in a Scott's Pi coefficient of intercoder reliability of .7931. Article prominence and direction scores were used in the calculation of a Media Vector for each newspaper, and Pearson correlations and regression analysis were used to identify connections between demographics and Media Vectors.

RESULTS

This study examined newspaper coverage of immigration reform, comparing Media Vectors from 21 large cities during the period of April 23, 2010, through November 12, 2013. The *Wisconsin State Journal* had the highest Media Vector at 0.6324, whereas the *Seattle Times* had the lowest Media Vector at −.4800. The range of Media Vector results was 1.1133, demonstrating wide variation in coverage of immigration reform. In the 21 sampled cities, 19 newspapers, or 90.48%, demonstrated favorable Media Vectors, whereas two, or 9.52%, demonstrated unfavorable Media Vectors. Table 1 offers a complete list of the Media Vectors scores found in this study, listed from most positive to most negative. To examine regional variations in coverage, Media Vector scores were averaged to aggregate each region's news-

TABLE 1
Media Vectors

City	Newspaper	Media Vector
Madison, WI	*Wisconsin State Journal*	.6324
Las Vegas, NV	*Las Vegas Sun*	.6027
Chicago, IL	*Chicago Sun-Times*	.4929
Philadelphia, PA	*The Philadelphia Inquirer*	.4729
St Louis, MO	*St Louis Post-Dispatch*	.4681
Cleveland, OH	*The Plain Dealer*	.4649
Buffalo, NY	*The Buffalo News*	.4646
Sacramento, CA	*The Sacramento Bee*	.4636
Atlanta, GA	*The Atlanta Journal Constitution*	.4422
Manchester, NH	*New Hampshire Union Leader*	.4047
Pittsburgh, PA	*The Pittsburgh Post-Gazette*	.3876
Minneapolis, MN	*Star Tribune: Newspaper of the Twin Cities*	.2988
San Antonio	*San Antonio Express News*	.2542
Portland, OR	*The Oregonian*	.2353
Memphis, TN	*The Commercial Appeal*	.2296
Mobile, AL	*Press Register*	.1390
Columbia, SC	*The State*	.1081
Charlotte, NC	*Charlotte Observer*	.0503
Salt Lake City, UT	*The Salt Lake City Tribune*	.0401
Boston, MA	*Boston Herald*	−.2561
Seattle, WA	*The Seattle Times*	−.4800

papers. Regional results (see Table 2) all reflected favorable coverage of immigration reform. The Midwest displayed by far the most favorable regional Media Vector, and the region that displayed the least favorable coverage of immigration reform was the West.

Pearson correlations were calculated using SPSS to search for connections between city characteristics and variations in newspaper coverage. For purposes of the Pearson correlations, researchers judged immigration reporting scores from the cities of Madison, Wisconsin, and Las Vegas, Nevada, to be outliers. The Media Vectors from these cities were divergent from all other cities and skewed otherwise reasonable correlation patterns. Thus, researchers did not include them in subsequent calculations of the observed correlations. These calculations are shown in Table 3.

TABLE 2
Media Vectors by Region

Region	Media Vector
Midwest	.47102
North	.2947
South	.2039
West	.1723

TABLE 3
Pearson Correlation Results

City Characteristic	Pearson Correlation	Significance Level
Percentage of people living below poverty line	.601	.003**
Women in the workforce	−.543	.008**
Crime rate	.490	.017*
Hate crimes	−.403	.048*
Foreign born	−.374	.057
Unemployment rate	.368	.061
African American	.358	.066
Homicide	.335	.080
Police reports	.326	.086
Physicians/100,000	−.317	.093
Municipal spending on healthcare	.313	.096
Professional occupational status	−.283	.120
Ages 18–24	−.276	.126
College educated	−.216	.187
Ages 25–44	−203	.202
Military veterans	.195	.212
Having children younger than 5	−.189	.219
Catholic	.180	.230
Having children 5–10	−.152	.267
Having children 11–15	−.143	.279
Ages 45–64	−.137	.288
Evangelical	−.124	.307
Mainline Protestant	.119	.313
Single parent household	−.112	.323
Republican	−.111	.326
Having children 16–18	−.091	.355
No. of hospital beds/1,000	−.087	.361
Devotional readers	−.073	.383
Hispanic	.073	.383
Democratic	−.028	.455
Ages 65 and older	.015	.476
Hunting license	−.005	.492

*Significant at .05 level, **significant at .01 level.

DISCUSSION OF SIGNIFICANT FINDINGS

Vulnerability Hypothesis: Percentage Below the Poverty Line Linked to Favorable Coverage of Immigration Reform (Confirmed)

Following the vulnerability hypothesis, it was predicted that the greater percentage below the poverty line, the more favorable the coverage of immigration reform. This hypothesis was confirmed, yielding the most significant positive correlation ($r = .6011$, $p = .003$). This finding is significant because it supports the notion put forth by the vulnerability hypothesis that newspapers mirror the interests of vulnerable groups such as those living below the poverty line. A reasonable explanation as to why those below the poverty line would be more favorable toward the issue of immigration reform is that many of those who make up this demographic may be immigrants themselves or have strong affiliations with other immigrants, leading to more sympathetic opinions toward immigration reform. Similar results were also found for vulnerable groups in studies done by Pollock and colleagues showing that the higher the proportion of those below the poverty line in a city, the more favorable coverage of both abortion legalization (Pollock, Robinson, & Murray, 1978) and of a Patient's Bill of Rights, and the less favorable coverage of capital punishment (Pollock, 2007). All of these results challenge the "guard dog" perspective of Donohue, Tichenor, and Olien (1995), which asserts that media typically reinforce or reflect the interests of powerful social, political, and economic elites.

Crime Rate Linked to Favorable Coverage of Immigration Reform (Confirmed)

Based on the vulnerability hypothesis, it was predicted that the higher the crime rate in a city, the more favorable the coverage of immigration reform. This hypothesis was also confirmed ($r = .490, p = .017$). A potential reason for this outcome was that more immigrants may live in high crime areas, and thus these areas would be more supportive of immigration reform.

Hate Crimes Linked to Less Favorable Coverage of Immigration Reform (Disconfirmed)

Using the vulnerability hypothesis, it was predicted that more hate crimes in a city would correlate with more favorable coverage of immigration reform. This expectation was disconfirmed ($r = -.403, p = .048$). Although inconsistent with predictions, one can theorize a reason behind this contradictory outcome. Perhaps residents who live in areas with high rates of hate crimes believe that illegal immigrants are connected to this issue. Alternatively, it could be theorized that areas with higher proportions of hate crimes might have greater levels of intolerance among their populations, thereby contributing to a general opposition to immigration reform.

Stakeholder Hypothesis: Females in the Workforce Linked to Opposition to Immigration Reform (Disconfirmed)

It was originally predicted that the larger proportion of females in the workforce, the more favorable the coverage of immigration reform, yet the findings were in the opposite direction ($r = -0.543, p = .008$). Perhaps some women in the workforce consider themselves threatened by immigrants joining the American workforce, offering more competition for jobs and pay. Alternatively, women in the workforce could be related to another "hidden" socio-political variable that could be driving this observed correlation with unfavorable coverage of immigration reform.

Regression Analysis

Regression analysis revealed that the percentage living below the poverty line was the most significant variable, accounting for 37.2% of the variance. The second most significant variable

TABLE 4
Regression Analysis

Model	R (equation)	R^2 (cumulative)	R^2 Change	F Change	Significance of F Change
Below poverty line	.610	.372	.372	9.483	.007
Below poverty and hate crimes	.750	.563	.191	6.537	.022

was the proportion of hate crimes in a city, accounting for 19.1% of the variance. The combined percentages of people living below the poverty line and the proportion of hate crimes in a city accounted for 56.3% of the variance. It is important to note that percentage living below the poverty line, the most powerful variable, reflected a positive correlation with favorable coverage of immigration reform, whereas proportion of hate crimes reflected a negative correlation, indicating that vulnerability categories are linked to varying coverage perspectives toward immigration reform. Regression results are displayed in more detail in Table 4.

CONCLUSIONS AND IMPLICATIONS FOR FURTHER RESEARCH

Immigration reform has been widely discussed in the news for years, and with renewed vigor since the passage of the "Show Me Your Papers Law" on April 23, 2010, in Arizona. This study on media coverage of immigration reform revealed several correlations between coverage and community demographics, the most significant of which was a positive correlation between percentage below the poverty line and favorable coverage of immigration reform. This pattern confirmed the vulnerability hypothesis, suggesting that immigration reform may speak more loudly to those in more disadvantaged communities. Additional significant correlations were found with crime rate in a city (linked to favorable coverage) and proportions of females in the workforce and proportion of hate crimes in a city (both linked to unfavorable coverage).

A noteworthy surprising finding is the "lack" of significant associations between political affiliation and coverage of immigration reform, perhaps because both parties seek to leverage the issue to garner support. Another surprising lack of significance was that higher percentages of Hispanics in a city did not correlate with coverage variations. Because immigration reform is generally linked to Latino Americans and their pathways to citizenship, as well as border security along the Mexican border, the absence of significant correlations was unexpected.

In regard to future research, additional studies could delve more deeply into the results associated with the vulnerability hypothesis. Specifically, researchers could examine several papers from the same city/county, particularly those in "vulnerable" areas, to probe the initial results related to this hypothesis. Researchers could also endeavor to include smaller publications from rural or less populated areas to address this sample's skew toward larger cities. Another option would be for researchers to sample newspapers cross-nationally to examine how immigration reform is covered internationally. As the political debate over immigration reform continues, it would be beneficial to investigate how coverage of immigration reform changes during the remainder of President Obama's term. The results from this initial sample period could then be compared with those from a subsequent time frame, or subsequent president's term, to reveal any shifts in city characteristics driving coverage of immigration reform.

REFERENCES

Abrajano, M., & Singh, S. (2009). Examining the link between issue attitudes and news source: The case of Latinos and immigration reform. *Political Behavior, 31*, 1–30.

Aguirre, A., Jr. (2008). Immigration on the public mind: Immigration reform in the Obama administration. *Social Justice, 35*, 4–11. Retrieved from http://search.proquest.com /docview/60025402?accountid=10216

American fact finder. (2010). Retrieved from http://factfinder2.census.gov/faces/nav/jsf/pages/index.xhtml

Association of Religion Data Archives. (2006). Retrieved from http://www.thearda.com.

Barnes, R. (2011, May 27). Hiring aliens may cost license-high rules in Arizona case. *The Pittsburgh Post-Gazette*, p. A-1.

Branton, R. P., & Dunaway, J. (2009). Slanted newspaper coverage of immigration: The importance of economics and geography. *Policy Studies Journal, 37*, 257–273.

Brayton, S. (2011). Razing Arizona: Migrant labour and the "Mexican avenger" of Machete. *International Journal of Media & Cultural Politics, 7*(3), 275–292.

Brunswick, M. (2013, June 12). On the beat-immigration-study gives context to immigrant debate. *Star Tribune: Newspaper of the Twin Cities*, p. 03B.

Caniglia, J. (2012, May 12). Immigration debated at CSU panelist's plan: Make U.S. 'inhospitable' to illegal immigrants. *The Plain Dealer*, p. B2.

County and city extra: Annual metro, city, and county data book. (2010). Lanham, MD: Bernan Press.

Donohue, G. A., Tichenor, P. J., & Olien, C. N. (1995). A guard dog perspective on the role of media. *Journal of Communication, 45*, 115–132.

Dunaway, J., Branton, R. P., & Abrajano, M. A. (2010). Agenda setting, public opinion, and the issue of immigration reform. *Social Science Quarterly, 91*, 359–378.

Edwards, J. A., & Herder, R. (2012). Melding a new immigration narrative? President George W. Bush and the immigration debate. *Howard Journal of Communications, 23*, 40–65.

Fixing our broken immigration system: The economic benefits of providing a path to earned citizenship. (2013, August). Retrieved from http://www.whitehouse.gov/sites/default/files/our-broken-immigration-system-august-2013.pdf

Gil de Zúñiga, H., Correa, T., & Valenzuela, S. (2012, December). Selective exposure to cable news and immigration in the US: The relationship between FOX News, CNN, and attitudes toward Mexican immigrants. *Journal of Broadcasting & Electronic Media, 56*(4), 597–615.

Grimm, J., & Andsager, J. L. (2011). Framing immigration: Geo-ethnic context in California newspapers. *Journalism & Mass Communication Quarterly, 88*(4), 771–788.

Hindman, D. B. (1999). Social control, social change and local mass media. In D. Demers & K. Viswanath (Eds.), *Mass media, social control, and social change: A macrosocial perspective* (pp. 99–116). Ames, IA: Iowa State University Press.

Jeong, G. (2013). Congressional politics of U.S. immigration reforms: Legislative outcomes under multidimensional negotiations. *Political Research Quarterly, 66*, 600–614.

Kiernicki, K., Pollock, J. C., & Lavery, P. (2012). Nationwide newspaper coverage of universal health care: A community structure approach. In J. C. Pollock (Ed.), *Media and social inequality: Innovations in community structure research* (pp. 116–134). New York, NY: Routledge.

Kim, E. (2013). Immigrants missing from immigration debate. *Extra!, 26*(6), 9–10.

Levasseur, D. G., Sawyer, J. K., & Kopacz, M. A. (2011). The intersection between deep moral frames and rhetorical style in the struggle over US immigration reform. *Communication Quarterly, 59*(5), 547–568.

Lifestyle market analyst: A reference guide for consumer market analysis. (2008). Des Plaines, IL: Standard Rate and Data Service.

Marquez, T., & Schraufnagel, S. (2013). Hispanic population growth and state immigration policy: An analysis of restriction (2008–12). *Publius: The Journal of Federalism, 43*, 347–367.

McLeod, D. M., & Hertog, J. K. (1999). Social control, social change and the mass media's role in the regulation of protest groups. In D. Demers & K. Viswanath (Eds.), *Mass media, social control, and social change: A macrosocial perspective* (pp. 305–331). Ames, IA: Iowa State University Press.

Mink, M., Puma, J., & Pollock, J. C. (2001, May). *Nationwide newspaper coverage of the reparation of Elian Gonzalez: A community structure approach.* Paper presented at the annual conference of the International Communication Association, Washington, DC.

Mishak, M. (2013, September 8). House immigration reform pushed by group Republicans. *The Huffington Post.* Retrieved from http://www.huffingtonpost.com/

Montero, D. (2012, April 2). Utah seeks to study costs, benefits of illegal immigration. *The Salt Lake City Tribune.* Retrieved from http://archive.sltrib.com/article.php?id=20407553&itype=storyID

Pollock, J. C. (2007). *Tilted mirrors: Media alignment with political and social change—a community structure approach.* Cresskill, NJ: Hampton Press.

Pollock, J. C. (2008). Community structure model. In W. Donsbach (Ed.), *International encyclopedia of communication* (pp. 870–873). London, UK: Blackwell.

Pollock, J. C. (Ed.). (2013). *Media and social inequality: Innovations in community structure research* (pp. 1–30). Mahwah, NJ: Routledge.

Pollock, J. C., & Branca, V. (2011). Nationwide-US newspaper coverage of handling water contamination: A community structure approach. *Ecos de la Comunicación, 4,* 93–121.

Pollock, J. C., & Haake, J. (2010). Nationwide newspaper coverage of same-sex marriage: A community structure approach. *Journal of PR, 1,* 13–40.

Pollock, J. C., & Koerner, M. (2010). *Cross-national coverage of human trafficking: A community structure approach.* Documento de Trabajo #2. Departamento de Derecho y Ciencia Política/Universidad Nacional de La Matanza (UNLaM), Buenos Aires, Argentina.

Pollock, J. C., Maltese-Nehrbass, M., Corbin, P., & Fascanella, P. B. (2010). Nationwide newspaper coverage of genetically-modified food in the United States: A community structure approach. *Ecos de la Comunicación, 3,* 51–75.

Pollock, J. C., Piccillo, C., Leopardi, D., Gratale, S., & Cabot, K. (2005). Nationwide newspaper coverage of Islam Post-9/11: A community structure approach. *Communication Research Reports, 22*(1), 15–24.

Pollock, J. C., Reda, E., Bosland, A., Hindi, M., & Zhu, D. (2010, June). *Cross-national coverage of climate change: A community structure approach.* Paper presented at the annual conference of the International Communication Association, Singapore.

Pollock, J. C., & Robinson, J. L. (1977). Reporting rights conflicts. *Society, 13*(1), 44–47.

Pollock, J. C., Robinson, J. L., & Murray, M. C. (1978). Media agendas and human rights: The Supreme Court decision on abortion. *Journalism Quarterly, 53,* 545–548, 561.

Pollock, J. C., Shier, L., & Slattery, P. (1995, November). Newspapers and the "Open Door" policy towards Cuba: A sample of major cities—community structure approach. *Journal of International Communication, 2,* 67–86.

Pollock, J. C., & Whitney, L. (1997). Newspapers and racial/ethnic conflict: Comparing city demographics and nationwide reporting on the Crown Heights (Brooklyn, NY) incidents. *The Atlantic Journal of Communication, 5*(2), 127–149.

Pollock, J. C., & Yulis, S. (2004). Nationwide newspaper coverage of physician-assisted suicide: A community structure approach. *Journal of Health Communication, 9,* 281–307.

Rodriguez, J. C. (2013, August 12). Bipartisan support for immigration reform strengthens during August recess. *The White House Blog.* Retrieved from http://www.whitehouse.gov/blog/2013/08/12/bipartisan-support-immigration-reform-strengthens-during-august-recess

Shear, M. D., & Preston, J. (2013, September 9). Immigration reform falls to the back of the line. *The New York Times,* pp. A1–A13.

State and metropolitan area data book. (2010). Retrieved from http://www.census.gov/prod/2010pubs/10smadb/2010smadb.pdf

Tamari, J. (2013, June 28). For Menedez and Chisea, vote has historic weight. *The Philadelphia Inquirer,* p. B01.

Tichenor, P. J., Donohue, G., & Olien, C. (1980). *Community conflict and the press.* Beverly Hills, CA: Sage.

Webb, J., Novick, F., Pagan, H., Villanueva, M., O'Gorman, E., & Pollock, J. C. (2010, November). *Nationwide coverage of the homeless: A community structure approach.* Paper presented at the annual conference of the National Communication Association, San Francisco, CA.

Zremski, J. (2013, June 6). Many hail Schumer for immigration bill's passage-but senate legislation faces hurdles in house. *The Buffalo News,* p. 1.

Nationwide Newspaper Coverage of Posttraumatic Stress: A Community Structure Approach

John C. Pollock, Stefanie Gratale, Angelica Anas, Emaleigh Kaithern, and Kelly Johnson

Department of Communication Studies
The College of New Jersey

This study utilized the community structure approach to analyze newspaper coverage of post-traumatic stress (PTS) in veterans in 26 U.S. cities. The study examined whether media placed responsibility for PTS treatment on government or society through a review of 353 articles from March 20, 2003, to March 20, 2013. Researchers coded articles for "prominence" and "direction" to produce a "Media Vector" for each paper, ranging from 0.8403 to −0.3592. Results showed that 25 of 26 Media Vectors (96%) supported government responsibility. Pearson correlations yielded nine significant findings. Results disconfirmed buffer hypotheses linking privilege with support for government responsibility (privilege defined by percentage of college educated, percentage of family income $100,000 or more, and percentage of professional/technical occupational status; $r = −.486, −.524, −.553$, respectively, significant at the .006 level). Stakeholder hypotheses were also disconfirmed; greater percentages of age 65 and older correlated with more emphasis on government responsibility ($r = .340, p = .048$), whereas greater percentages of age 25 to 44 correlated with less emphasis ($r = −.342, p = .047$). The only confirmed hypothesis linked percentage of age 45 to 64 with less emphasis on government responsibility ($r = −.559, p = .002$). A regional finding was noteworthy: Media in the Midwest supported government responsibility more than other regions. Regression analysis revealed three variables influencing coverage most significantly: Family Income $100K+ (26% of variance), Percentage of Hispanic (8%), and Professional/Technical Occupational status (5%). It must be noted that nearly all newspapers yielded positive Media Vectors. This indicates that coverage in major cities generally favors government responsibility for veterans' PTS treatment, and Pearson correlation results may represent differences in the degree of support and demographic characteristics influencing this support.

INTRODUCTION

For those who have served in the Armed Forces, returning home does not necessarily mean leaving the war for good. Since the Vietnam War, it has been documented that many soldiers face the challenge of posttraumatic stress (PTS). PTS was not always recognized as a medical condition, and controversy surrounds whether it is a disorder. Over the past few years, PTS has garnered extensive media coverage, potentially as a result of recent wars. One facet of this coverage is public scrutiny over who is primarily responsible for PTS treatment for veterans: government or society.

Media coverage of PTS utilizes two primary frames. In journalism, framing is defined as "the activity of organizing events into a coherent story, presenting some perspectives as more reasonable" (Pollock, 2007, p. 1). One frame that media have embraced in the discussion of PTS is that the U.S government is primarily responsible for aiding veterans in their transition into mainstream civilian life. Through this lens, media assert that the government owes veterans for their service and thus should be responsible for helping treat their PTS. The alternative frame in PTS coverage depicts PTS as the veteran's own responsibility or the responsibility of social charities or nonprofit organizations, thereby representing an overall societal responsibility frame.

This study specifically examines coverage of PTS in newspapers, utilizing a community structure approach to investigate the manner in which community characteristics are linked to reporting on the issue. Building upon previous community structure approach research, the study analyzes the relationship between specific community demographic indicators and newspaper coverage of responsibility for PTS treatment in veterans in order to address the following research questions:

RQ1: How much variation exists in newspaper coverage of PTS in veterans in major United States cities?

RQ2: How closely is the variation in coverage linked to differences in community characteristics?

To test these research questions, this study offers several hypotheses regarding the connection between city characteristics and newspaper coverage of PTS treatment.

LITERATURE REVIEW

Several fields such as sociology, nursing, and psychology have extensively studied PTS in veterans. They have debated where the responsibility for treatment lies in a manner relevant to the nature of those fields. However, searches in communication studies databases reveal that similar attention to this topic is curiously scarce, as the literature has generally overlooked the topic of media coverage of PTS, arguably pertinent to the field.

Initial searches in communication studies databases for articles on PTS in veterans yielded few results. As a result, the researchers added the term "disorder" to return as many results as possible. Searching "post-traumatic stress disorder veterans" in Communication and Mass Media Complete returned 157 results. Most of the results focused on issues that veterans face as a result of PTS, such as unemployment or substance abuse, which is not pertinent to this study. Few articles examined media coverage of PTS in veterans.

The articles found discussed a variety of studies unrelated to media coverage. They covered such topics as the relationship between PTS symptoms and marital intimacy among Israeli war veterans (Solomon, Zerach, & Dekel, 2008), and "mechanisms for the [transmission] of trauma symptoms and [strategies] for interventions" (Grillo, 2009). Two articles, however, were particularly relevant. One discussed efforts to help veterans assimilate upon their return (Jankowski, Major, & Myrick, 2011). Another article studied the way that PTS was covered in the media, as well as "the absence and presence of common mental health themes" (Shevory, 2013). Although these results began to explore PTS from a communication studies context, the field produced few relevant results regarding coverage of PTS. However, searches within sociology, nursing, and psychology databases yielded more results specific to their fields and more discussion of responsibility for PTS treatment.

A search of the Sociological Abstracts database for "post-traumatic stress disorder" yielded 580 results, and narrowing the search to "post-traumatic stress disorder veterans" yielded 83 results, examining such topics as the recognition of PTS as a medical condition and the significance of government assistance for veterans with conditions such as PTS. In the nursing field, the terms "post-traumatic stress disorder veterans" yielded 3,139 results in the PubMed database, covering issues such as vocational aid for veterans with PTS and the effect of medications on veterans with PTS. Similarly, in a search of the PsycINFO database, the term "post-traumatic stress" yielded more than 6,000 related results, including articles on such topics as how PTS affects the lives of veterans, how it can lead to substance abuse and dangerous behaviors, and how PTS treatment varies across nations.

In effect, the sociology, nursing, and psychology fields all explored PTS in a manner relevant to their disciplines. Yet research within communication studies has yet to examine PTS in veterans to a degree commensurate with its explorations elsewhere. Research is particularly scant relating to media coverage of PTS in veterans. This study seeks to help bridge the attention gap by considering the aforementioned research questions. Exploring links between community demographics and variations in coverage of PTS, this study explores several hypotheses.

HYPOTHESES

This study applied the community structure approach and previous research in the development of 27 hypotheses examining coverage of PTS. The hypotheses can be divided into three umbrella groups: buffer, vulnerability, and stakeholder.

Buffer Hypothesis

The buffer hypothesis states that "cities with relatively large proportions of privileged groups may be linked to relatively sympathetic media coverage of groups or group representatives making rights claims" (Pollock, 2007, p. 61). Greater proportions of privileged groups are expected to correlate with more supportive media coverage of human rights issues. Privilege is generally measured in terms of percentage with college education, family income of $100,000 or more, and professional occupational status (Pollock, 2007).

The buffer hypothesis has been confirmed in many prior case studies. A nationwide newspaper study of same-sex marriage by Pollock and Haake (2010) found that higher proportions of privileged groups correlated with more favorable coverage of same-sex marriage. Coverage of the Clarence Thomas–Anita Hill hearings regarding gender discrimination illustrated a strong correlation between favorable coverage of Hill and higher levels of college educated, family income, and particularly professional or technical occupations in a city (Pollock, 2007, pp. 62–75). Moreover, a multicity case study conducted by Pollock, Shier, and Slattery (1995) on the coverage of the "open door" policy toward Cuba found that the higher the proportion of privileged groups, the more favorable coverage of Cubans seeking asylum in the United States. Finally, in a study about the acceptance of homosexuals in the Boy Scouts of America, researchers found that higher percentages of college-educated individuals in a city correlated with more favorable coverage (Pollock, 2007). These case studies reinforce the buffer hypothesis's assertion that communities with greater "privilege," more buffered from uncertainty, will report more favorably on human rights issues, and thus will more likely support government intervention to protect them. The buffer hypothesis can be applied to media coverage of veterans with PTS with the following hypotheses:

H1: The greater the percentage of college educated in a city, the more media support for government responsibility for PTS (Lifestyle Market Analyst, 2008).

H2: The greater the percentage of families with incomes of $100,000 or more, the more media support for government responsibility for PTS (Lifestyle Market Analyst, 2008).

H3: The greater the percentage of those with professional/technical status, the more media support for government responsibility for PTS (Lifestyle Market Analyst, 2008).

Health care access. In addition to traditional definitions of privilege, the concept of privilege can also be represented through additional indicators, such as access to health care. Pollock (2007) asserted that health care access can be measured "by the proportion of the municipal budget that a city spends on health care" and "the availability of hospital beds and physicians" (p. 93). Based on the measure of physicians per 100,000 people, a study examining coverage of embryonic stem cell research revealed a "positive correlation between access to health care and favorable news coverage" on the issue (Pollock, 2007, p. 93). Thus, it can be hypothesized that in communities with greater access to health care or higher proportions of government spending on health care, the population and the media will be more sympathetic to human rights claims. In regard to care for veterans with PTS, the following can be predicted:

H4: The greater the number of physicians per 100,000 people, the more media support for government responsibility for PTS (State and Metropolitan Area Data Book, 2010).

H5: The greater number of hospital beds per 100,000 people, the more media support for government responsibility for PTS (County and City Extra, 2010).

H6: The greater the percentage of municipal spending on healthcare, the more media support for government responsibility for PTS (County and City Extra, 2010).

Vulnerability Hypothesis

The vulnerability hypothesis suggests that media may represent issues and events from the perspective of the vulnerable, such as poor, the unemployed, and those living in high crime communities (Pollock, 2007). Conventional wisdom has long supported the "guard dog" perspective of Donohue, Tichenor, and Olien (1995), which expects that media typically reinforce or reflect the interests of powerful social, political, and economic elites. More recent research, however, such as a nationwide study on coverage of capital punishment has supported the vulnerability hypothesis, finding that "the greater the percentage below the poverty level, the less favorable the coverage of the death penalty" (Pollock, 2007, p. 142). In a nationwide study examining newspapers and racial/ethnic conflict, it was found that "the higher the poverty or unemployment levels in a city, the more 'pluralistic' the coverage in newspapers nationwide, appreciating the claims of both Caribbean Americans and Hasidic Jews" (Pollock & Whitney, 1997). A nationwide study regarding a Patient's Bill of Rights revealed a correlation between the proportion of city residents below the poverty line and more positive coverage of the Patient's Bill of Rights (Pollock, 2007). The aforementioned studies depict how media coverage in communities with large proportions of "vulnerable" citizens correlates with more empathic media coverage of human rights issues. Besides the indicators just discussed, another measure of vulnerability is crime rate. Eitzen and Zinn (2009) connected crime rate to poverty and rising unemployment and argued that in some cases, crime may even be viewed as a necessary means of survival in vulnerable communities. As a result, it can be expected that greater crime rates may be associated with more liberal media perspectives on human rights issues. Thus, the following hypotheses can be applied to media coverage of veterans with PTS:

H7: The greater the percentage of people living below the poverty line, the more media support for government responsibility for PTS (American Fact Finder, 2010).

H8: The greater the percentage unemployed in a city, the more media support for government responsibility for PTS (American Fact Finder, 2010).

H9: The greater the crime rate in a city, the more media support for government responsibility for PTS (County and City Extra, 2010).

H10: The greater the percentage of single-parent households in a city, the more media support for government responsibility for PTS (County and City Extra, 2010).

Stakeholder Hypothesis

According to Tichenor, Donohue, and Olien (1973, 1980), media in more populated cities often reflect a greater proportion of progressive and pluralistic viewpoints (Pollock, 2007). In addition, McLeod and Hertog (1992, 1999) asserted that the greater the size of a protest group, the more attention and favorable coverage that group will receive in mass media. Expressed more globally, it is reasonable to assume a "link between stakeholder size and relatively favorable coverage of stakeholder concerns" (Pollock, 2007, p. 172). Thus, the community structure approach can be applied to explore the relationship between specific city demographic categories and media reporting (Pollock, 2007). The stakeholder categories to be considered when examining media coverage of veterans with PTS are ethnic identity, belief system, political identity, generation, and position in lifecycle.

Ethnic identity. African Americans, Hispanics, and foreign-born citizens have a stake in the issue of PTS because they may be more likely to experience social injustice and difficulty in securing government aid for medical care. According to Noonan (2009), the unemployment rate among African Americans and Hispanics is considerably higher than the national average, and most of those unemployed are also uninsured. Therefore, they may be more likely to support government responsibility for veterans with PTS. In addition, Kiernicki, Pollock, and Lavery (2013) found that higher percentages of Hispanics in a community correlated with more favorable coverage of universal healthcare. Further, a study by Pollock and Branca (2011) illustrated that higher proportions of Hispanics in a city may correlate with favorable coverage of governmental regulation of drinking water contamination "rather than simply relying on 'society' to self-regulate" (p. 104). Cities with a high percentage of African American population and higher poverty levels were also found to more favorably cover the issue of legalizing abortion during the *Roe v. Wade* Supreme Court abortion decision in 1973 (Pollock, Robinson, & Murray, 1978). The higher the percentage of foreign-born in a city, one study found, the less favorable the coverage of Islam in the year after 9/11 (Pollock, Piccillo, Leopardi, Gratale, & Cabot, 2005). Based on the findings of several studies, it is evident that minority groups are significant stakeholders in media coverage of human rights issues. Therefore, the following is expected:

H11: The greater the percentage of African Americans in a city, the more media support for government responsibility for PTS (County and City Extra, 2010).

H12: The greater the percentage of Hispanics in a city, the more media support for government responsibility for PTS (County and City Extra, 2010).

H13: The greater the percentage of foreign-born in a city, the more media support for government responsibility for PTS (County and City Extra, 2010).

Belief system. As with ethnic identity, belief systems and religious values can also potentially influence coverage of critical issues in newspapers. Using the community structure approach, Pollock et al. (1978) found that higher percentages of Catholics in a city correlated with less favorable coverage of elective abortions during the *Roe v. Wade* case. However, in more recent research, it was revealed that a higher percentage of Catholics in a city was associated with favorable coverage of same-sex marriage and same-sex adoptions (Pollock & Haake, 2010). In addition, Catholic support for successful legalization of same-sex marriage in Spain was associated with appreciation for the role of gay couples in adopting children. Other studies found that the greater the percentage of Mainline Protestants in a city, the more favorable the news coverage of the Occupy Wall Street movement before the protesters were removed from Zuccotti Park (Pollock, 2013, pp. 1–30), and the greater the support for detainee rights at Guantanamo (Zinck, Rogers, Pollock, & Salvatore, this issue), suggesting that Catholics and Mainline Protestants may, in some cases, lean in a more liberal direction on selected social issues.

By contrast, cities with higher proportions of devotional readers and other religions that rely on literal interpretations of the Bible, like Evangelicals, were found to have less favorable coverage of gays in the Boy Scouts (Pollock, 2007, p. 241). Moreover, devotional readers, who hold traditional views about the origin of life, are accordingly associated with coverage opposing embryonic stem cell research (Pollock, 2007, p. 98). Historically, some Evangelicals and devotional readers have regarded mental illnesses as conditions that can be cured through prayer and may believe that secular therapists threaten their beliefs (McLatchie & Draguns, 1984). Clearly, belief systems and religions may represent complex stakeholder positions that can impact media coverage. In terms of media coverage of veterans with PTS, the following is hypothesized:

H14: The greater the percentage of Evangelicals in a city, the less media support for government responsibility for PTS (Association of Religion Data Archives, 2006).

H15: The greater the percentage of devotional readers in a city, the less media support for government responsibility for PTS (Lifestyle Market Analyst, 2008).

H16: The greater the percentage of Mainline Protestants in a city, the more media support for government responsibility for PTS (Association of Religion Data Archives, 2006).

H17: The greater the percentage of Catholics in a city, the more media support for government responsibility for PTS (Association of Religion Data Archives, 2006).

Political affiliation.   Another stakeholder issue is political affiliation. In cities, the population is often divided into two main political parties, Republicans and Democrats, and media may reflect the political interests of these parties. In a study about oil drilling in the Arctic, it was found that higher proportions voting Republican were linked to coverage supporting drilling, whereas higher proportions voting Democratic were associated with coverage opposing drilling (Pollock, 2007, p. 192). In a study regarding trying juveniles as adults, higher percentages voting Democratic in the 1996 elections correlated with less media support (Pollock, 2007, p. 204). Although both parties support veterans, Republicans traditionally see government-funded programs as social welfare, which they often do not support, evidenced by their legendary disapproval of welfare and universal healthcare. Thus, the following is predicted:

H18: The greater the percentage voting Republican in the last presidential election, the less media support for government responsibility for PTS.

H19: The greater the percentage voting Democratic in the last presidential election, the more media support for government responsibility for PTS.

Generation.   As a result of the social environments in which they were raised and resulting distinct perspectives, different generations may have contrasting views on social issues. As a result, the generational configuration of a community can affect its media coverage. In a study about affirmative action, Brechman and Pollock found less favorable media coverage in communities with greater proportions of 18- to 24-year-olds (Pollock, 2007). When studying coverage of legalization of physician-assisted euthanasia, Pollock and Yulis (2004) found greater proportions of citizens older than 75 correlated with less favorable coverage.

Unfortunately, stigma is often affiliated with mental illness. Specifically, PTS is commonly perceived to be tied to violent behavior and instability. Curiously, research indicates that individuals in their teens to early 20s and those older than 50 express the most negative attitudes toward mental health disorders including PTS (Alonso, 2009; Crisp, 2005). As a result, the following is hypothesized:

H20: The greater the percentage of 18- to 24-year-olds in a city, the less media support for government responsibility for PTS.

H21: The greater the percentage of 25- to 44-year-olds in a city, the more media support for government responsibility for PTS.

H22: The greater the percentage of 45- to 64-year-olds in a city, the less media support for government responsibility for PTS.

H23: The greater the percentage of 65-year-olds and older in a city, the less media support for government responsibility for PTS.

Position in life cycle. Newspaper coverage may also reflect the interests of families in a community. Previous research has indicated in communities with higher percentages of people with young children, media coverage tends to reflect the interests and protection of families. In a study about trying juveniles as adults, Pollock found that in areas with more families with young children, coverage more often supported trying juveniles as adults, potentially because of the desire to protect children from dangerous teens (Pollock, 2007). Furthermore, in a study examining coverage of Cuban immigrant Elian Gonzalez, Mink, Puma, and Pollock (2001) found that in cities with more families with children roughly the same age as Gonzalez (ages 5–7), newspaper coverage favored the repatriation of Gonzalez to his biological father in Cuba. Because individuals with PTS are sometimes interpreted as being violent or disturbed, parents of young children might perceive these people as a threat or danger. Therefore, the following is predicted:

H24: The greater the percentage of families with children younger than the age of 5 in a city, the more media support for government responsibility for PTS.

H25: The greater the percentage of families with children ages 5 to 10 in a city, the more media support for government responsibility for PTS.

H26: The greater the percentage of families with children ages 11 to 15 in a city, the less media support for government responsibility for PTS.

H27: The greater the percentage of families with children ages 16 to 18 in a city, the less media support for government responsibility for PTS.

METHODOLOGY

To strategically analyze media coverage of veterans with PTS, researchers selected a nationwide sample of 26 newspapers from the NewsBank database; the sample included all articles of relevant content with 500 words or more in the sample period, yielding 353 articles in total. The selection included the following publications: the *Atlantic Journal Constitution*, the *Boston Herald*, the *Buffalo News*, the *Charlotte Observer*, the *Cincinnati Post*, the *Dallas Morning News*, the *Denver Post*, the *Deseret News*, the *Hartford Courant*, the *Houston Chronicle*, the *Las Vegas Sun*, the *Lexington Herald-Leader*, the *New Hampshire Union Leader*, the *Omaha-World Herald*, the *Oregonian*, the *Orlando Sentinel*, the *Philadelphia Inquirer*, the *Pittsburgh Post-Gazette*, the *Plain Dealer*, the *San Francisco Chronicle*, the *Seattle Times, St. Louis Post Dispatch*, the *Sun Herald*, the *Times Union*, the *Wichita Eagle*, and the *Wisconsin State Journal*. Newspapers with nationwide readership including the *Los Angeles Times*, the *New York Times*, the *Wall Street Journal*, and *USA Today* were not included because they target national rather than local audiences.

The newspaper articles studied span a 10-year period, from March 20, 2003, through March 20, 2013. March 20, 2003 marked the first U.S. invasion of Iraq, and the Iraq War is among the most recent U.S. wars with documentation about PTS. To gather a sufficient number of articles, the end date was set exactly 10 years later, which was also after the official end of the Iraq War on December 15, 2011.

Article Coding and Procedures

The researchers coded each article for prominence and direction to convey the article's issue projection in the newspaper. The prominence score represents how significantly editors positioned the article in the paper, and direction conveys the way the content was framed: government responsibility, societal responsibility, or balanced/neutral. Coverage emphasizing government accountability in treatment of veterans with PTS, or focused on the positive impact of government initiatives, was coded as "government responsibility." An article in the *Deseret News* articulated a clear case for government responsibility, citing a report under the Bush administration that

> urged Congress to "enable all veterans who have been deployed in Afghanistan and Iraq who need post-traumatic stress disorder care to receive it from the VA." Only recently has the VA acted to add mental health counselors and 24-hour suicide prevention services at all facilities. (Yen, 2007, p. A2)

Another article in the *San Francisco Chronicle* covered a lawsuit against the Department of Veterans Affairs, quoting a law firm:

> The lawsuit focuses on the VA's handling—or [mishandling]—of PTSD disability claims and their repeated failures to provide medical care to returning veterans as required by federal statute. Plaintiffs' attorneys estimate the class could include between 320,000 and 800,000 veterans. (Stannard, 2007, p. A6)

These articles stressed government responsibility in treating veterans with PTS.

Conversely, coverage that favored placing primary responsibility for treatment of veterans with PTS on society and private assistance was coded as "societal responsibility." A 2011 article in the *Lexington Herald-Leader* covered the story of a man who started "a non-profit group . . . to engage veterans in public service—as a way of helping them heal" (Dao, 2011, p. C10). Similarly, a 2012 article from the *Dallas Morning News* discussed "Heroes on the Water, a nonprofit organization [that organized] kayak fishing outings for veterans who are suffering from war disabilities" (Booke, 2012, p. B1). Both of these articles portrayed society as the primary actor assuming responsibility for veterans' PTS treatment.

Coverage of PTS treatment for veterans was coded as "balanced/neutral" if it did not lean toward either government or societal responsibility but rather discussed both options equally or simply discussed the issue without assigning responsibility. A 2008 article in the *Buffalo News* discussed the effects of PTS on female veterans, stating, "With the wars in Iraq and Afghanistan, women also are suffering the emotional wounds from battle" (Michel, 2008, p. A1). Another article published on November 16, 2011, in the *St. Louis Post Dispatch* covered a veteran's battle with PTS, explaining, "He ended up in a psychiatric hospital. . . . He was diagnosed with post-traumatic stress disorder" (McClellan, 2012, p. A11). Neither article conveyed preference for government or societal responsibility, thus leading to their classification as balanced/neutral.

A total of 194 of 353 articles (55%) were read by two coders, resulting in a Scott's Pi coefficient of intercoder reliability of 0.758. The prominence and direction scores for all articles were utilized in the determination of a Media Vector score for each newspaper. Researchers then used Pearson correlations to identify which city characteristics were most significantly related to the Media Vectors, and regression analysis to reveal the importance of each individual variable.

RESULTS

This study examined U.S. newspaper coverage of veterans with PTS by comparing newspaper coverage and resulting Media Vectors from 26 major cities. Results showed that the *Sun Herald*, printed in Biloxi, Mississippi, had the highest Media Vector, at 0.8403. In contrast, the *Dallas Morning News* had the lowest Media Vector, at −0.3592. The range of Media Vector results was therefore 1.1995, illustrating the spectrum of coverage that major metropolitan newspapers displayed regarding treatment of veterans with PTS. Media Vectors that supported government responsibility for PTS comprised 96.1% of the newspapers analyzed. Only 3.8% (one newspaper) had a Media Vector that favored societal responsibility for PTS. A complete list of all 26 Media Vectors can be found in Table 1.

In addition to representing individual city differences, Media Vectors were also averaged by region. Table 2 displays regional Media Vector results. The range of Media Vectors based on region was 0.198. Regionally-averaged Media Vectors showed that all regions placed the responsibility for treating PTS on the government. The Midwest region had the highest Media Vector, at 0.289, whereas the West had the lowest Media Vector, at 0.091. The high Media Vector for the Midwest suggests that it is a more progressive-minded region regarding some human rights issues, which may not have been expected. Previous community structure studies using regional analysis have yielded similar findings. Consistent with regional findings in recent studies of coverage of detainee rights (Zinck et al., this issue) and of the Occupy Wall Street movement (Pollock, 2013, pp. 1–30), the Midwest is capable of showing high levels of support for government responsibility for human rights issues. Therefore, this study on coverage of PTS reinforces an emerging pattern that newspapers and perhaps public opinion in the Midwest are likely to support government responsibility for selected human rights claims.

DISCUSSION OF SIGNIFICANT FINDINGS

To measure connections between city characteristics and variations in newspaper coverage, Pearson correlations were calculated. Results of the calculations are shown in Table 3.

Buffer Significant

Percentage with professional/technical occupations, percentage of families with income of $100,000 or more, and percentage of college educated all correlated with less media support for government responsibility for PTS.

TABLE 1
Media Vectors

Newspaper	City	Media Vector
The Sun Herald	Biloxi, MS	0.8403
The Lexington Herald-Leader	Lexington, KY	0.5836
The Wichita Eagle	Wichita, KS	0.4793
The Omaha-World Herald	Omaha, NE	0.4324
The Cincinnati Post	Cincinnati, OH	0.3359
The New Hampshire Union Leader	Manchester, NH	0.2889
The Pittsburgh Post-Gazette	Pittsburgh, PA	0.2495
The Buffalo News	Buffalo, NY	0.2376
The Plain Dealer	Cleveland, OH	0.2200
St. Louis Post Dispatch	St. Louis	0.1976
The Boston Herald	Boston, MA	0.1975
The Hartford Courant	Hartford, CT	0.1716
The Deseret News	Salt Lake City, UT	0.1496
The Charlotte Observer	Charlotte, NC	0.1395
The Oregonian	Portland, OR	0.1190
The Houston Chronicle	Houston, TX	0.1171
The Las Vegas Sun	Las Vegas, NV	0.1169
The Seattle Times	Seattle, WA	0.1107
The Orlando Sentinel	Orlando, FL	0.1023
The Times Union	Albany, NY	0.0779
The Wisconsin State Journal	Madison, WI	0.0741
The Atlantic Journal Constitution	Atlanta, GA	0.0687
The Denver Post	Denver, CO	0.0420
The Philadelphia Inquirer	Philadelphia, PA	0.0276
The San Francisco Chronicle	San Francisco, CA	0.0105
The Dallas Morning News	Dallas, TX	−0.3592

Percentage with professional/technical occupations (disconfirmed). Pearson correlations showed that the percentage of professionals in a city correlated negatively with newspaper coverage of government responsibility for treatment of PTS, disconfirming the original hypothesis for this variable ($r = -.553$, $p = .002$).

Percentage with family income of $100,000 or more (disconfirmed). Pearson correlations revealed that newspapers in cities with higher percentages of families with incomes of

TABLE 2
Media Vectors by Region

Region	Media Vector
Midwest	0.289
South	0.213
Northeast	0.178
West	0.091

TABLE 3
Pearson Correlations

City Characteristic	Pearson Correlation	Significance
45–64	−0.559	.002**
Professional/technical occupation	−0.553	.002**
Family income $100K+	−0.524	.003**
College educated	−0.486	.006**
Foreign born	−0.467	.008**
Hispanic	−0.410	.019*
25–44	−0.342	.047*
Democratic	−0.340	.048*
65+	0.340	.048*
Republican	0.327	.055
Homicide rate	−0.283	.085
Devotional reader	0.255	.104
Hospital beds	0.243	.116
Unemployed	−0.203	.160
Municipal spending	−0.198	.167
Children ages 16–18	0.185	.188
Evangelical	0.177	.194
Single-parent households	0.159	.219
Below poverty	0.139	.254
Children ages 11–15	0.095	.326
Protestant	0.082	.345
African American	−0.073	.362
Children younger than 5	−0.057	.393
18–24	0.056	.396
Children ages 5–10	0.049	.409
Crime rate	−0.044	.418
Female work	0.027	.447
Catholic	−0.013	.475
Hate crime rate	−0.011	.480
Physicians	−0.003	.495

*Significant at .05 level, **significant at .01 level.

$100,000 or more were less likely to emphasize government responsibility for veterans' PTS treatment ($r = -.524$, $p = .003$). This finding disconfirmed the original hypothesis regarding this variable.

Percentage of college educated (disconfirmed).   It was predicted that greater percentages of college educated in a city would correlate with more media support for government responsibility for PTS. However, this hypothesis was disconfirmed, as the indicator correlated with less media emphasis on government responsibility for PTS ($r = -.486$, $p = .006$).

Curiously, all significant results related to privilege were in the opposite direction as predicted. Privilege, as it turned out, correlated with less media emphasis on government responsibility for veterans with PTS. Perhaps greater privilege in some metropolitan areas may be affiliated with a more active social sector and thus a more empowered populace that is confident of its own ability to effect change, rather than rely on government efforts.

Stakeholder Significant

Percentage of foreign born, percentage of Hispanic, and percentage voting Democratic all correlated with less media support for government responsibility for PTS.

Percentage of foreign born (disconfirmed). The hypothesis that greater percentages of foreign-born would correlate with more media support for government responsibility was disconfirmed; instead, a higher percentage of foreign-born correlated with less emphasis on government responsibility for treatment of PTS in veterans ($r = -.467$, $p = .008$).

Percentage of Hispanic (disconfirmed). The initial hypothesis regarding the percentage of Hispanics in a city was also disconfirmed. Instead, Pearson correlations illustrated that greater percentages of Hispanics in a city correlated with less media emphasis on government responsibility for treatment of PTS ($r = -.0410$, $p = .019$).

Percentage voting Democratic (disconfirmed). Originally, it was predicted that cities with higher percentages voting Democratic would correlate with more media support for government responsibility for PTS treatment. Yet Pearson correlations revealed that the higher the percentage voting Democratic in a city, the less media coverage emphasizing government responsibility for treatment of PTS ($r = -.340$, $p = .048$).

Once again, significant results contradicted original predictions. Perhaps one reason for the results could be a distrust of government efforts on the part of some groups that may have felt marginalized in society, such as those who are foreign-born.

Stakeholder Generation Significant

Generations of ages 45 to 64 and 25 to 44 correlated with less media support for government responsibility for PTS, whereas the generation of age 65 and older correlated with more media support for government responsibility for PTS treatment.

Percentage of 45- to 64-year-olds (confirmed). The researchers hypothesized that the greater the percentage of 45- to 64-year-olds in a city, the less media support for government responsibility for PTS. Pearson correlations confirmed this hypothesis, with a highly significant and highly negative correlation ($r = -.559$, $p = .002$). Along with the indicator of professional occupational status in a city, this association was the study's most highly significant finding.

Percentage of 25- to 44-year-olds (disconfirmed). Although it was predicted that this generational group would support government responsibility for PTS, results indicated the opposite. Instead, in communities with greater percentages of individuals ages 25 to 44, media coverage reflected less support for government responsibility for treatment of PTS in veterans ($r = -.342$, $p = .047$).

Percentage of 65-year-olds and older (disconfirmed). Correlations involving this stakeholder group were also found to be in the opposite direction as predicted ($r = .340$, $p = .048$).

TABLE 4
Regression Analysis

Model	R (equation)	R^2 (cumulative)	R^2 Change	F Change	Significance of F Change
Family income $100k+	0.513	0.264	0.264	7.877	0.010
Family income $100k+, Hispanic	0.586	0.344	0.080	2.556	0.125
Family income $100k+, Hispanic, Professional/ technical occupation	0.627	0.393	0.050	1.636	0.216

Although it was hypothesized that the greater the percentage of 65-year-olds and older in a city, the less media support for government responsibility for PTS, higher proportions of this stakeholder group actually correlated with more media support for government responsibility.

The somewhat unexpected generational findings may be related to generational differences regarding war. Particularly, the 65 and older generation experienced the Vietnam War and may be more sympathetic to veterans' rights than younger generations never subjected to a draft. Older generations may also view the military and government intervention more favorably, whereas younger generations might favor a more active social sector and grassroots efforts.

Regression Analysis

A regression analysis of significant variables as defined through the Pearson correlations showed that the percentage of families with incomes of $100,000 or more was the most significant variable, accounting for 26.4% of the variance. The second most significant variable was percentage of Hispanics in a city (8% of the variance), and the third most significant variable was the percentage of professionals in a city. The three variables accounted for 39.3% of the variance. All three of these variables had negative correlations with newspaper coverage emphasizing government responsibility for treatment of PTS in veterans (see Table 4).

CONCLUSIONS AND IMPLICATIONS FOR FURTHER RESEARCH

After more than a decade of military engagement overseas in Afghanistan and Iraq, American soldiers continue to return home. The issues and subsequent health conditions they face as a result of war, including PTS, are not easily resolved. The question of responsibility for treatment of PTS in veterans has been debated nationwide but not sufficiently covered by communication scholars, and this study attempted to bridge that gap. This study has shown that across major metropolitan areas, media coverage emphasizes government responsibility for treatment of veterans with PTS.

The study revealed several significant correlations, yet most were in the opposite direction than predicted. All three of the buffer hypotheses were disconfirmed, finding that the higher the percentage of professionals, families with incomes of $100,000 or more or college educated in a city, the less the media emphasis on government responsibility for treatment of veterans with PTS. In addition, the hypothesis concerning Democratic political affiliation was also disconfirmed. This study found that the higher percentage voting Democratic in a city, the less coverage emphasized government responsibility. Although this study revealed a number of significant correlations, the percentage voting Republican was not a significant variable. Researchers expected that this variable would be tied to media coverage of PTS treatment, as political affiliation guides considerable discourse in this country regarding multiple public issues. Yet results in the Pearson correlations and regression analysis suggest that the issue of responsibility for treating veterans with PTS may not be a partisan issue. Rather, coverage of PTS may be more closely related to socioeconomic status and stakeholder groups.

Pearson correlations also showed that the higher the percentages of both 25- to 44-year-olds and 45- to 64-year-olds in a city, the less media support for government responsibility for treatment of veterans with PTS. Conversely, the higher the percentage of 65-year-olds and older in a city, the more media support for government responsibility. This generational finding could be due to ingrained generational values and experiences. The Vietnam War spanned from 1959 to 1975 and had a draft that rendered, at a minimum, any male born between January 1, 1944, and December 31, 1950, eligible (Angrist, 1990). Virtually every family had a stake in U.S. wars because the lottery put all eligible men in the same group; all were equal and connected in that they were affected by the lottery. Today, these men would be between the ages of 63 and 69. Veterans of the Vietnam War and all those in that generational group may be more inclined to support governmental responsibility for treating PTS due to their experiences during the war. As there is no draft today, younger men have a choice regarding war. This absence of universal stakeholding could explain why newspapers in cities with greater proportions of younger people tended to have less media emphasis on government responsibility for PTS treatment.

The significant findings of this study warrant further discussion. The disconfirmation of the buffer hypothesis, although at first surprising, may indicate that areas with greater privilege support alternative means of assisting veterans, through more active social efforts. Regarding the stakeholder hypotheses, perhaps the generational findings are reflective of overall support for veterans and the military among the 65+ generation, due to their experiences with war, whereas younger generations might support more social sector efforts.

Ultimately, it must be acknowledged that nearly all newspapers had Media Vector results indicating support for government responsibility. Thus, the significant findings do not actually indicate any substantial resistance to government responsibility for PTS treatment in veterans but rather differing degrees of support among demographic variables. This finding in itself is telling, as it indicates that treatment of veterans with PTS may be an issue that transcends typical demographic differences among cities and instead garners widespread support in major cities.

Future research should look more closely at privileged groups in society to investigate why the buffer hypotheses were disconfirmed. Researchers should also evaluate possible correlations between cities with higher proportions of veterans and/or active military personnel and media coverage of the issue to further test the stakeholder hypothesis. Furthermore, future research should compare media coverage in larger cities with that in smaller towns in order to explore any effects related to city and newspaper size. This potential approach could be applied to other community structure studies. A final avenue of future research could involve a new demographic dimension requiring more in-depth city-level study. Specifically, researchers could attempt to identify demographic indicators related to social sector activity. If relevant data are available, researchers could compile a "social sector index" or "social capital index" as a score representing how active and prominent social organizations are. This index, if available, could be utilized in Pearson correlations that could inform some of the unanticipated results of this study.

ACKNOWLEDGMENT

A previous version of this article was presented at the annual conference of the New Jersey Communication Association in April 2014, where it won the award for best HJCA conference undergraduate paper.

REFERENCES

Alonso, J. (2009). Perceived stigma among individuals with common mental disorders. *Journal of Affective Disorders*, *118*, 180–186.

American fact finder. (2010). Retrieved from http://factfinder2.census.gov/faces/nav/jsf/pages/index.xhtml

Angrist, J. D. (1990, June). Lifetime earnings and the Vietnam era draft lottery: Evidence from Social Security administrative records. *The American Economic Review, 80*, 313–336.

Association of Religion Data Archives. (2006). Retrieved from http://www.thearda.com

Booke, E. (2012, May 25). Vets cast troubles adrift. *The Dallas Morning News*, p. B1.

County and city extra: Annual metro, city, and county data book. (2010). Lanham, MD: Bernan Press.

Crisp, A. (2005). Stigmatization of people with mental illnesses: A follow-up study within the Changing Minds campaign of the Royal College of Psychiatrists. *World Psychiatry, 4*, 106–113.

Dao, J. (2011, November 3). Offering vets a chance to serve communities helps them heal. *The Lexington Herald-Leader*, p. C10.

Donohue, G. A., Tichenor, P. J., & Olien, C. (1995). A guard dog perspective on the role of media. *Journal of Communication, 45*, 115–132.

Eitzen, D. S., & Zinn, M. B. (2009). *Social problems* (11th ed.). Boston, MA: Allyn and Bacon.

Grillo, C. (2009). DCS facilitation of fear extinction and exposure-based therapy may rely on lower-level, automatic mechanisms. *Biological Psychiatry, 66*, 636–641.

Jankowski, S. M., Major, L. H. & Myrick, J. G. (2011, May). *Framing post-traumatic stress disorder: A look at twenty years of television news coverage.* Paper presented at the annual conference of the International Communication Association, Boston, MA.

Kiernicki, K., Pollock, J. C., & Lavery, P. (2013). Nationwide newspaper coverage of universal health care: A community structure approach. In J. C. Pollock (Ed.), *Media and social inequality: Innovations in community structure research* (pp. 116–134). New York, NY: Routledge.

Lifestyle market analyst: A reference guide for consumer market analysis. (2008). Des Plaines, IL: Standard Rate and Data Service.

McClellan, B. (2012, November 16). Veteran winning battle with stress. *St. Louis Post-Dispatch*, p. A11.

McLatchie, L. R., & Draguns, J. G. (1984). Mental health concepts of evangelical Protestants. *The Journal of Psychology: Interdisciplinary and Applied, 118*, 147–159.

McLeod, D. M., & Hertog, J. K. (1992). The manufacture of public opinion by reporters: Informal cues for public perceptions of protest groups. *Discourse and Society, 3*, 259–275.

McLeod, D. M., & Hertog, J. K. (1999). Social control, social change and the mass media's role in the regulation of protest groups. In D. Demers & K. Viswanath (Eds.), *Mass media, social control, and social change: A macrosocial perspective* (pp. 305–331). Ames, IA: Iowa State University Press.

Michel, L. (2008, March 24). Healing deep psychic wounds—From battlefield trauma to sexual assaults, stress is a nightmare, and VA is trying to respond better. *The Buffalo News*, p. A1.

Mink, M., Puma, J., & Pollock, J. (2001, May). *Nationwide newspaper coverage of the repatriation of Elian Gonzalez: A community structure approach.* Paper presented at the annual conference of the International Communication Association, Washington, DC.

Noonan, K. (2009, April). *Health care: Economic crisis worsens racial and ethnic health disparities* [Web log post]. Retrieved from http://www.newamerica.net/blog/new-health-dialogue/2009/health-care-economic-crisis-worsens-racial-and-ethnic-health-disparities-10

Pollock, J. C. (2007). *Titled mirrors: Media alignment with political and social change—A community structure approach.* Cresskill, NJ: Hampton Press.

Pollock, J. C. (Ed.). (2013). *Media and social inequality: Innovations in community structure research.* New York, NY: Routledge.

Pollock, J. C., & Branca, V. (2011). Nationwide-US newspaper coverage of handling water contamination: A community structure approach. *Ecos de la Comunicación, 4*, 93–121.

Pollock, J. C., & Haake, J. (2010). Nationwide newspaper coverage of same-sex marriage: A community structure approach. *Journal of PR, 1*, 13–40.

Pollock, J. C., Piccillo, C., Leopardi, D., Gratale, S., & Cabot, K. (2005, February). Nationwide newspaper coverage of Islam post-September 11, 2001: A community structure approach. *Communication Research Reports, 22*, 15–27.

Pollock, J. C., Robinson, J. L., & Murray, M. C. (1978). Media agendas and human rights: The Supreme Court decision on abortion. *Journalism Quarterly, 53*, 545–548, 561.

Pollock, J. C., Shier, L., & Slattery, P. (1995). Newspapers and the "Open Door" policy towards Cuba: A sample of major cities—community structure approach. *Journal of International Communication, 2*, 67–86.

Pollock, J. C., & Whitney, L. (1997). Newspapers and racial/ethnic conflict: Comparing city demographics and nationwide reporting on the Crown Heights (Brooklyn, NY) incidents. *Atlantic Journal of Communication, 5*, 127–149.

Pollock, J. C., & Yulis, S. G. (2004). Nationwide newspaper coverage of physician-assisted suicide: A community structure approach. *Journal of Health Communication, 9*, 281–307.

Shevory, K. (2013). Saving Sargent Nickel. *Pacific Standard, 6*, 24–25.

Solomon, Z., Zerach, G., & Dekel, R. (2008). The relationships between posttraumatic stress symptom clusters and marital intimacy among war veterans. *Journal of Family Psychology, 22*, 659–666.

Stannard, M. (2007, July 24). Veterans' rights groups sue VA, seeking better care for injured troops. *San Francisco Chronicle*, p. A6. Retrieved from NewsBank database.

State and metropolitan area data book. (2010). Retrieved from http://www.census.gov/prod/2010pubs/10smadb/2010 smadb.pdf

Tichenor, P. J., Donohue, G., & Olien, C. (1973). Mass communication research: Evolution of a structural model. *Journalism Quarterly, 50*, 419–425.

Tichenor, P. J., Donohue, G., & Olien, C. (1980). *Community conflict and the press.* Beverly Hills, CA: Sage.

Yen, H. (2007, July 26). Broad changes in vet care urged. *The Deseret News*, p. A2. Retrieved from NewsBank database.

Index

INDEX